CHRISTIAN BIBLICAL ETHICS

From Biblical Revelation to Contemporary Christian Praxis: Method and Content

Written and edited by
Robert J. Daly, S.J.

in cooperation with
**James A. Fischer, C.M.
Terence J. Keegan, O.P.
Anthony J. Tambasco**

with additional contributions by
**L. John Topel, S.J.
Frederick E. Schuele**

in consultation with the
**Catholic Biblical Association
Task Force**

**PAULIST PRESS
NEW YORK/RAMSEY**

ACKNOWLEDGMENTS

As we indicate in "The History of This Book" in our Introduction below, not just dozens but perhaps hundreds of persons could be mentioned as having contributed in one way or other to this book. Important contributions extend far beyond those mentioned on the title page or in occasional footnotes. The most important of these are the Catholic Biblical Association of America which provided a home for the continuing seminar and task force that eventually led to this book, and the members itself of the task force. It is true that the book itself became the special project of the method sub group, and that only the individual names mentioned on the title page can be spoken of as its authors in the strict sense. On the other hand, it is quite clear to these "authors" that there simply would be no book—certainly not this book—without the task force and the interest and commitment of its members. Their commitment to our common project made the book possible in the first place and contributed much to what is good in it. Most of all, and in ways which we feel that they may not be aware of, they contributed much to the "education" of those who eventually wrote the book. Those who made this contribution by serving at one time or another on the task force are, listed alphabetically: Thomas Aquinas Collins, O.P., Richard J. Cassidy, Cassian Corcoran, O.F.M., Lawrence Frizzell, Paul Jurkowitz, Neil J. McEleney, C.S.P., Jerome Murphy-O'Connor, O.P., Justin A. Pierce, Stanley M. Polan, Patrick Henry Reardon, Joseph Zalotay.

Library of Congress
Catalog Card Number: 83-61906

ISBN: 0-8091-2592-7

Published by Paulist Press
545 Island Road, Ramsey, N.J. 07446

Printed and bound in the
United States of America

CONTENTS

A. The History of this Book 3

**B. The Purpose and Goals of
the Task Force and this Book** 7

Part One

Christian Biblical Ethics: Method

I. Approaches to the Bible 13
The Bible and Revelation; Reading and Inter-
preting the Bible; The Historical-Critical
Method; The Controversy about the Historical-
Critical Method

II. The Bible and Theology 35
The General Situation; The Christocentricity of
Christian Theology and Christian Ethics; Some
Basic Positions on the Relationship of the Bible
to Christian Theology; Some Methodological
and Hermeneutical Observations; From the Bible to Doctrine

III. The Bible and Ethics 66
Transitional: From the Bible and Theology to
the Bible and Ethics; The Christocentricity of
Christian Ethics; The Normativity of the Bible
for Christian Ethics; The Distinctiveness of
Christian Ethics; Biblical Commands and Par-
enesis. Literary Form and *Sitz Im Leben;* Bibli-
cal Paradox (FISCHER); Law and Wisdom
(FISCHER); The Science and the Art of Christian
Biblical Ethics; Excursus: Where have all the
Stories Gone?; First and Third World Ethics
(TAMBASCO)

iii

IV. Story and Image (FISCHER) **156**
Human Life as Story; The Bible as Ethical Story

Part Two

Christian Biblical Ethics: Some Attempts

Introduction **173**

I. The Christian Ethics of the Lukan Sermon (TOPEL) **179**
Past Research on the Lukan Sermon; Future Directions of Research

II. Living up to Matthew's Sermon on the Mount: An Approach (SCHUELE) **200**

III. The New Testament Love Command and the Call to Non-Violence **211**

IV. Paul's Dying/Rising Ethics in 1 Corinthians (KEEGAN) **220**

V. 1 Cor 7:8–24—Marriage and Divorce (FISCHER) **245**

VI. Dissent within a Religious Community: Romans 9—11 (FISCHER) **256**

VII. Politics and Biblical Ethics: Romans 13:1–7 (FISCHER) **266**

VIII. Human Sexuality and Christian Biblical Revelation **278**

Appendix **287**

Epilogue **297**

Indexes **302**

Introduction

A. THE HISTORY OF THIS BOOK

Although modest in size and obviously incomplete in terms of some important aspects of its topic, this book has been in the making for a period of nine years and has involved the written and/or oral contributions of many dozens of scholars. It began in 1975 when Pheme Perkins, who was in charge of organizing the continuing seminars for the general meeting of The Catholic Biblical Association of America (CBA), asked her colleague at Boston College, Robert Daly, S.J., to run a continuing seminar on the subject of New Testament ethics. Having no idea he would still be working on the project nine years later, he innocently accepted the assignment. The continuing seminar was successful, at least in the sense that eight or nine of its participants decided to continue it for a second year and consider the possibility of forming a "task force" which would be able to meet annually at the general meetings of the CBA for a period of up to five years. That first meeting at the Iliff School of Theology in Denver was thus followed by a second meeting at Duquesne in 1976, after which the continuing seminar requested and was granted status as a task force. At that time the core group numbered about twelve.

In the course of the ensuing annual meetings of the CBA, at the University of Detroit in 1977, the University of San Francisco in 1978, Boston College in 1979, the College of St. Scholastica (Duluth) in 1980, and the University of Seattle in 1981, the task force, with a fairly stable core group, went about formulating and reformulating its goals and methods, while at the same time attempting to "apply" or use them. This resulted in some fifty or so written contributions ranging from very brief working papers to substantial articles, some of which have already been published in biblical and theological journals. The name of the task force was fairly early modified to "Christian Biblical Ethics:

3

Method and Content" in order to reflect more accurately its concerns and goals. There were three major focal points which are also reflected in the contents of this book: (1) method and hermeneutics, (2) 1 Corinthians, (3) the Matthaean Sermon on the Mount and the Lukan Sermon on the Plain. These three foci developed in this chronological order. The work of the group began with methodological questions. But even as the focus was shifting from "method" to "content," theological methodological concerns seemed to retain, for a group of biblical scholars, an unusual degree of dominance which is obviously reflected in the contents of this book. This dominance seemed to correspond to the interests of most of the most active members of the task force, but it was also inevitably heightened by the fact that its moderator, Robert Daly, is actually more of a theologian than a biblical scholar. However, not all in the task force were equally interested in the same things. Thus, in order to serve both the divergent and common interests of the task force, it divided into three sub groups for the last two years of its operation. Group I concentrated on the Sermon on the Mount, Group II on Method, and Group III on a specific issue, viz. family and sexual ethics. Thus, in the 1980 and 1981 meetings, the task force met as a whole only at the beginning and at the end of the time allotted to the task forces, while each sub group continued its own work in between.

It was also during these final years of the task force that the idea of producing a book matured and became identified as the special project of the method sub group. Its work was the most advanced, for it was with questions of method that the whole project had begun. In addition, its four central members, Daly, Fischer, Keegan and Tambasco had held additional meetings in the summer and fall of 1979. This history helps explain the listing of authors, editors and contributors found on the title page and in the Acknowledgments. For all practical purposes, only those mentioned on the title page bear responsibility for what is in the book. However, the credit for it also extends far beyond them to the many dozens of theologians and exegetes who commented on and discussed different parts of this work in its various stages of development. The lion's share of this credit goes to the other members of the task force whose interest, faithfulness to the project and encouragement made the conception of this book possible in the first place.

It was also during these final years that the editorial principles and the appointment of Robert Daly as the principal editor of the book were agreed to. Consultation with prospective publishers supported the impression that it would be preferable to produce as unified a book as possible, even if that meant extensive editing, rather than merely patch together a group of essays. This editorial activity is most obvious in Part One, where most of the material was first formulated by Daly before going through its various stages of discussion and reformulation in the task force and method sub group. The exceptions are those parts of Chapter I, Section 4, "The Controversy about the Historical-Critical Method" first formulated by Jurkowitz, Chapter III, Section 6, "Biblical Paradox," and Section 7, "Law and Wisdom" and Chapter IV, "Story and Image," first formulated by Fischer and Chapter III, Section 9 "First and Third World Ethics," first formulated by Tambasco. But although most of the writing and editing of this material was done by Daly, its conception, development and final shape were so influenced by the task force, especially Fischer, Keegan and Tambasco, that they must be mentioned with Daly as its co-authors and co-editors. Unless otherwise indicated at the beginning of a particular chapter or section, or in an appropriate footnote, this is how the book was written.

An important step toward the eventual production of the book was taken in the August 1982 CBA general meeting at Siena College where a panel discussion based on an early draft of Part One took place. Robert Daly, S.J. represented the task force (most specifically the method sub group), Daniel Harrington, S.J. represented the CBA (as a biblical scholar not part of the task force), and Charles E. Curran represented the Catholic Theological Society of America (as an ethicist from outside the CBA). The moderator was Pheme Perkins. The discussion and interest occasioned by this panel confirmed the impression of the editors that they had something worth publishing. It also had the important practical effect of attracting the interested attention of several publishers and led to the discussions which resulted in our agreement with Paulist Press.

The panel members and several others were able to

point out a number of areas where the proposed book appeared to be incomplete or in need of further improvement and clarification. Some of these criticisms and suggestions have been accepted and worked into the book. Other very important ones have indeed been accepted as valid but, for lack of time and/or ability on the part of the authors/editors, they have not been worked into the final draft of the book. Among these still-to-be-done tasks is the need to pay more attention to the following: (1) the social ethos of the early Christians; (2) some recent sociological research on the idea and dynamics of tradition (it is not yet clear to us whether these suggestions would best be taken up by adding another major chapter entitled, e.g., "The Bible and Society" or by seeing to it that sociological perspectives properly permeate the whole work, as at least to some extent they already do); (3) feminist theology (one rightly asks why liberation theology is given some attention and feminist theology is not); (4) a systematic or representative select bibliography.

The neglect of these important aspects of the task in no way reflects a value judgment on them. What it reflects are the capabilities and limitations of the book's authors and editors. We recognize that for this book to be complete, or "representative," or even to be an adequate description of the present state of this question, the topics we have just mentioned, and probably others as well, would have to be given their proper place. Our decision not to take on these additional tasks is based simply on the recognition that we would be unable to do them justice within a reasonable period of time. An important consideration behind this decision was also our realization that this task force and the energies and inspiration that supported it had just about run their course. If our results, however imperfect and incomplete, were to be of help beyond the narrow circles of the task force members, we would have to package our "product" now as best we could and present it as a consciously incomplete but also hopefully helpful and important contribution. If our work is judged successful in this limited sense, then we or others can consider ways to complete and improve it.

The final writing and editing was done in a ten-week period from February through April, 1983.

B. THE PURPOSE AND GOALS OF THE TASK FORCE AND THIS BOOK

Precisely speaking, one might distinguish between the goals of the task force and the goals of the authors and editors of this book. The latter, smaller group all came from the task force, of course; but as the book itself became a project, its authors and editors worked more and more independently of the task force as a whole. However, this articulation of goals goes back to a time when the task force was working as a unit without sub groups. Thus, to the extent that there may be real differences here, they will probably lie less in the formulation of goals than in the way one attempts to reach them.

The words "Christian Biblical Ethics" in our title thus describe the goal toward which we are striving rather than a goal achieved. But each of these three words expresses an essential element of what the task force came to realize was its task. *Christian,* because we are conscious of working precisely as Christian theologians on a theme that is central to Christian life itself. How to live our *life in Christ* is, ultimately, what we are talking about. *Biblical,* and not just "New Testament" which is, in fact, our dominant material focus, in order to express our awareness of the unity of the two Testaments, and of the unintelligibility of the New without the Old, and to emphasize that the whole of the Bible, or "Christian biblical revelation" as we will define it below (14), is the central formal object of our study. *Ethics* has been the one constant term in the title of the project from the beginning. But it, too, took on specific connotations for us. That is, we have attempted not just a scientific study of the moral teaching of a specific biblical author or book, or even (to the extent that it may even be possible to speak this way) of the Bible as a whole, but also and especially, a study of the way Christians should try to live a biblically grounded and centered ethic.

In the later stages of producing this book, we came to realize that we were also attempting to work out the methodological relationships between the *non*-technical-theological ways in which the vast majority of Christians make moral decisions and the technical-theological ways in which Christian ethicians attempt to work out consistent methods of decision-making and commitment which do justice to "Christian biblical revelation" (see below 14). Another way of expressing this, as we shall see below (114–138), is to say that our concern is not just for ethics as a "science" but also and especially (for this has been much neglected) for ethics as an "art."

In 1977, the task force formulated its goals substantially as follows:

(1) *To develop in theory and test in practice the methods of doing Christian biblical ethics.* This would involve two levels:

    (a) The specifically exegetical or biblical-theological level of identifying and investigating those passages and aspects of the Bible, especially in the New Testament, which have moral content or relevance.

    (b) The methodological or hermeneutical level of working out and articulating an over-arching method or context or organizing principle within which the specifically exegetical work of (a) can go forward more efficiently and contribute more productively to the larger task of (1).

(2) To work out, articulate and (as far as possible) begin to implement the building of bridges to the other theological and academic disciplines which are also needed in order to develop a truly contemporary method of *doing Christian ethics from the perspec-*

> tive of and fully consistent with Christian biblical
> faith.

These have remained our goals. Over the years we have become increasingly aware of the demanding nature of the relationship between the two levels of (1). There is a tension here which we have tried not to evade. We have tried to keep this an *inter*-relationship so that exegesis and theology/methodology would mutually influence each other and not just each go its own comfortable way. This is difficult to achieve because individuals very often have interests and ability on just one of these levels. Genuine competence in one individual on both levels is, in fact, quite rare.

Within this task force, while we have tried to operate simultaneously on both levels, the methodological, as we explained above (3–5), has dominated. The two levels, however, are clearly reflected in the basic structure of this book. Part One is methodological, hermeneutical and theological. Part Two is more specifically exegetical or biblical-theological. There we will present some at least initial attempts to demonstrate what effect our "method" (at least our attempt to work toward a method) might have on exegesis and biblical theology. With regard to the goals formulated in (2), there has been a significant amount of individual activity by members of the task force, especially in the method sub group. In the past few years we have paid increasing attention to coordinating these attempts and to integrating them, as far as possible, into a coherent theory and method.

We have in fact, from the beginning, been very aware of the theologically interdisciplinary nature of our task. Although the CBA is a society primarily of exegetes who work mostly with the historical-critical method, the members who formed this task force immediately recognized the validity of the statement first made when the task force was still operating as a continuing seminar: "To say 'New Testament ethics' is to make a systematic theological statement." This becomes even more true when one says "Christian biblical ethics." One inevitably gets involved with, or at least must acknowledge that one is operating within the context of, a whole host of meta-exegetical and meta-ethical questions. Biblical exegesis, fundamental and systematic theology, and Christian ethics are the central skills involved. But the more thoroughly one gets involved in the task, the more deeply one is also involved with philosophy, literature and the social sciences.

Part One

CHRISTIAN BIBLICAL ETHICS:
METHOD

APPROACHES TO THE BIBLE

1. THE BIBLE AND REVELATION

We use the term *Bible* in its normal sense as referring to that collection of books which Christians revere and look to as their primary foundational document. This "Bible" or "Scripture" or "Sacred Scripture" has three main divisions. (1) *The Old Testament* or *Hebrew Bible:* the sacred foundational writings of the Jewish people, written (in its presently existing literary forms) in Hebrew and between the tenth and first centuries B.C. Its main divisions are the Law, the Prophets, and the Writings (historical and wisdom books). (2) *The New Testament* was written in Greek from the middle of the first to the beginning of the second century A.D. It is made up of the four Gospels and the Acts of the Apostles, the letters of Paul and other early Christian figures, and the Apocalypse of John or Book of Revelation. These, together with the Old Testament, are the sacred foundational writings of the Christian Church. (3) *The Apocrypha and Pseudepigrapha.* The Apocrypha consist mostly of those writings which appear in the Septuagint (the "official" third to second century B.C. Greek translation of the Bible) but not in the Hebrew Bible itself. Since the Council of Trent (1546) they have been accepted by Catholics and generally rejected by Protestants as belonging to the full canon of the Bible. The Pseudepigrapha are a varied collection of largely pseudonymous religious writings dating from about 200 B.C. to 100 A.D. Although not accepted as part of the canonical Bible, they provide invaluable background for the understanding of the New Testament.

Revelation, in its most general religious meaning, signifies God's self-disclosure to humanity, whether to communities or individuals, publicly or privately. *Biblical revelation* refers either (1) to the event of, or (2) to the written record (in the Bible) of God's self-disclosure to the faith-communities of Judaism and Christianity.

In our work we gradually came to articulate and then to apply throughout this book the following definition or description of "Christian biblical revelation":

> *Christian Biblical Revelation* (as we will see more fully below in Chapter Two 45–54) is the written record and faith-recollection of particular entrances of the divine into the realm of the human as recorded by the Jewish and Christian faith communities which experienced them and continue to live by them. Thus, *Christian Biblical Revelation* is that written history and recollected experience, not only as it has been recorded in the Bible, but also as it is *now* being appropriated (continuing revelation) in the human and religious experience, knowledge and understanding of those living in a Christian faith community, i.e., in people attempting to live according to the reality and consequences of these divine entrances into the realm of the human.

[handwritten margin note: or "divine self-disclosure"]

2. READING AND INTERPRETING THE BIBLE

That any reading of the Bible involves some kind of interpretation of it should be fairly obvious. Even the biblicist attempt just to "let the Bible speak for itself" is itself a kind of interpretation. The way the Bible has been interpreted through the ages makes a fascinating history that can help put our own work into context. These are a few high points of such a history.

Biblical interpretation was already a reality deep with-

in the Old Testament. The Yahwist and Elohist accounts
(tenth to eighth centuries B.C.) are already interpretations
of earlier events and accounts. This is even more true of the
later biblical authors, the Deuteronomists, Prophets, Priestly Writers, Psalmists, and the Chronicler. All of them, in
various ways, were interpreting already existing sources
which, at least in the later years, were already looked upon,
at least to some extent, as "Scripture." The Qumran sectari-
ans who produced the Dead Sea Scrolls very obviously interpreted Scripture in the light of their own vision of reality.
Except that the vision was different, this too is exactly what
Jesus did, and the New Testament writers after him.

As we follow this history of biblical interpretation
through the first few Christian centuries when the New
Testament writings themselves gradually came to be recognized as Sacred Scripture, it is fascinating to see our fore-
bears in faith struggling with very much the same kinds of
problems with biblical interpretation that trouble us even
today.

The lack of perfect harmony between the Gospels was
apparently noted and struggled with very early, as attested
by the great popularity of Tatian's *Diatessaron,* the first
serious attempt (shortly after A.D. 150) to harmonize the
Gospel differences. Translation problems were there even
before the New Testament was written. Jesus spoke and
preached in Aramaic, which was apparently also the moth-
er-tongue of the apostles; and yet the entire New Testament
is written in Greek, the lingua franca of the ancient Medi-
terranean world. Moreover, these New Testament authors
apparently knew the Old Testament only (or at least predominantly) in the Septuagint Greek translation, or some
variation of it. Greek-speaking Jews and, as far as we can
determine, most early Christians looked upon this translation as "inspired." Finally, no less and perhaps much more
than we, the early Christians had their literalist-fundamen-
talist versus spiritualist-rationalist tensions. The most fam-
ous focus of this tension was Origen of Alexandria and
Caesarea who emphasized the spiritual (= in Christ) meaning that gives life over against the merely literal or historical (= "Jewish") meaning that kills. But to many of his
fellow Christians, Origen's spiritual interpretations, which
sometimes developed into highly imaginative allegory, did

not adequately safeguard the literal, historical truth of the Bible. The battle was on.

Ultimately, both sides and all of Christianity for many centuries were the losers. Origen was forced to move from Alexandria under pressure, and long after his death he was condemned as a heretic (if that was done with *any* justice at all has been seriously questioned by recent historical study). In the polarization of the positions that followed—the Logos theology, divinization themes and allegorism of the Alexandrians over against the incarnationalism and literal-historical interpretation of the Antiocheans—much of the worst of both positions was preserved. What was not preserved were two particular skills whose absence helps account for the fact that biblical exegesis seems to be a relative newcomer to the theological scene. These skills were Origen's meticulous care (not equaled again until the renaissance) for the philological foundations of exegesis, and his consistent sensitivity (not surpassed until the rise of modern redaction-criticism) to the theological importance of the differences between the Gospels and other possible parallel texts.

The fact that the Antiochean historical-literal camp won the field and held it so strongly until modern times helps account for the agonizing difficulty that so many now have in accepting the Christian validity of a historical-critical approach to Scripture. The spiritual roots of all the major Christian confessions go back to a time when a literal-historical approach was taken for granted as the only way for a Christian to read and interpret the Bible. The early Christians, of course, did not have the burden of this long history, but neither did they have access to what has become for us the central key to the achievements of modern exegesis: methods for unraveling the history of how the biblical books came to be written the way they are.

These methods presuppose the development of modern text criticism whose major beginning we owe to the Renaissance humanists. But the major breakthrough began some two hundred years ago when the enlightenment began to subject the Bible to rational criticism. The battle lines that were then drawn, biblical faith versus scientific skepticism or unbelief, still mar the landscape of biblical reading and interpretation. The nineteenth century myth that true history means total, pure objectivity, free of presuppositions and subjectivity and of every influence of fantasy and imagination (which rationalists tended to equate with religion and faith), has only recently been demolished, theoretically at least, by modern hermeneutics. With scientific scholarship demonstrating ever more massively that a purely literal interpretation of the Bible cannot stand, and while both sides still assumed that the Bible, and especially the Gospels, were to be read as history, even a theoretical solution was hard to come by.

Now, some two hundred years after the Enlightenment began to cast its rationalizing, analytic eye on the Bible, scholars have succeeded in gradually developing genuinely scientific methods of studying the origins, context, nature and original meaning of biblical texts. These methods constitute what is commonly referred to as the *historical-critical method.* Not all scholars agree on these methods and their application, and there remains strong criticism, especially from the conservative biblicist or fundamentalist branches of Christianity, as to whether such scientific (i.e., "secular") methods are appropriate or even possible ways of approaching Sacred Scripture and of making it accessible as nourishment for the living faith of the Christian community. Nevertheless, the historical-critical method remains the most common means (and for many the only respectable means) of an intellectually critical scholarly approach to the Bible. Since it is the overwhelmingly dominant approach among biblical scholars, and especially in the CBA, it must obviously be central in the work of this task force even if some aspects of it, or the claims that some make for it, may be subject to challenge.

3. THE HISTORICAL-CRITICAL METHOD

The term "historical-critical method" is often used in such a way as to assume that the reader knows what the author means by it. However, it can have a whole variety of meanings ranging from just the particular technical skills (philological, literary, historical, etc.) an exegete uses to approach the biblical text to a full-scale philosophy and theology. In the former sense, we are referring specifically to the technical tools available to the exegete regardless of his or her hermeneutical (= philosophical-theological) inclinations. This is the sense in which we will use the term in this section. In the latter sense, "historical-critical method" signifies a full-scale hermeneutic, a "higher method" expressing the author's whole Weltanschauung. This is the meaning which the word "method" has in such things as Lonergan's *Method in Theology* or Gadamer's *Truth and Method.* This is the meaning we will primarily have in mind as we discuss the controversy about the historical-critical method in the next section. This distinction is not intended to suggest that there can be such a thing as a supposition-less use of the technical tools of exegesis, but more about that later. Perhaps we may find it convenient to refer to the former meaning with the phrase "historical-critical tools" and leave the well-known phrase "historical-critical method" to its more hermeneutical, higher-method range of meanings.

a. TEXT CRITICISM

This refers to the methods used to determine what is the most original, purest form of the biblical text. Except for the Qumran scrolls and a few papyrus fragments, no extant text of the Bible, Old or New Testament, stands any closer to the original than the fourth century A.D. For all that, the Bible is the most thoroughly witnessed document to come from the ancient world. But this very wealth is sometimes a problem; not all the codices and manuscripts agree in every detail; and in a few instances the differences affect important points of meaning. Since it is the *original text* that most Christians hold to be the inspired text, the intensively demanding philological analysis used to establish the biblical text as accurately as possible is the beginning of all biblical scholarship.

b. PHILOLOGY *language (word) study*

Beyond the study of Hebrew and Greek, at least a dozen other ancient Near Eastern languages have relevance in subsidiary but important ways for our understanding of the biblical text. Just as every exegete must be able to use at least the results of text criticism, so too must every exegete be enough of a philologist, at least in the principal biblical languages, to have a comfortable control over the tools of philology as they relate to biblical exegesis (familiarity with the structure and grammar of the languages, lexica, concordances, etc.).

c. SOURCE CRITICISM

This studies, by means of analysis of its probable or possible earlier forms of literary sources, how the biblical text came to take its present form. The best known examples of this are, in the Old Testament, the identification and study of at least four major sources (Jahwist, Elohist, Deuteronomist, Priestly) which went into the formation of the Pentateuch. Best known in the New Testament is the "two-source theory" which studies the way the Gospels of Matthew and Luke were apparently composed in large part from two previously existing sources: the Gospel of Mark and a hypothetical collection of 230–250 verses, usually designated as Q, of the sayings of Jesus. Source criticism, both in the Old Testament and the New Testament, has proven its usefulness over many years of fruitful exegetical results that have contributed significantly to our knowledge and understanding of the Bible. Ultimately, however, no matter how useful and well-established, these methods remain, for the most part, not absolutely proven fact but theories arrived at by extrapolation from the existing texts.

d. TRADITION CRITICISM

Similar to and sometimes used as a synonym for source criticism, tradition criticism can, in fact, be complementary to or in competition with source criticism. It studies specifically the processes of transmission, most especially oral transmission, which led to the formation of the text as it now is. It has a variety of names: oral transmission, tradition history, history of traditions, or the German words

Traditionsgeschichte or *Überlieferungsgeschichte.* When applied to the Old Testament it can be an invaluable auxiliary tool for unlocking the meaning of a text or for affording a glimpse into the events that stood behind or accompanied the formation of the text. In the New Testament it can be used in conjunction with source criticism or, especially among scholars of conservative or biblicist leanings, as an alternate explanation of how the Gospels took their present form. Like source criticism, this method produces not facts but, by extrapolation and comparison, explanations and theories which have varying degrees of possibility or probability.

e. FORM CRITICISM

This is a study of the particular literary forms of literary genres found in the Bible: narrative (historical or fictional), law texts, cult legends, proverbs, hymns, parables and similitudes, paradigms, miracle stories, dialogues, dominical sayings, editorial comment by the biblical writer, etc. A certain common-sense awareness of literary forms has always at least implicitly accompanied every intelligent reading of the Bible; e.g., a normal human being instinctively recognizes the difference between a parable and an historical account (or between a detective story and a police report), although not necessarily in every instance. However, beyond this common-sense awareness, form criticism, especially in the study of the Gospels, has been developed in this century into a sophisticated tool for identifying and then studying the primary units or building blocks (pericopes) which make up the biblical text. In itself, form criticism can be relatively neutral in its presuppositions. In fact, however, it was developed first by scholars with strong existentialist (at times also rationalist or reductionist) leanings who dismissed the search for the historical Jesus as irrelevant and were interested primarily in how the faith of the primitive communities formed the Gospels. This led some to look on form criticism not as a helpful tool for study but as an insidious tool in the service of an anti-faith, rational reductionism.

f. REDACTION CRITICISM

This studies the editorial contribution or the specific "theology" of the individual biblical writers. Its most intensive application has been to the four Gospels. In many ways it is a logical further development from form criticism which enables the exegete to identify and study more intensively those passages, elements and aspects of a Gospel which seem to be due specifically to the particular evangelist or community from which the evangelist comes. As a methodological tool it can be either relatively free of, or heavily freighted with, presuppositions.

g. STRUCTURAL CRITICISM *recent in its application to biblical studies*

This studies the biblical text, much as any other literary text would be studied, in terms of the patterns and structures of human thinking, imagining and feeling contained or reflected in it. It is used predominantly by those who have a basically structuralist view of human reality (i.e., that human reality and experience takes place according to recognizable a-temporal and transcultural patterns of thought and experience that are basic to the human condition as such). Whether it can be a fruitful exegetical tool also for those unsympathetic to a structuralist view of reality is not yet clear.

h. LITERARY CRITICISM. RHETORICAL CRITICISM

Among biblical scholars, "literary criticism" has generally been used to refer to what we have called source criticism and tradition criticism. Only recently has it come also to be used to refer to the application to the Bible of the methods of literary analysis used in profane literary criticism. Rhetorical criticism is also a fairly new term in biblical scholarship. It seems to refer specifically to the use of the methods of literary criticism to study the rhetorical structure or logical, meaning-content of biblical texts. At present it seems to be used primarily by Old Testament scholars.

i. HISTORY OF RELIGIONS. THE COMPARATIVE STUDY
   OF RELIGION

This is an auxiliary discipline for biblical studies. Its most precise title is the German *Religionswissenschaft* for which there is no precise English equivalent. The discipline, which studies the similarities and relationships between the forms and practices of different religions, is represented by a great variety of conceptions and "schools," not all of which find a respectable balance between the normative and the descriptive. In the early part of this century, many scholars, on the basis of often superficial and faulty historical analyses, attempted to prove the dependence of the Old and New Testaments on the non-biblical religions of their natural environment. However, the application of the discipline to the Bible has gradually outgrown what was often a relatively superficial reductionism and become an important, and in some cases indispensable, tool of exegesis. The Scandinavian and British branches of the "Myth and Ritual School" have developed from it. Today it is most often associated with the highly regarded contributions of such scholars as A. E. Jensen and M. Eliade in which the phenomenological and historical methods converge to form a "morphology of the sacred."[1]

j. SOCIOLOGICAL ANALYSIS. SOCIOLOGICAL EXEGESIS

Over the past decade or so, biblical scholars have increasingly been attempting to improve the historical-critical method by paying greater attention to the social dimension of the biblical text. Until recently, attention to social factors tended to be subsumed under analyses of historical diachronic sequences to the neglect of social synchronic interaction. But scholars have recently begun to study the *social facts,* the *social history,* the *social organization, forces* and *institutions,* and the *social worlds* of the communities which produced the different parts of the Bible. Gerd Theissen in Germany and John Gager in the United States seem to be the leaders on their respective continents. Elliott suggests that in addition to sociological *analysis* of social facts, social history, etc., there is also needed a sociologically oriented *exegesis* of individual *texts.* Doing this involves a method to which he gives the more comprehensive designation: "literary-historical-sociological-theological analysis."[2]

4. THE CONTROVERSY ABOUT THE HISTORICAL-CRITICAL METHOD

(As part of the work of the task force, Paul Jurkowitz described and analyzed current disagreements about the usefulness of the historical-critical method—disagreements which surfaced among the members of the task force—and presented reasons for his personal position. We have used his research and analysis extensively in this section, although our analysis and our position differ somewhat from his.)

There has always been a certain amount of controversy connected with the historical-critical method. In recent years, however, this controversy has intensified. Some, who were formerly proponents and users of the method, or who at least tolerated it silently, now openly challenge its adequacy or speak of its failure. Much of this challenge and accompanying controversy can be helpfully clarified by distinguising between the "historical-critical tools," as we have suggested calling them, and the historical-critical method taken as a whole hermeneutic or total Weltanschauung. This enables us to pinpoint some of the causes of the controversy:

1. the sheer complexity of the method, even of the "tools" of the method;

2. fundamental differences between seeing the historical-critical method on the one hand as a set of methodological tools, and on the other hand as an embodiment or expression of one's total hermeneutic or Weltanschauung;

3. confusion or lack of consistency in speaking about the immediate practical purposes and functions of the method.

(1) The sheer complexity of the tools of the historical-critical method which we have just described is an obvious cause of controversy. Who but highly trained exegetes can even begin to use such a method? One might well be tempted to concede the method's theoretical validity, but in the end reject it as too complicated to be of use to ethicists, let alone the ordinary Christian. This is a real problem, not just something that bothers the lazy and the inept. For even the most gifted and energetic of Christian ethicists have been unable to integrate the historical-critical method and its results effectively and consistently into their own work. However, common sense forbids us to reject nuclear medicine just because it can be practiced only by a small number of highly trained specialists with sophisticated equipment. So too with the historical-critical method; it may present us with massive problems of theological communication; but if it works, if it brings us closer to the meaning of the Bible and the events of biblical revelation, and if it is the best humanly accessible method we have for doing this, then the answer is surely not to reject it.

(2) The historical-critical method, as we have indicated in the previous section, can be taken not just as a collection of methodological tools but also as an embodiment and application of one's total philosophical and theological hermeneutic. Theologians and exegetes in traditions which emphasize or identify themselves with a *sola Scriptura* principle very often have no ecclesiology or theological system to fall back on when the Bible, or rather, as the logic of their presuppositions dictate, when their method of interpreting the Bible does not seem to provide the answers they need to certain theological and religious questions. The Bible cannot be at fault; therefore it must be the method of interpreting it. But to call the method in question, which one must do if it does not seem to be doing its "job," is to call into question all that one is as a theologian and exegete. For among those with a "lower" ecclesiology, some have a tendency to make the historical-critical method do all by itself

what, to a large extent, Church and ecclesiastical teaching authority does in communities with a high ecclesiology, namely, mediate the Word of God to the people. Others, however, would reject from the outset a hermeneutic that attempts to mediate the Word to the people. For those who accept the mediating role of the historical-critical method, there is tremendous pressure to find answers in the Bible somewhere, to force the method to try to do things it is not equipped to do. Thus, for someone in this position, calling the method into question cannot be done without great courage, anxiety and desperation.

All of this, however, is much less of a problem for those who adhere to a "higher" or "Catholic" principle of ecclesiology, or have a philosophy or Weltanschauung which is not, for all practical purposes, identified with the way they interpret the Bible. Catholic exegetes, for example, have not only been accustomed to an approach to God that employs numerous intermediaries, they are also part of a theological tradition that has used Scripture as only one of several norms. Exegetes in this tradition are not as disturbed by a method whose complexity restricts its use to a learned few. They are also accustomed to being members of a large theological and religious team whose other sections and members can be expected to take the responsibility of providing what the Bible does not seem to have. They are thus under far less pressure to find answers in the Bible somehow.

However, recent developments in Catholic theology, which now sees Scripture and tradition not as separate sources of revelation but as different aspects of *one* source, are bringing the "Protestant" and "Catholic" positions much closer together than one often realizes.[3] Before this development, a Catholic could, with a seemingly cavalier lack of concern, look to the tradition to provide whatever seemed to be lacking in the Bible or one's interpretation of it. In fact, it was not uncommon for Catholics not even to look to the Bible at all. This has now all been changed, at least on the level of theory and official teaching. For it seems that Catholic theologians on the whole have still not dealt effectively with the far-reaching consequences of seeing Scripture *and* tradition, *together,* as *one* source of revelation. When they do, they will probably find themselves sharing more of the anxiety and desperation which accompanies the Protestant's questioning of the perceived inadequacies of the historical-critical method.

Thus, the fundamentally "Catholic" stance from which we write this book causes us to look negatively on the tendency to make the historical-critical method serve as a total Weltanschauung or hermeneutic. At best, that would be forcing the method to do or provide what it cannot; at worst, it would be method arrogating totally to itself an essential function of the whole Church: mediating the Word to the people.

(3) In addition, there are different conceptions about what the historical-critical method does or should do. We can quickly list at least three distinct roles or functions which can be attributed to the method:

a. Reconstructing the events connected with the words of the Bible.

b. Discerning the meaning intended by various human speakers/authors/editors.

c. Discerning what we can about the origin, nature and purpose of the biblical texts without either neglecting or one-sidedly emphasizing a. or b.

(a) Now if successfully reconstructing the events connected with the words of the Bible is considered to be the purpose of the historical-critical method, then it is clear that the method has failed, at least in the sense that it has achieved only limited success. These successes, however, have been real, and in some instances quite significant. We know vastly more than we did one hundred years ago about the events connected with the words of the Bible, and this knowledge has made possible the development of biblical theologies which have already taken their place in or had significant influence on not just the theological life but also on the spiritual, pastoral and homiletic life of the Christian communities. How, then, can one speak of failure? The answer stems from one's expectations. If, for example, one accepts the premise that Scripture will, if approached cor-

rectly, provide us with helpful or usable answers to our
current theological or ethical questions, and this is not happening, then the conclusion is inevitable that the method
must be at fault.

> Many Christians, by reason of their theological po-
> sition or confessional stance, are committed to this
> premise. In many cases, they are looking for some
> kind of direct access to the events recorded in bibli-
> cal revelation because with that, they would be in
> contact with divine revelation in such a way as to
> make superfluous all mediating interpretations of
> the biblical word. Many find the historical-critical
> method makes them even more distant from the
> events connected with the words of the Bible, that it
> undermines the (often uncritical, biblicist) view of
> biblical history on which their faith was built with-
> out replacing it with anything positive. Such per-
> sons cannot but look upon the historical-critical
> method as bankrupt, a failure, if not also a danger-
> ous perversion. We have been associating these
> problems with the unrealistic expectations which
> an uncritical biblicist would typically have of the
> historical-critical method. But such unrealistic ex-
> pectations and their ensuing negative attitudes to-
> ward the historical-critical method, for which
> incautious exegetes are themselves sometimes to
> blame, can actually be found in one form or another
> all across the theological and confessional spec-
> trum.

(b) Similar but quite distinct from the goal of reconstructing the events connected with the words of the Bible is
that of discerning the meaning intended by various human
speakers/authors/editors. This is a more realizable goal,
and the historical-critical method can indeed claim considerable success here. It also seems to be more important and
promising for theological work. In addition, it has special
importance for members of the Catholic Biblical Association because of the way both Pius XII and the Second Vatican Council emphasized that it was the special responsibility of the interpreter of Sacred Scripture to search for and

investigate the "literal" sense of the Bible, that is, "the sense which the human author directly intended and which his words convey."[4]

Recent developments associated with the names of Hans Georg Gadamer, Paul Ricoeur and David Tracy make it advisable to point out that this "literal" sense is *not* two different senses (first, what the author intended, and second, what his words convey) but one sense: i.e., the author's intended meaning *which his words convey.* Gadamer, Ricoeur, Tracy and many others are now correctly pointing out that texts have a life of their own.[5] They reject approaches to the Bible which attempt to discover the text's meaning "by a psychological process of 'empathy' or 'divination' of the author's intention."[6] For, as Ricoeur puts it, "A work of discourse, as a work of art, is an autonomous object at a distance from its authorial intention, from its initial situation (its *Sitz im Leben*), and from its primitive audience. For this reason it is open to an infinite range of interpretations."[7]

We are in sympathy with a position which rejects or at least has strong reservations about a psychological or romantic type of interpretation (as, e.g., proposed by Schleiermacher and Dilthey) which maintains that the reader's/interpreter's goal is to *relive* the inner/outer experience out of which the author produced the text.[8] However, if this approach is seen as an attempt to learn as much as possible about the experience out of which the author produced the text, this is clearly a valid goal for the historical-critical method, for such knowledge enables us to understand better "the sense which the human author directly intended," or the meaning which a text had when it left the author's/redactor's pen.

But Gadamer, Ricoeur and Tracy are indeed right in insisting that biblical texts, like any others, have

a life of their own and that they are in themselves
open to a plurality of interpretations. It is our opinion that any theory of biblical interpretation which
attempts to ignore or reject this is essentially trun-
cated. Now much of the controversy associated with
this discussion stems from an actual or perceived
exclusivity of the respective positions, that is, insisting that this *and this alone* is the way for a Christian to interpret the Bible, or insisting that
investigating the literal sense of the Bible is the
only route to follow.

But if they are not to be exclusive, then we are faced
with the question of the relationship between these
and other methods and approaches. Or, to point the
question, which method or approach has the primacy? To claim that for Catholics this question has
been settled once and for all by the declarations of
Pius XII and the Second Vatican Council is neither
good history nor good theology. When those declarations were made, it was particularly necessary for
the Church to emphasize the independent integrity
of scientific biblical studies and to charge exegetes
with the primary responsibility of scientifically
searching for the sense directly intended by the
human biblical authors. This was needed to reduce
the widespread proof-texting abuse of the Bible in
theology and to make it possible for Catholic theology to be more faithfully in contact with its biblical
foundations. Much progress has been made in this
direction, but the job is far from finished. Indeed it
is hard to foresee a time when investigating the
literal sense (however it may come to be defined)
will not be an indispensable task for the Christian
exegete. And in a certain sense, it may always be
"primary" in the sense that it, or something like it,
must somehow first be established in order to provide some means of discerning which ones of a
"plurality of interpretations" are expressive of or
consonant with Christian biblical revelation. But
even this assessment must be qualified by the obser-

vation that it may imply an understanding of "meaning" in biblical texts which is too narrowly propositional to do justice to the Bible.

In their panel discussion devoted to this issue on August 20, 1980 during the CBA general meeting, David Tracy and Sandra Schneiders explained their carefully nuanced application to the Bible of the principle that texts have a life of their own and are in themselves open to a plurality of meanings. It is obvious that their preferred terminology (at some distance, it seems, from Ricoeur) is not an "infinite range of interpretations" but "openness to a plurality of meanings." They are obviously concerned to reject arbitrariness in determining valid meanings. Much of the discussion with this panel centered around the question of how one judges the validity (this is preferred to the traditional word "truth") of an interpretation. In this context Schneiders pointed out that one of the criteria for a relatively adequate interpretation is the historical-critical method. It also became clear from this discussion that if the traditional teaching about the primary purpose of biblical scholarship were being formulated today, it would probably speak not so restrictedly about "the meaning intended by the human author" but rather or also about the meaning the text or book had when it left the hands of its authors or redactors. The former formulation now seems too narrow, as Brown suggests (see the note at the end of this section). The latter formulation preserves continuity with the traditional teaching while freeing us from attempting the impossible, for modern hermeneutics and sociological analysis are making it increasingly clear that to uncover the meaning intended by the human author of a biblical text may not be a very realistic or practical goal.

In other words, the tools of the historical-critical method are reasonably well suited to investigate the literal meaning of the Bible. The method is effective in investigating what the biblical texts *meant* when they were spoken/written/edited. However, the method is, of itself, not particularly well suited to tell us what the text means now, or how the meaning from then becomes present and active in the world of now, or how the text from then becomes alive and active in the world of now, or what sense to make of meanings which the human author may not have directly intended but which do seem to be consistent with biblical revelation, or how the Bible can be used to help answer questions which were not the questions of its human authors, etc. These questions, which cannot be adequately answered by the historical-critical method alone, are fundamental to a biblically grounded Christian ethic. Christian theology obviously needs to find methodical ways of dealing with them.[9]

In the face of such complexities, some may prefer to stay with the traditional definition of the exegete's task to investigate the sense which the human author directly intended. But that by no means simplifies the task. Take, for example, a text in the Book of Isaiah. What is its literal meaning? Is it what the original redactors of Isaiah's sermons probably meant, or what later redactors meant? Is it what Matthew meant when he used the passage? Is it the meaning that various Christians found in the passage at the time when the Book of Isaiah was accepted as a canonical statement of their faith? It is thus very important, and often not very easy, when talking about the "meaning" of a biblical text, to make it perfectly clear what "meaning" one is talking about. Even phrases like "the literal meaning of the text" and "the canonical form of the text" are ambiguous and require further clarification. But in the end, even if all these safeguards and distinctions could be applied, it would still seem that to try to restrict or channel the role of the historical-critical method solely to search for the meaning intended by the various human speakers/authors/editors is simply too narrow and confining. It seems to imply that "meaning" is something discursive, something that can be reduced to or expressed in propositional or logical form.

The inadequacy of this implication becomes particularly obvious when we look at some of the poetic passages and some of the stories and parables of the Bible.

(c) It is for this reason that we would like to delineate a third role or function of the historical-critical method, one that goes beyond reconstructing, as far as possible, the events connected with the words of the Bible, and one that also goes beyond discerning the meaning intended by various human speakers/authors/editors. We want to see the role of the historical-critical method as something that subordinates these functions to the broader function of discerning what we can about the origin, nature and purpose of the biblical texts. Thus we prefer to see the historical-critical method not as something which makes absolute claims and to which allegiance must be professed or denied, but as a proven, highly useful and also indispensable means of studying both the biblical text and what we have defined more broadly as "Christian biblical revelation" (see above 14). It is a key part of the total process of doing Christian Biblical Ethics which we are attempting to clarify and study in this book. Confer how this fits in with the way we outline this process below in Chapter Three, Section 8, "The Science and the Art of Christian Biblical Ethics" (114–138).

Notes

1. Cf. F.P. de Graeve, "Religion, Comparative Study of," *NCE* 12 (1967) 250–54.

2. Cf. the "Introduction" of John H. Elliott, *A Home for the Homeless: A Sociological Exegesis of 1 Peter, Its Situation and Strategy* (Philadephia: Fortress, 1981) 1–20.

3. The central reference point for these developments is the 1965 Vatican II Dogmatic Constitution on Divine Revelation, *Dei Verbum:* "Sacred tradition and Sacred Scripture, then, are bound closely together and communicate one with the other. For both of them, flowing out from the same divine wellspring, come together in some fashion to form one thing, and move toward the same goal" (*Dei Verbum* 9; *Vatican Council II,* A. Flannery, O.P., General Editor; Collegeville: Liturgical Press, 1975, p. 755). "Sacred tradition and Sacred Scripture make up a single sacred deposit of the Word of God, which is entrusted to the Church.... Yet this magisterium is not superior to the Word of God, but is its servant. It

teaches only what has been handed on to it. At the divine command and with the help of the Holy Spirit, it listens to this devotedly, guards it with dedication and expounds it faithfully. All that it proposes for belief as being divinely revealed is drawn from this single deposit of faith.... Sacred tradition, Sacred Scripture and the magisterium of the Church are so connected and associated that one of them cannot stand without the others" (*Dei Verbum* 10, Flannery 755–56).

4. This formulation is from R. Brown, "Hermeneutics," *The Jerome Biblical Commentary* (Englewood Cliffs: Prentice-Hall, 1968) No. 71:10; II, 607. Vatican II's *Dei Verbum* (Flannery 757) puts it this way: "Seeing that, in Sacred Scripture, God speaks through men in human fashion, it follows that the interpreter of Sacred Scripture, if he is to ascertain what God has wished to communicate to us, should carefully search out the meaning which the sacred writers really had in mind, that meaning which God had thought well to manifest through the medium of their words." Cf. Pius XII's 1943 "Divino afflante Spiritu" Nos. 23–27 (Denzinger-Schönmetzer, *Enchiridion Symbolorum* 3828 [2293] (33rd ed.; Freiburg/New York: Herder, 1965). As we will see below, recent developments in hermeneutics and sociological analysis suggest that this literal sense might be better expressed in terms of the meaning a text had when it left the hands of its author or final redactor.

5. For H.G. Gadamer, cf. *Truth and Method* (trans. and ed. from the 2nd German ed. by G. Barden and J. Cumming; New York: Seabury, 1975). For P. Ricoeur, cf. *Interpretation Theory: Discourse and the Surplus of Meaning* (Fort Worth: Texas Christian University, 1976); "The Task of Hermeneutics" and "The Hermeneutical Functions of Distanciation," *Philosophy Today* 17 (1973); "Philosophy and Religious Language," *Journal of Religion* 54 (1974) 71–85. For D. Tracy, cf. *Blessed Rage for Order: The New Pluralism in Theology* (New York: Seabury, 1975) esp. 44, 49, 74, 76, 78; *The Analogical Imagination: Christian Theology and the Culture of Pluralism* (New York: Crossroad, 1981) esp. 115-24.

6. D. Tracy, *Blessed Rage for Order* 76.

7. "Philosophy and Religious Language" 75.

8. Gadamer describes Schleiermacher's psychological interpretation (as compared with his grammatical interpretation) in this way: "It is ultimately a divinatory process, a placing of oneself within the mind of the author, an apprehension of the 'inner origin' of the composition of a work, a re-creation of the creative act. Thus understanding is a reproduction related to an original production ... a reconstruction that starts from the vital moment of conception, the 'germinal decision' as the composition's point of

organization" (*Truth and Method* 164). "... [for Schleiermacher]
the ultimate ground of all understanding must always be a divinatory act of corresponding genius, the possibility of which depends
on a pre-existing connection between all individualities" (*Truth
and Method* 166).

9. The best treatment of these and related problems is to be
found in R.E. Brown, *The Critical Meaning of the Bible* (New
York/Ramsey: Paulist, 1981) esp. Chapter Two, "What the Biblical
Word Meant and What It Means" 23–44. Brown distinguishes three
levels of meaning: (1) the *literal sense* "which a book has when it
has left the pen of the author (and/or redactor)"; (2) "the *canonical sense* which it has when seen in the context of its Testament or
of the whole Bible, especially when the change of meaning is
substantial" (p. 32). (3) The third level is the *"biblical meaning,"*
the meaning which a biblical text comes to have in the life of the
Church and which may be quite different from the literal sense.
Brown contends that "the way in which the Church in its life,
liturgy, and theology comes to understand the Bible [this process
has continued from the moment of canon formation to the present
moment] is constitutive of 'biblical meaning' " (p. 34).

Chapter Two

THE BIBLE AND THEOLOGY

This chapter is integrally related to the next: "The Bible and Ethics." The reasons for dividing the material into two chapters are methodological, strategic and practical. Methodologically, *this chapter relates to the next as the whole to a part. It will try to provide the broader theological context for the more specific approaches of the next chapter.* Strategically, *the authors are very conscious that their work is an incomplete and defective document. But they also hope that it will serve as a catalyst for clarifying, correcting and amplifying discussion among a broad range of theologians. We think that this might be more easily achieved by a document whose skeletal structure is somewhat exaggerated rather than by something too neatly packaged into a supposedly integrated and definitive whole.* Practically, *although we have become increasingly aware that the whole first part of this book should ideally be presented in a more integrated way, we decided not to attempt at this time the extensive rethinking and rewriting that this would entail, in order not to delay any further the appearance of this (essentially interim) report.*

1. THE GENERAL SITUATION

The interrelationship of the Bible and theology is obviously central in Christian theology. It is something with

35

which every age must come to terms, especially our own age
in which the context of theology, or what we understand as
exegesis, hermeneutics, culture and history, is undergoing
considerable change. In terms of a geopolitical metaphor,
the former "colonial-imperialist" domination of the biblical
sciences by dogmatic theologians has been replaced in recent times by the successful counterattack of modern biblical science which has exposed the ignorant misuse of the
Bible by dogmatic theologians, established its own autonomy, and fairly effectively sealed off the territory of biblical
studies as an area into which only the exegete is allowed to
enter. One might now describe the relationship between the
camps of dogma and exegesis as one of jealously guarded
"detente." There are no ongoing hostilities, but anyone ven-
turing into the other's airspace may not receive a gentle
welcome. Yet, more and more theologians and exegetes are
aware that both our Christian and our scholarly vocation
calls us to work not only toward supportive cooperation, but
also beyond that to a genuine integration of the biblical and
theological sciences. Right now, however, we are falling far
short of the goal.

As a result, a whole range of fundamental theological
questions (which the theologian, without the technical
skills and methodological attitudes of the exegete, cannot
adequately handle, and with which the exegete, without the
systematizing expertise of the theologian, cannot cope) are
suffering neglect. The themes of revelation, inspiration, tradition, authoritative sources and guides of interpretation
don't seem to command much attention. Among Roman
Catholics, for example, most theologians are not even aware
that as many as half of the texts cited or referred to in the
documents of Vatican II seem not to be used or applied in a
manner consistent with their "literal sense" as that is determined by the norms of modern scientific exegesis in accordance with the directives of *Divino afflante Spiritu* and
several authoritative documents since then (see above 33
n.4). *Mysterium Ecclesiae*—a document from the Sacred
Congregation for the Doctrine of the Faith (6/24/73) cf. *The
Pope Speaks* 18/2 (1973) 145–57—points out the need for
attention to the hermeneutical problem. Granted, the constantly shifting terrain of hermeneutics makes this task

doubly difficult. Nevertheless, the reality of ongoing interpretation and the fact and propriety of reinterpretation has been recognized even in circles as conservative as the Roman congregations. However, as Roland Murphy points out, there remains a severe time lag from both a pastoral and theological point of view.[1]

What is needed is a change in climate, on both sides, so that the theologian or exegete thrashing about awkwardly in strange territory will not be treated as an incompetent intruder (which might indeed be the case) but welcomed supportively, even affectionately, as the long-lost brother, Joseph. This will be anything but easy because, in welcoming bumbling brothers and sisters, one must also find constructive and non-threatening ways of pointing out the inadequacies of their positions. A fuzzy irenicism is not the answer.

Beyond a change in climate, a change in tactics is also called for. This refers specifically to the way exegetes and theologians plan their work, and particularly to the use they make of the opportunities for collaboration afforded by the existence of strong and active professional societies in the various disciplines. This is too important a task to leave to the private initiative of those individuals who might feel the urge to barge in where no angel dares tread.

And, finally, a long-term change in strategy is also needed. This might well begin with a serious rethinking of the theories and priorities of theological, ministerial and pastoral education. Two major problem areas immediately come to mind: (1) the general education in theology of those being prepared for ministerial work of various kinds in the Church, and (2) the specialized education of those preparing for academic careers in one or other of the theological disciplines. In an age of increasing specialization, are we doing enough to see to the development and continuance of a body of scholars who are even *able* to function in a coordinating and integrating way among the various theological disciplines? This too will not be easy to bring about. How can the drawbacks of superficiality be avoided? The more obvious immediate answers involve degrees of involvement in and commitment to what we might call a "community of scholarship" that few of us have seriously thought about.

[handwritten marginalia:] Is this pro-scholar insistence needing a balance with the biblical human experience of non-scholars?

[handwritten footnote:] ✻ Irenics = Theology dealing with the promotion of peace and unity among the churches.

2. THE CHRISTOCENTRICITY OF CHRISTIAN THEOLOGY AND CHRISTIAN ETHICS

Jesus Christ dying and rising, yesterday, today and tomorrow, the Alpha and the Omega, the one mediator for all, the head of the body whose members we are, into which body we are baptized so that we become living stones in the temple which is his body, the Church, etc.; this Jesus Christ is the way, the truth and the life—in short, the total reality of all Christian existence. This is a truth so obvious that it hardly needs to be mentioned to an educated Christian. And it is the living core and heart of what we have been calling "Christian biblical revelation." Yet we know from experience how easy it is, as we work our way into the increasingly complicated tasks of Christian theology and ethics, to lose sight of this central reality. We must keep him constantly before us, even when dealing with those who do not recognize Jesus Christ as Lord. In those instances, the challenge is to discover ways of conceiving and formulating our tasks that will be supportive of and not alienating to their search for truth and the good life. For the one who calls them is the same Lord who calls us.

But also, as we work out the Christocentricity of Christian theology and ethics, we should be aware that not all Christian theological traditions look on this in the same way. Eastern Orthodox Christianity is, by contrast, much more Trinitarian. Some Orthodox, for example, would look on Western Christian ethics as being Christocentric to the point of being Christo-monist.

Theocentric - presence too of Father + Spirit

3. SOME BASIC POSITIONS ON THE RELATIONSHIP OF THE BIBLE TO CHRISTIAN THEOLOGY

We have already given above (14) a broad definition of "Christian biblical revelation" which encompasses the three major "moments" of Christian theology: that of revelation (biblical revelation in the strict sense), that of history and tradition, and that of the present looking to the future. As already remarked, the central reality, event, person in all of these "moments" is Jesus Christ who is, or has been, present to them, but in different ways. This presence is strongest or, more accurately perhaps, most extensive in the "moment" of biblical revelation, and especially in the New Testament which centers around the reality of the historical incarnation. Thus, this first "moment," the biblical "moment," in which God's self-disclosure takes place in a concreteness and fullness that essentially distinguishes it from every other kind of revelation, private, ongoing, continuing, or whatever, contains not only the starting point but also the very heart and center and, in a certain way, also the ultimate goal of all Christian theology. It will thus be helpful to have a basic overview of the different ways in which Christians can conceive of the relationship between their theology and the Bible. As we come to those positions which we think are more adequate to the realities of Christian theology, the reader will note that our term of reference is not just the Bible narrowly conceived, but "Christian biblical revelation" in the broad sense we have described above.

Accepting some unavoidable oversimplification, we can distinguish four basic positions. We do not conceive them as wholly distinct positions but rather as distinguishable stages of a single movement or continuum.

1. The attitude of biblicism, or strictly literal interpretation, or what we might call a kind of pre-Nicene fundamentalism. It holds that Christian theology is essentially evangelical preaching. It holds that a theology which departs from the language and concepts of the Bible is invalid, or simply not Christian.

2. Christian theology is basically systematized exegesis. In other words, all really Christian theology is basically, or ultimately, biblical theology.

3. Christian theology must be at least foundationally biblical, i.e., its *ultimate, real* center and foundation is biblical (regardless of whether or not the connec-

tion to that foundation is explicit, or consciously made).

4. Christian theology is theology done in a Christian context, i.e., it does not actually or really have a foundation in biblical revelation. (Some who are doing this kind of theology may really *think* that it has such a foundation.)

The first position sins by excess, and the fourth by defect. Further, while not wholly rejecting the second position, it seems to us that the third position comes closest to defining what Christian theology should be.

The *first position* takes the place of the Bible in Christian theology so seriously that it does not allow theology to express itself in anything but the propositions, images and concepts of the Bible. Since this, in its strict form at least, is not a live option among critical theologians, we pass over it without further comment.

The *second position,* that Christian theology is *systematized exegesis,* has much to be said for it. It takes seriously the relationship between theology and the Bible, and also manages a kind of unity or identity between them. Happily then, all truly Christian theology is also biblical theology. However, on further reflection, a whole series of fundamental questions arise which eventually call into question the adequacy of conceiving Christian theology as only systematized exegesis. If indeed systematized exegesis, then by what system? If exegesis, then by what hermeneutics? If such questions are answerable, likely enough it will be by one who is already in possession of a traditionally tried and proven coherent system, and who has a basic understanding of the tools of exegesis, but who is also largely unaffected by the more prickly problems of modern hermeneutics. Can theology, if it is only systematized exegesis, be truly open to the realities and problems of contemporary human experience, and to the ways in which God's Spirit is now working in the world? It seems to us that theology conceived as systematized exegesis will ultimately fall short of expressing the fullness of what theology is or should be in the modern world.

The *third position* defines Christian theology as at least

foundationally biblical, and insists that its ultimate and real foundation must actually be biblical. It attempts to overcome the restrictive limitations of the second position while still maintaining the reality of the relationship to biblical revelation. But this relationship need not be explicit or consciously made.

This is the position which comes closest to expressing adequately and accurately the necessary relationship of Christian theology to biblical revelation. We will return to it shortly.

The *fourth position* defines Christian theology merely as that which is done in a Christian context. It seems to err as much by deficiency as does the first position by excess, for it affirms that, essentially, theology is not grounded in biblical revelation. In rejecting this position we are, in effect, labeling as "not Christian" most of what is generally understood as philosophical theology or natural theology. No derogation is intended, but only the insistence that in terms of specifically Christian theology and the specifically Christian theological question of the relationship between the Bible and theology, this fourth position seems to rest outside the pale. We are, then, questioning whether any theological analysis or study which does not have a real and at least implicit relationship to biblical revelation really merits the name of Christian in the strict sense in which we are using it here.

But to return to the third position: within it, one can distinguish three ways in which biblical revelation can be related to theology:

POSITION 3/1: THE BIBLE PROVIDES THE SOURCE,
           BUT IS NOT INVOLVED IN THE PROCESS
           OF THEOLOGICAL INVESTIGATIONS

The Bible, or Christian biblical revelation, provides the source, foundation, starting point or background for theology in general or for a particular doctrine or theological problem. However, once the process of theological investigation is underway, exegesis or biblical theology no longer, for all practical purposes, plays an active part.

It is possible to ask whether this does justice to the ideal of a truly biblical Christian theology. Is it enough to have the Bible merely provide the starting point, but not be involved in the theological process itself? A provocative question, since few theologians command the skill to incorporate exegesis into their theology. Regardless of how one reacts to it, some theological problems do not seem to be solvable only (or adequately only) on this level.

POSITION 3/2: THE BIBLE PROVIDES THE SOURCE AND
                IS ALSO INVOLVED IN THE PROCESS
                OF THEOLOGICAL INVESTIGATION

> Not only does the Bible, or biblical revelation, provide the source, foundation, starting point or background for theology in general, or for a particular doctrine or theological problem, but exegesis or biblical theology is also actively involved *in the very process* of theological investigation.

> This means much more than just taking up a problem or doctrine from some biblical source, studying it according to one or more of the various methods available to the theologian, and then reflecting on how the conclusions reached relate to the evidence of the Bible. For this would be an instance of *Position 3/1* in which one begins with the Bible, and perhaps returns to it, but in between is not involved with the Bible.

This is the ideal position. When (and if) it is realized, Christian theology can be fully Christian and fully biblical. But is this realistic and feasible? *Realistically,* it does not seem possible to ground all theological doctrines and problems, and certainly not all the problems that a Christian theologian should deal with in the world today, directly on the Bible. And of course it is also possible that some Christian theological problems may not require that exegesis or biblical theology be present in the process of their solution.

Thus, if this is the ideal, it has to be prefaced with the qualification "to the extent applicable." In terms of *feasibility,* one cannot avoid the practical question: Who can live up to this ideal? The normal course of education for a career in academic theology does not supply one with the needed skills. But would it not at least be possible so to reform theological education, so to stimulate cooperation and cooperative work between theologians and exegetes, that we narrow the now widening chasm between theology and exegesis?

POSITION 3/3: THE BIBLE DOES NOT PROVIDE THE SOURCE, BUT IS INVOLVED IN THE PROCESS OF THEOLOGICAL INVESTIGATION

This position assumes that there are Christian theological problems which do not originate in the Bible, but in whose investigation exegesis or biblical theology should be actively involved.

This is also an ideal position, along with *3/2.* All that has been said regarding the reality and feasibility of *3/2* would seem, mutatis mutandis, to apply here. This is the particular position which overcomes the major limitation of *Position 2* (systematized exegesis); for one would not want to define as outside the pale of Christian theology that significant complex of doctrines and problems which seem to take their origin more from tradition, history and human experience than directly from the Bible.

At the risk of falling into a kind of biblical reductionism, let us propose that *the touchstone of whether or not theology is genuinely Christian in the fullest sense of the word is the question of whether or not exegesis or biblical theology is involved in its process.* This is not an attempt to define out of existence those cases where the involvement of exegesis or biblical theology in the theological process does not seem to apply. In such cases one can only insist that the theologian be alert to compare or confront the results of the investigation with biblical revelation to the extent applicable and possible. But in those cases where exegesis/

biblical theology *can* be involved in the theological process, we insist that it also *should.*

We are proposing something more than a process whereby, at every step along the way, the theologian stops to compare and confront with biblical revelation the interpretation of the evidence, the argument itself, and its final conclusions. The ideal is to have *exegesis and biblical theology be internal to the process of theological argumentation,* not just an external point of comparison or confrontation. This implies that the mark is being missed rather badly by those theologians who think that the problem might be solved if only exegetes would make their findings available in a reasonably intelligible fashion. It is important, of course, that exegetes do this, and that theologians make conscientious use of this information. But that alone is far from enough (although it would be a marvelous improvement over the present situation). Failure to allow the Bible its proper role *within* the process of theological argumentation can result in theological conclusions which are inadequate and even erroneous.

and scarey

A comment on the (biographically) continuous nature of these typical positions: A fairly common developmental pattern is to begin with the *first position,* reading the Bible literally and uncritically. (For example, the great majority of entering college students seem to be biblicist/fundamentalist in orientation—or at least think that this is the faith-position their Church expects them to have.) But as one matures personally and intellectually, one often enters into or passes through a stage corresponding to our *second position* in which theology (or preaching) could be characterized as systematized exegesis. But, as one becomes more aware of the inadequacies of this position, there is a tendency to move to one or more of the phases of our *third position* in which the Bible provides, if possible, the *source,* and is also involved in the *process* of theological investigation. But, in some circumstances and for some people, even this does not seem to be possible (or worth struggling for), and one moves, or slips, into a *fourth position* in which one does not attempt to ground one's theology or ethics in Christian biblical revelation. It is also possible to move in the reverse direction, or to shift positions without necessarily or obvi-

a developmental overview

ously passing through the intermediate steps. Education and personal experience, especially experiences of conversion (intellectual and/or moral and/or religious), usually serve as a catalyst for changes.

But what is happening to one's faith and one's understanding in all this? The process of moving from position one is obviously a movement toward greater intellectual sophistication. Ideally, it should also be a movement toward greater spiritual and intellectual integration in the Christian person. However, this movement could also be one in which faith and belief in the Bible as the foundation of Christian life plays less and less a role in one's theology and life. Development toward greater intellectual, critical and methodological sophistication is not the cause of a weakening or loss of faith—if anything, quite the opposite. But these are so often parallel phenomena that it is easy to understand how one could come to the idea that the histori-cal-*critical* method is detrimental to Christian faith and life. But this leads us to the themes of faith development and character development as foundational starting points for Christian ethics, themes which we cannot enter into at this point.

[handwritten marginal note: thought provoking!]

4. SOME METHODOLOGICAL AND HERMENEUTICAL OBSERVATIONS

We will attempt here only to tidy up a few of the more obvious loose ends that have thus far been left dangling. As is by now obvious, we have been proceeding from the assumption of the existence of a *Christian biblical revelation* sufficiently concrete and accessible to provide a necessary internal component for Christian theological reflection. This is not the place to provide the warrants for this assumption, but it is appropriate at least to call to mind again what we understand by "Christian biblical revelation." It is more than just exegesis or biblical studies as these are commonly understood, for it encompasses the three major "moments" of theology mentioned above (39): revelation,

history and tradition, present and future, and it is not unrelated to what even conservative theology is increasingly
aware of as "continuing revelation."

> *Christian biblical revelation,* as described above,
> (14) is the written record and faith-recollection of
> particular entrances of the divine into the realm of
> the human as recorded by the Jewish and Christian
> faith communities which experienced them and
> continue to live by them. Thus, *Christian biblical
> revelation* is that written history and recollected
> experience, not only as it has been recorded in the
> Bible, but also as it is *now* being appropriated (con-
> tinuing revelation) in the human and religious ex-
> perience, knowledge and understanding of those
> living in a Christian faith community, i.e., in people
> attempting to live according to the reality and con-
> sequences of these divine entrances into the realm
> of the human.

Another reason for favoring the term "Christian biblical revelation" is that it can more easily encompass the
point of Kelsey's remark that the theologian's task is not so
much to answer the question "What does the Bible say? but
rather the question "What is God using the Bible to say?"[2]
The point is that the theologian should be trying to draw
attention to the dynamic function of the Bible, "to 'what God
is using the Bible for,' viz., shaping Christian existence."
This involves far more than just translating the Bible. It is a
matter of the way one perceives and experiences, in and
through the Scriptures, God's saving activity. However, as
Kelsey asserts:

> Shaping is abstract. Every actual set of theological
> proposals (i.e., every "theological position") is given
> its peculiar shape by some concrete construal of the
> mode in which that "shaping" takes place. And that,
> we have suggested, is an imaginative act, not an
> exegesis of the "meaning" of what God "says"
> through the Bible (Kelsey 214).

To expand this a bit, note how Kelsey accounts for differences in theological positions:

> They are the result of irreducible differences among imaginative construals of the mode of the presence of God;[3] and they are evidence that this act of the imagination is decisive for the particular characteristics that give a theological position its particular specificity and most deeply separates it from other "theological positions" (Kelsey 163).

As a result, the reasons why and the ways in which theologians use the Bible "are never 'theological-position-neutral.' They always derive their force from a logically prior imaginative judgment about how best to construe the mode of God's presence. That is, they always presuppose a prior decision about what it is to be a Christian" (Kelsey 166).

Exegesis, Kelsey remarks (pp. 198–201), involves studying biblical texts either as *texts* or as *Scripture*. Taking them as texts, one may study a biblical text:

i. *as an historical source* which itself has historical sources, or

ii. *as it stands,* i.e., how it was understood by its original audience (= approximately what Roman Catholic theology understands as the "literal sense" of the text; cf. above 28).

But when one studies a biblical text

iii. *precisely as Christian Scripture,* one is involved in something much more than what is commonly understood as scientific exegesis.

> Such an exegesis would result in judgments about it precisely as used in certain rulish and normative ways in the Church's common life to help nurture and reform her self-identity. Taken that way, an exegetical judgment is part of the theological task. It

[handwritten margin note: If tradition is never unscriptural, not ordaining women is not true tradition. [etc.!]]

is guided in important ways by theological judgments about the nature of the Church's task and
about just how Scripture ought to be used in the
Church's common life to help keep her faithful to
that task. In particular, it involves a judgment about
which of several patterns in Scripture are normative for doing theology and ought therefore to be the
principal subject of the exegesis. And those judgments, I have been arguing, are decisively shaped
by an imaginative judgment about the mode in
which God makes himself present in and through
those uses of scripture, a judgment that is logically
prior to any exegetical judgments about the text
(Kelsey 198–99).

In other words, the beginning of the whole process is
theological, or, more accurately, *theological-imaginative.*
The beginning is a *discrimen* which is a prior act of the
imagination, a theological vision which determines the patterns to be studied. Thus, in a real way, and inevitably,
theology sets the agenda for exegesis. We are back within
the inevitable hermeneutical circle. Is there any escape
from it? Recent theology and exegesis can suggest perhaps a
cautious optimism. For not only are theologians increasingly alert to the relativity and historical contingency of the
discrimen, the imaginative-theological vision from which
they operate, and thus are more open to a broadening and
development of that vision, but also theologians and exegetes are now accustomed to distinguish fairly easily *exegesis iii* (texts studied *precisely as Christian Scripture*) from
exegesis i and *ii. Exegesis i* and *ii* are relatively free of the
narrowing, aberrational effects of the hermeneutical circle.
Scholars who do not share the same *discrimen* can with
relative ease come to common conclusions regarding the
results of studying a biblical text as a historical source
(*exegesis i*) or as it was understood by its original audience
(*exegesis ii*). From there, it is possible to move to levels of
agreement in studying biblical texts precisely as Christian
Scripture (*exegesis iii*) which were not possible even a few
decades ago.[4] Thus, it has already been proven that the ideal
of bringing together theology and exegesis is clearly realizable, at least to a significant extent.

*(The remainder of this section was written by L. John To-
pel, S.J., originally as part of his "The Christian Ethics of
the Lukan Sermon" which appears below in Part Two
179–199.)*

A fine example of the way in which theologians are
becoming increasingly aware of both the general and particular hermeneutical context in which they are working
can be found in the way Peter Chirico begins his study of
infallibility.[5] He begins his interpretation theory from the
observation that each person possesses an experiential continuum divisible into five aspects:

1. an aspect of experience explicitly understood, as
   when one recognizes that one is lazy, tender, etc.;

2. an aspect not yet explicitly understood, but potentially understandable, as when a series of moral faults
   can be subsequently grasped as adding up to a knowledge of a characteristic vice. This is material which
   can be expressed only through the artistic preconscious in symbol, and so the psychologist can help us
   discover ourselves in dream images;

3. an aspect which is of itself unintelligible and inco-
   herent, as when one's conduct is an unreflected-upon
   and unresolved bundle of contradictions. The only
   expression of this aspect is the inverse insight that
   one is dealing with a <u>surd</u>; ✳

4. an aspect which is the dynamic process unifying the
   three prior aspects, as when one dimly grasps an
   element of one's personality which had seemed mysterious or unintelligible and begins to act and think
   out of an implicit awareness of that quality (moving
   from the third to the second aspect), or later through
   analysis explicitly grasps the quality which had previously only dimly surfaced in dreams and metaphors (moving from the second to the first aspect);

5. an aspect unifying the first four, finally arriving at
   the level of invariance or certitude (P. Chirico, *Infallibility* 12–15).

✳ surd: ① A sum, as √2 + √3, containing one or more irrational
roots of #s ② A voiceless sound in speech

Now it is a commonplace of psychology that we act out of all aspects of our experience, so that what is only implicitly understood nevertheless affects not only how we act (defensively or openly), but also how we conceive of ourselves ("O.K." or "not O.K.") or reality (as hostile or friendly), etc. Thus our self-expression is structured not only by what we can explicitly formulate, but also by our preconscious or unconscious apprehension of reality which will show up in the images and figures of speech we will use.

Further, what we can immediately express are the more superficial and quantifiable aspects of our being. Deeper understanding of our being in the world as persons in communion with a tri-personal God we can only dimly grasp and express mutely through symbol and ritual.[6] Yet these deeper aspects of our being are precisely the center of our sense of identity and of our sense of how we should act in our world. In short, it is in what is implicitly known that the inchoative grasp of one's ethic resides.[7] Of course the educated person continues to reduce these deeper transcendental relationships (by Chirico's aspect 4) to the explicit formulations of a metaphysics. Then one arrives at the grounding of one's ethics (now a system!) in a systematic metaphysics. But where such formulation is lacking, as in the ethic of an aesthetic mode of expression such as a Gospel, the interpreter can still seek and find the underlying unity in the author's diverse commands. In this sense one must go beyond the author's explicit formulations to what is implied in his thought if one is to adequately interpret even the explicit formulations.

Consequently, when Chirico comes to discuss the qualifications and acts of the interpreter, he begins by suggesting:

> The successful interpreter necessarily possesses in his being an experiential continuum and a differentiated understanding that corresponds to the subject matter of the text ... moreover, his source of meanings as constituted by that existential continuum and differentiated understanding must be superior to its counterpart in the author of the text (Chirico, *Infallibility* 24).

inchoative (in-kō-ə-tiv) ① In an initial or early stage; just beginning; incipient ② Immature, imperfect

The "ought" is built upon the "I".

This follows from the three tasks the exegete must perform.

First, the exegete must grasp <u>what the author of the text</u> <u>explicitly understood and intended to express</u> in his text (or, more cautiously formulated, the meaning the text had <u>when</u> <u>it left the hands of its author or final redactor</u>). Now because the author lived in a different age, with a different thought world (much of which has been lost to us), and because no author can put all the tools of the communication process (e.g., gestures, tone of voice, etc.) into a written text, the exegete has to proceed like a detective from clues in the text to hypotheses drawn from his or her own experiential continuum to a rigorous process of confirmation of one from a probable range of meanings (cf. the discussion of "plurality of meanings" above 28–32). This process demands an exegete with wide experience and ingenious interpretative skills.

Second, "the interpreter is called upon to make explicit that understanding which is only implied in the text," i.e., the interpreter must unify by an hypothesis that which the original author either could not unify or did not unify textually (Chirico, *Infallibility* 25–26). The reason for this is that only by proceeding to the underlying meanings, the inchoate "system" in the mind of the author, can the exegete verify one of his or her various hypotheses about the explicit meanings of the text. Further, it will happen that in a given author, one text will seem to contradict another. Only by arriving at a higher synthesis, presumably unexpressed, can one see a whole in which both statements are compatible and true.

Third, it may also be true that statements of the same author may be incompatible, and then one has arrived at the <u>surd</u> in the third aspect of the author's experiential continuum. <u>The task of the exegete here will be to "complement and correct that aspect of the text which reflects the</u> <u>*ex se* unintelligible aspect of the author's experience."</u>[8] But this can happen only by going through the author's implied meanings to the surd involved in his or her incomplete interaction with an incomplete world, and that involves intelligence of the highest order in the exegete.

In conclusion, then, contemporary interpretation theory indicates that the interpreter not only can, but *must* probe

beneath the text's explicit formulations of ethical commands to the underlying *Weltanschauung* which orders and
contextualizes the imperatives if he or she is to understand
their real meaning.[9] Such a conclusion has been anticipated
by New Testament exegetes in their phrase "the Christian
imperative flows from the Christian indicative": what
Christ has done for us affects the way Christians now live
and act. This expression leaves vague the kind of causality
Christ's life has on the Christian's. Catholic exegetes sometimes specified that causality by reference to the philosophical principle *agere sequitur esse*. This principle would
explain Christ's influence on Christian life by a (quasi-)
formal causality: in faith and baptism the Christian is incorporated into Christ in such a way as to be "divinized,"[10]
and so interiorly empowered to live a new mode of life. It
would be, then, a new mode of existence which would make
possible the radical new demands Christ makes on his hearers in the Beatitudes, imperatives, and parenesis of the
Sermon on the Mount/Plain.

Now we are not suggesting that the exegete import such
a systematic ethical principle into exegesis of a non-system-
atic work. That would be to mix up the levels of awareness
and expression which Chirico has laid out in our interpretation theory. We are suggesting, however, that the exegete
probing the images used in New Testament texts might
discover that a preconscious awareness of some relationship between Christian existence and Christian action
might be part of the second aspect of its author's experiential continuum. In other words, the images used throughout
the New Testament might indicate that a dim perception of
that relationship was not foreign to the New Testament
authors. Consider, among many others, the following texts:

John 15:1–11, where abiding (*menein*) in Jesus, as
the branch vitally exists in and from the vine,
causes the disciple to bear much fruit (and sets the
context and possibility for the love commandment
in 15:12!);

1 Cor 12:27, where being members of the Body of
Christ explains unity in the charisms that Corinthi-

an Christians possessed (and sets the context for the exhortation to Christian love which follows immediately in ch. 13!);

2 Cor 5:17, where anyone in Christ is a new creature (*kainē ktisis*), reconciled to God. Two verses later God was in Christ (*en Christō,* just as *en Christō* was used in 5:17), here speaking of more than an intentional union. The ethical consequence of such union is found in v. 21, "so that in him we might become the righteousness of God";

Rom 8:12–17, where through the Spirit we are ~~sons~~ *children* of God, able to address the Father with Jesus' own intimate title, "Abba," and so we are free from both sin and Law in our ethical conduct;[11]

Eph 4:22–24, where Christians are to put off the old ~~man~~ *person* (*ton palaion anthrōpon*) with its deceitful lusts and put on the new ~~man~~ *person* (*ton kainon anthrōpon*) with its true righteousness.

Here, then, are three different New Testament authors[12] who have used literary figures or symbols (vine and branches, Body of Christ, ~~sons~~ *children* of God, baptism, the new ~~man~~ *person*, the new creature) to describe a personal bond (*menein, eis Christon, en Christō*) with Christ so real as to constitute a new being (new creature, new ~~man~~ *person*) who is to effect a radically new Christian action. But this is exactly what contemporary philosophical interpretation theory, developed from the actual practice of literary authors and secular interpreters, should have alerted us to expect: an author roots his aesthetic description of appropriate human action in his preconscious sense of the ontological structures of the human person, and he expresses this preconscious sense through symbols and figures of speech. When such a personal bond seems to be followed by ethical contact quite unattainable by normal human striving, we have an obligation to probe into the nature of that bond, asking what ontological relationships might ground such new action.

SUMMARY

Contemporary interpretation theory has vindicated the exegete's task of probing for systematic ontological relationships beneath an author's aesthetic expression. We ourselves have briefly adverted to the fact that New Testament authors have used images of the Christian life which imply new ontological structures grounding new modes of human ethical conduct. This has given us the clue for the method by which such probing might be done in New Testament exegesis—analysis of the images an author uses (see below in the introduction to Part Two 173–177).

5. FROM THE BIBLE TO DOCTRINE

We conclude this chapter with an attempt to sketch out something of the process of moving from biblical revelation to doctrinal affirmation. We begin with the fairly obvious assumption that the Bible is, to a large extent, a *story*. More exactly, it is a collection of stories, told, and frequently retold and reshaped, by many different authors in different ages—stories which are sometimes so different, even when talking about the same thing, that they cannot be harmonized. Yet all of them, when taken together, are perceived by Christians as basically one. It is in fidelity to that story and to their own perceived role in it that Christians make sense of their lives as Christians. What we are attempting here is to understand the process of going from (biblical) story to credal affirmation and Christian praxis, and to the ethical reflection which is a part of and a consequence of this process.

Behind this attempt is the view that, as Amos Wilder put it, telling a story is a means of "imaginatively objectifying" one's experience, and that a story can thus report reality, that it can be a window into the way things objectively are.[13] The stories implicitly or actually produced by Marx and Freud, Nineham reminds us (and we can add Sophocles, Plato, Hobbes, Locke, Rousseau, Hegel, Kierkegaard,

Nietzsche, Dostoevski, Roots, Star Wars, E.T., Gandhi, and a countless host of film and TV dramas), all purport to tell us something about the way things are or should be.

The ancient biblical writers primarily told stories and clothed their law-giving texts in a narrative framework. From our point of view we can see that they, probably without being conscious of it, were doing two distinct things: (1) they were giving an account of the course of this world, and (2) they were telling a story about it (Nineham 181). And it is fairly easily documented that, as their experiences and perceptions changed, so too did their stories. The New Testament writers, in their turn,

> told a story, *prima facie* in historical form, of how God had a Son, a pre-existent supernatural being, distinct from Yahweh, who at a certain point entered the course of history, lived a human life in it for a while under the name of Jesus, died a redemptive death on man's behalf and then was raised again to his proper place at God's right hand to exercise control of the universe, from then onward, on God's behalf (Nineham 18–20).

This generalized summary, not found or necessarily agreed to in every detail by each and every New Testament author, does nevertheless sketch out what is generally understood as the "story" told by the New Testament authors. But the evangelists and other New Testament writers (and Christians after them) do not merely report what they perceive to be an historical event, e.g., the birth of Christ; they also go on to "speak of the birth as the means by which a pre-existent heavenly being made his entry into history." In doing that, they are "in effect placing an interpretation on that historical event, they are embedding it in a context of story" (Nineham 187).

> One of the valuable contributions of form-criticism has been to bring home to us that every *pericope* partakes of this dual character; insofar as it is historical at all, it is precisely history *and* story—history embedded in a context of interpretative story.

... the early Christians ... not only mingled history
and story inextricably together, but it must be con-
fessed they sometimes allowed the demands of the
story to modify the details of the history. ... This
does mean that it is very often impossible for us to
get back to the history and see what *our* reaction
would have been.

And further:

So far as the early Christians were Jews, they were
not so much *telling* a story as [continuing or] com-
pleting a story ... their imaginative objectification
of experience rested back on, and was largely con-
trolled by, the objectifications in which countless
earlier generations had sought to give expression to
their experience. Still more significant in determining their story was the impact and teaching of Jesus
himself (Nineham 187–89).

Thus, however differently we, or others, might have responded, the early Christians, right from the pre-New Testament beginnings, responded by producing poetry and
telling stories (cf. Nineham 190).

For our task, we have only to remind ourselves of that
commonplace of literary criticism that a poem cannot really be translated without changing it, that the "message"
extracted from a parable does not express the full, or necessarily even an accurate part of the meaning of the parable,
and that the "lessons" or "teachings" drawn from a story are
not the same as the story itself, in order to be aware of the
magnitude and complexity of the problems faced by theologians of the hermeneutical, post-McLuhan age who want to
figure out how we get from the Bible to doctrine.

This is, of course, by no means just a contemporary
problem. The attempt to draw out of the Bible an essential,
central core of Christian doctrine, or "constant quantum of
truth" (Shirley Jackson Chase) to which all could adhere,
whether conceived of as something valid for all time, or
even more modestly as something valid just for each particular generation, has never really been successful. (This does
not, of course, discredit the whole historical-critical meth-

od, as is argued by Gerhard Maier who concludes from "the abortive search for a canon in the canon" to the bankruptcy of the method itself. He does not deal with the obvious rejoinder that one is here simply putting a good method to an improper use.[14])

> There never was a time when the Bible could be left to explain itself in such a way as to produce universal agreement about what it has to teach. It was not so before the coming criticism. Fundamentalism cannot restore to us a happy past that never was. The critical wave broke in upon the Church in which the successors of the tractarians were still disputing with the heirs of the evangelical revival while Presbyterians, Congregationalists, Baptists, Friends and Methodists (and, we may add, Roman Catholics) had their differing interpretations of biblical theory. . . . The followers of Calvin, Zwingli, Melancthon *et al.,* not to mention the theologians of the Council of Trent and the Orthodox Church of the East, all claimed to be the true interpreters of the Bible in their differing understandings of the Christian faith (Leonard Hodgson, *The Bible and the Training of the Clergy* 12–13 as quoted in Nineham 199–200).

We can contribute this obvious failure to differences in what Kelsey calls the *discrimen,* the theologian's imaginative vision which determines the patterns in Scripture to be studied. This *discrimen* represents the counterpart, at this end of the interpretative continuum, of that storied vision of reality (God's/Christ's presence in the world/Church) which gave rise to the biblical author's story in the first place. In other words, *exegesis iii* (the interpretation of biblical texts *as Scripture*—see above 47–48[15]) and biblical theology (to the extent that it really is theological) tends to be an imagination-dominated interpretation of what was predominantly a product of the imagination in the first place. Awareness of this, in any of the various ways in which hermeneutics and critical historiography might lead one to express it, makes possible a whole series of fruitful distinctions which can contribute (and in some cases already has)

"religious imagination"

Value of imagination has been appreciated more in recent years.

to a dismantling of the theological and credal Tower of Babel that characterizes modern Christianity. But, as we have pointed out (above n. 3), one must go beyond Kelsey's notion of irreducibility to achieve much in this direction.

To look now more closely at the continuum we perceive to exist between the biblical story and our own story in the modern world, a number of *modes* and *phases* can be distinguished.[16]

One can distinguish *four modes* in which Christian existence (or Christian biblical revelation) is preached or communicated by Jesus Christ himself, by the New Testament, and by the Christian communities of faith in the past and present. These are (1) *indicative* mode, (2) *imperative* and *parenetic* (exhortatory) mode, (3) *parabolic* mode, and (4) *mystical* mode.

(1) INDICATIVE MODE

In the indicative mode the Christian story is told. It is a story that has its center in biblical revelation and the Gospel (the story of Jesus Christ), but it also is a continuing story that both antedates and will postdate all human history. Most significantly, it is also a story in which we all have a part. For example, as Origen of Alexandria would point out, the real significance of the Passover is that it refers not just to Christ's "passing over" but also to our "passing over" with him.

(2) IMPERATIVE/PARENETIC MODE

In the imperative mode are found the various biblical do's and don'ts. All these prescriptions and exhortations are part of the ongoing history of salvation, and none of them can be separated from their place in the story. Some of them have been superseded because the story has moved to another stage. Others (i.e., some biblical imperatives) retain their prescriptive validity for us to the extent that the story in which they have their setting remains or has become our story. Still other (non-biblical) imperatives have prescriptive value for us because they have a place *in our story* within the fullness of the Christian story. In other words, the Christian story or "salvation history" (but be careful of the connotations!) supplies the medium of continuity between biblical imperatives and post-biblical Christian imperatives. Thus it is not precisely the fact that an imperative is biblical, or even from the Lord, that gives it its prescriptive value, but rather its place within the Christian story and its relation to our individual and communal places in that story. This helps explain why Christians who are aware of historicity as well as of the Christian story are comfortable with fewer moral absolutes than previously. It reduces neither to a situation ethic nor to a merely individualistic ethic. For Christian ethics remains ever an ethic of community and for the community, and in which charity always has the primacy. Ultimately, it is only from within the broad context of the Christian story and the more particular context of each one's Church community that one can begin to interpret and apply the different kinds of moral imperatives, exhortations and counsels of the Bible.

(3) PARABOLIC MODE

In the parabolic mode the Gospels report Jesus as communicating Christian existence in *parables.* We can consider them as *stories within a story.* Already having a place in the Christian story, we are challenged to enter psychologically or imaginatively into the story of the parable in order to enable ourselves to enter even more fully into the Christian story (which for us is our own existential, individual and communal entering into the life of Christ). One cannot, as is now commonly recognized, conceptualize or rationally explain a parable without killing it. But beyond this, what the parable effects (our fuller incorporation into Christ) transcends the natural level and thus the merely rational means of dealing with it. Pursuing this further, we can see that story and parable are not only a means of expressing the Christian story, they are also a primary means of access to Jesus Christ, the very center of the Christian story. Thus their role in the dynamic of Christian existence (coming to be in Christ) is significant. In this dynamic we can distinguish *three phases:*

a. *The first phase* of the parabolic mode establishes the foundations, principles, values and goals of one's existence; what many authors call "Christian intentionality." For Christian existence, this foundational *Weltanschauung* (Kelsey's *discrimen,* or Curran's "stance"[17]) is mediated to us primarily by means of story, the Christian story. Because this story is the Word of God as well as of human beings, the process of coming to know and enter into this story involves both faith and reason. In contrast to this, for merely natural existence (i.e., one which does not seem to include faith) the foundational *Weltanschauung* is mediated to us primarily by reason and human experience. Story may play an important part, as in the myths of Plato or the "stories" of Marx, Freud, etc., but the process does not become transcendent; it remains a human one carried out with human capabilities.

b. In the *second phase* in the dynamic of the parabolic mode, one applies this *Weltanschauung/discrimen* to one's concrete mode of existence. A person operating without faith, or attempting to prescind from faith, will do this usually by means of deduction and inference. The Christian will use these same rational means, but will characteristically also rely on a general appeal to the place that this particular situation has in the overall Christian story, as well as rely on a particular use of parable (story within a story) to illuminate the concrete situation. A person without a faith-existence can make a similar use of story and parable but, if indeed without faith, will have no access to the transcendent dynamism of the faith-existential process of coming-to-be in Christ.

c. The *third phase* of the parabolic mode involves the realization and application of the first two phases to specific human situations. It is the stage of living out not only intellectual and moral conversion, but also religious conversion—Christian metanoia. It is the final stage of decision and commitment where (speaking ethically) merely rational ethics becomes particularly inadequate and where faith ethics makes an increased use of story and parable in order to stimulate religious conversion. For the problem is not so much to *know* the good (which is, difficult as it often is, *relatively* easy), but also to transcend one's individual and communal moral impotence and find the wherewithal actually to do the good. We achieve this by existentially entering into the Christian story. This leads to the fourth mode in which Christian existence is communicated by Jesus Christ, by Christian biblical revelation, and by the living Christian communities: the *mystical mode.*

(4) MYSTICAL MODE

In the mystical mode, the actuality of Christian existence or being-in-Christ is (inceptively, partially, or more fully) realized. The indicative, imperative and parabolic modes, although they have aspects which are existentially contemporary, focus on the historical center of the Christian story: Jesus and the New Testament. But the mystical mode, while remaining in continuity with the other three, focuses nevertheless on what is taking place now: our individual and communal incorporation into Christ.

Although we can conceptually distinguish these four modes, functionally they are never completely separate from each other. The Christian who listens to the story, hearkens to the commands, and enters into the parables of Jesus is the same Christian who has been and is being incorporated into Christ.

This is not easy to summarize. But the following seem to be of central significance: With regard to the two main poles of this discussion, the *Bible* and *theology*, it is now seen that *imagination* plays a part that is far more extensive and pervasive than has previously been the custom to admit. This applies both to the origins, formation and transmission of biblical revelation, as well as to its reception, assimilation, formulation and affirmation on the credal, doctrinal and theological levels. The biblical authors themselves lived by and expressed themselves by their own *discrimen* (imaginative construal of the mode of God's presence and activity in their world). But no less do modern theologians also live by and express themselves by their own particular and possibly quite complex *discrimen.*

Bultmannian demythologization would seem of itself to be an inadequate methodological response to this situation, because it tended to presume that an imaginative *discrimen* was at work only at the biblical pole of the discussion and not also at the pole of the modern scientific theologian. Demythologization, as it was commonly understood, tended to presume the possibility of moving from an imaginative mode of construing reality to a (purely?) rational-intellectual mode of construing reality. But modern hermeneutics has fairly effectively dismantled this presumption.

This implies that the theologian (or, at least, the theological enterprise) now out of necessity, not choice, must become involved with problems and disciplines formerly regarded as somewhat peripheral to the central tasks of theology. These are, to begin naming them, literary criticism, linguistics, psychology, sociology, analysis of myth, ritual and symbol, structuralism, etc.

Further exploration of the way "story" variously functions to bring us from the Bible to doctrine, from the "then" of biblical revelation to the "now" of moral life in Christ, is obviously called for. However, one should not rush to the story motif as a theological panacea. In concentrating on one's own faith-story and the faith-story of one's community, one could easily evade responsible attention to the truth question, or think it possible to evade the work required by the vigorous analyses of the historical-critical method. If one completely evades the question "Is it a true story?" one moves into a different orbit than that of the historian and the exegete. The Christian biblical theologian cannot be just a descriptive thinker, evading the critical truth questions. But the opposing danger, that of encapsulating one's religion in the theology one is learning, or attempting to do this, remains perhaps the greater danger for the modern theologian.

Notes

1. Roland E. Murphy, "Vatican III—Problems and Opportunities of the Future: The Bible" in *Toward Vatican III: The Work That Needs To Be Done,* eds. D. Tracy, H. Küng and J. B. Metz (New York: Seabury, 1978) 24. R. Brown, *The Critical Meaning of the Bible,* provides a graphic description of this time lag.

2. David H. Kelsey, *The Uses of Scripture in Recent Theology* (Philadelphia: Fortress, 1975) 213. Another way to put this question is: "What are the ways in which the Bible speaks?" Thus the theologian's task, as distinct from that of the exegete narrowly conceived, is to study the ways in which the Bible speaks to others than exegetes.

3. But note that a more profound use of theological method (e.g., Lonergan's) can show that a basic theological position (*discrimen*) is not as irreducible as Kelsey supposes. Cf. C. Hefling, "Lonergan on Development: *The Way to Nicea in Light of His More Recent Methodology* (diss.; Boston College, 1982) 305–357.

4. We have in mind such things as the several publications from the series *Lutherans and Catholics in Dialogue,* esp. *III: The Eucharist as Sacrifice* (U.S. Catholic Conference, Washington, D.C.; U.S.A. National Committee for Lutheran World Federation, New York, 1967); R. E. Brown, K. P. Donfried, J. Reumann, *Peter in the New Testament* (Minneapolis: Augsburg; New York/Toronto: Paulist, 1973; R. E. Brown, K. P. Donfried, J. A. Fitzmyer, J. Reumann, *Mary in the New Testament* (Philadelphia: Fortress; New York/Toronto: Paulist, 1978); L. Swidler (ed.), *The Eucharist in Ecumenical Perspective,* a special issue of the *Journal of Ecumenical Studies* 13:2 (Spring 1978).

5. Peter Chirico, *Infallibility. The Crossroads of Doctrine* (New York: Sheed, Andrews and McNeel, 1977), 3–29, is a reliable synthesis of the work of a host of thinkers on interpretation theory, including especially the theories of Collingwood and Mandlbaum on historical knowledge, and of Heidegger, Gadamer, Polanyi, Betti, and Coreth on the philosophical grounds of interpretation methods. Like Chirico, we are personally most indebted to B. Lonergan, *Insight* (New York: Philosophical Library, 1958) and his disciples, M. Lamb and F. Lawrence, for our own interpretation theory.

6. This is why Lonergan calls myth the uneducated person's philosophy; cf. also his description of the move from an implicit to an explicit metaphysics in *Insight,* 396–401 and his understanding of the relation between metaphysics, mystery, and myth in pp. 531–49.

7. Cf. how R. McCormick expresses this when speaking of the "Origins of Moral Judgment" in "Does Religious Faith Add to Ethical Perception?" in C. E. Curran and R. A. McCormick, *Readings in Moral Theology No. 2. The Distinctiveness of Christian Ethics* (New York/Ramsey: Paulist, 1980) 164–67. This pre-reflective grasp of the basic principles of one's moral reasoning is, of course, the ethical correspondence of what we have just described as the *discrimen* (above 57–62).

8. Chirico's example (p. 26) is Paul's perception that slavery was permissible in the Christian community. Cf. also the way L. Schottroff consciously moves beyond what is possible by exegesis alone in order to make sense of the apparent incompatibility between the New Testament commands to non-violence and the non-resistance to evil on the one hand, and on the other hand to love one's enemies and not passively accept their involvement in evil without attempting to help them and rectify the evil (see below 217). Another example of this is the way Schuele discusses Grundmann's "going beyond the text" (see below 202–203).

9. Compare with "The Science and the Art of Christian Biblical Ethics" (below 125): "But with everyone ... this involves at least an imaginatively construed, pre-discursive awareness (*discrimen*) of who and what one is, of whether and how God is present and active in the world."

10. In the words of the Greek Fathers such as Clement of Alexandria (*Pedag.* 1.6; 3.1), Origen (*Contra Celsum* 5.23), Cyril of Alexandria (*On Hosea* 4), Augustine (*Expos. on the Pss,* Ps 49:2).

11. Note that Romans 8:2, introducing our pericope (8:12–17), links the work of the Spirit to the liberation from sin/self, death, and the Law, which had been the burden of 4:25—7:25. All of these are liberations which free and affect Christian action. Indeed, this same relationship between union with Christ and our action is taken up twice in Romans 6—7: Romans 6:1–4 indicates that being baptized into Christ's death is being baptized into Christ Jesus (*eis Christon Iēsoun*) in such a way that one may no longer sin (vv. 5–14). The same type of argument about dying to the Law in Romans 7:1–5 has the consequences that we now serve in newness of Spirit in 7:6.

12. We have by no means exhausted such symbolic use in these three authors: cf. Eph 2:13–16, and esp. Gal 6:15 for another usage of *kainē ktisis* (clearly indicating a new mode of existence). We believe that the relationships these three authors point to can be found in the images of most of the New Testament authors.

13. Cf. Amos Wilder, *New Testament Faith for Today* (London: SCM, 1956) 59–71, as reported by D. Nineham, *The Use and Abuse of the Bible. A Study of the Bible in an Age of Rapid Cultural*

Change (London: S.P.C.K., 1978) 205–06. Stanley Hauerwas shows how it is possible, and indeed necessary, to relate one's ethics to one's foundational stories and, from that basis, attempt to construct one's Christian ethics. Cf. S. Hauerwas with R. Bondi and D. R. Burrell, *Truthfulness and Tragedy: Further Investigations into Christian Ethics* (University of Notre Dame, 1977), and S. Hauerwas, *A Community of Character: Toward a Constructive Christian Social Ethic* (University of Notre Dame, 1981). And, of course, see below, Part One, Chapter IV: "Story and Image" (156–169).

14. Gerhard Maier, *The End of the Historical-Critical Method* (St. Louis: Concordia, 1977) 27 and passim. Cf. the critical rejoinder in Peter Stuhlmacher, *Historical Criticism and the Theological Interpretation of Scripture* (Philadelphia: Fortress, 1977) esp. 66–71. Most helpful on this problem, as we have already mentioned (34) is R. Brown, *The Critical Meaning of the Bible* (New York/Ramsey: Paulist, 1981) esp. Chapters I and II, pp. 1–44.

15. This understanding of biblical texts *as Scripture* somewhat parallels what R. Brown speaks of as the "biblical meaning," i.e., what the Bible *means* as distinct from what it *meant* in either its "literal sense" or "canonical sense." Of this "biblical meaning" Brown contends: "The way in which the Church in its life, liturgy and theology comes to understand the Bible [and Brown does speak of this as process, as we do] is constitutive of 'biblical meaning' because it is chiefly in such a context that this collection is serving as the Bible for believers" (*The Critical Meaning of the Bible* 34). This is, of course, another way of expressing what we mean by "Christian biblical revelation."

16. What follows is basically an abbreviated form of what appeared in R. Daly, "Towards a Christian Biblical Ethic," in *Critical History and Biblical Faith: New Testament Perspectives* (The Annual Publication of the College Theology Society, ed. by Thomas J. Ryan; Villanova, Pa.: The College Theology Society, 1979) 223–29.

17. C. E. Curran, *Moral Theology: A Continuing Journey* (Notre Dame University, 1982) 38–44.

Chapter Three

THE BIBLE AND ETHICS

The purpose of this chapter is to arrange a great variety of material which comes under this heading in such a way as to clarify and contextualize the issues and thus provide a basis for further fruitful discussion. Many of the divisions we have chosen overlap and interpenetrate each other. We tried to strike a helpful balance between the impossibility of saying everything all at once, and that compartmentalizing which conceals the real interrelatedness of things.

Sections 1–4 could be classified as "fundamental ethics," Sections 5–7 as a discussion of some central fundamental questions in Christian biblical ethics, Sections 8 and 9 as attempts to integrate all that has gone before. Section 8 attempts to bring it all together in a systematic methodological statement to the effect that Christian biblical ethics is an art as well as a science. Section 9 attempts to bring all this to bear on the practical and theoretical situation created by the rise of a specifically third world approach to Christian biblical ethics.

1. TRANSITIONAL: FROM THE BIBLE AND THEOLOGY TO THE BIBLE AND ETHICS

All that has been said about the Bible and theology can, mutatis mutandis, be said about the Bible and Christian ethics. This is so, formally speaking, because Christian ethics is a part or division of Christian theology, relating to it as

66

a part of the whole. In particular, the definition of Christian biblical revelation given above on pp. 14 and 46 has been formulated specifically with a view to the needs of this project on Christian biblical ethics. But before getting underway, two remarks are in order.

The first concerns the strong assumption we share generally with Roman Catholic ethics or moral theology of the congruence between reason and ethical systems. This means, negatively, that what is irrational or contrary to reason will not be accepted as ethical or moral. Positively, this is based on the doctrine of the convertibility of the ontological transcendentals, the One, the Good, the True and the Beautiful, and on a rejection of any kind of a theory of double truth such as proposed by Siger of Brabant and the Aristotelians of the thirteenth century. Epistemologically, it locates us in that broad band of the spectrum which is called moderate realism. The human being *can* attain to true knowledge, theoretical and practical, and from external human experience. In more specifically religious terms, we stand in a positive relationship to the doctrine that the human being *can* by human reason know the truths necessary for salvation (as, e.g., defined in Vatican I). In other words, human reason is, if one has to speak in minimal terms, at least *one* valid source of ethical knowledge.

The second remark concerns sources. It is customary to distinguish three sources of Christian ethics: (1) Scripture, (2) tradition, (3) human reason/human experience, both actual and ideal. Note how clearly this parallels the three "moments" of Christian theology we referred to above (39). "Scripture" should, if our project is on target and our definition of biblical revelation is valid, express not just the Bible as a source from the past but also as handed on through the tradition and lived in a forward-looking present. "Tradition" would then express primarily the faith and practice of the Christian community. This is where magisterium or authoritative Church teaching is located. "Human reason/human experience" expresses not just rational-ethical thinking and decision-making, but also, in terms of content, (a) some concept of the "normatively human" or "natural law," and (b) the empirical sciences.

In the practical situation, there is almost always some tension between these sources. If unable to integrate them, as is usually the case, some consistent way of prioritizing them is needed. (Note that asking the question of priority is a good first step in locating differences between various Christian-ethical stances.) Our prioritization of the sources is approximately as we have already listed them, i.e.:

1. Scripture (esp. in the full sense of "Christian biblical revelation");

2. tradition (and "Tradition");

3. human reason/human experience:

    a. some concept of the "normatively human" or "natural law";

    b. the empirical sciences.[1]

Before moving on, let us emphasize that we are not searching precisely for consensus on the prioritization of Christian ethical sources. That is needed only as a fall-back position to help us to some kind of consistency in our flawed human existence. Our real goal is to find ways of integrating the sources so that they all can have their proper place and influence in totally integrated Christian moral reflection and action. That is why our definition of Christian biblical revelation reaches out to encompass the three major "moments" of Christian theology and, when applied to ethics, the principal sources of Christian biblical ethics. If we must prioritize, perhaps the more helpful word-concepts are not in terms of primary and secondary, but rather in terms of what is more or less encompassing of the reality of an integral Christian life.

2. THE CHRISTOCENTRICITY OF CHRISTIAN ETHICS

If one understands Christian ethics as the science and the art of reflecting on and living out the practical aspects of existence in Christ, then the title of this section is an obvious tautology.* But since in much of the ethics done by Christians (e.g., Kantian, or natural-law ethics), Christ has little or no place, let alone the central place, we have to try to make some sense of this apparent contradiction, inconsistency or paradox. A similar challenge comes from the fact that, materially speaking, at least the great majority of all that is dealt with in Christian ethics is not distinctive of Christian ethics in any exclusive sense. And many of the best Christian ethicists, including Catholics, hold that there is nothing exclusively Christian in any of the material of Christian ethics. Thus the Christocentricity of Christian ethics is not an obviousity. However, all we can do in this section is present some of the elements that contribute to the complexity of the situation. The arrangement is as follows: *first,* we will comment on the significance of life in Christ as the hermeneutical center of Christian ethics, and on some things which immediately follow from this; *second,* we will briefly comment on the problem of the historical Jesus and some related questions; *third,* we will comment on those Christian ethical approaches which focus on Christ as exemplar and model, and which emphasize character-formation as the proper activity of Christian ethics.

First, since the ultimate goal of Christian existence is union with God in and with and through Jesus Christ, the hermeneutical center of Christian ethics (which is, of course, ordered to this ultimate goal) must somehow be integral to a genuine movement toward this goal. Our assumption is that the hermeneutical center of the Christian ethics which we do and live, and want to do and want to live, is our experience of Christ as living Lord, an experience that we have both as individuals and in community. This Christ, through, with and in whom we have access to the Father, is Christ dying and rising. In other words, our experience of Jesus is identical with our experience of the paschal mystery: our passing over with Christ through life and death to resurrection and glory. We experience this, however, not so much as a fait accompli, or as something perceptibly happening to us; we experience it rather as *call.* We perceive ourselves as called to this passing over with Christ and thus also to live accordingly. This is the heart of our Christian ethics, that we perceive ourselves and all men and women as called to "pass over" with Christ. This means

*tautology: needless repetition of the same sense in different words; redundancy

[margin handwritten note: ♡ of Xn Bible]

a call to self-transcending love of God and neighbor, of neighbor and God. If there is anything like a "canon within the canon" in the Christian Bible, this has to be the heart of it. Thus it is that Christian ethics at its best and truest will be characterized, paradoxically perhaps, both by ontonomy (*agere sequitur esse/credere*—we act according to what we are and believe ourselves to be) and by a modified consequentialism (because of their call to self-transcending love of neighbor and God, Christians can never prescind from the effects of their actions on their neighbor).

Our conviction that all, and not just Christians, are called to this self-transcending love helps locate the problem of the distinctiveness of Christian ethics which we will take up below. It is an obvious experiential fact that human beings experience this call in quite different circumstances and contexts. Further, not all realize that they are being called in this way, and some who presumably do realize it try to keep it outside of their ethical system (e.g., Kantian ethics). And of course, there are also those who in various ways and degrees resist or reject the call. This can and does result in an almost infinite variety of ethical positions, both theoretical and practical. Many or perhaps even most of these can be resolved by dialectic and hermeneutical analysis. Where they cannot, we are faced with a surd, as we mentioned above (51). When faced with a surd, there is the further disquieting realization that we have no way of knowing whether we are dealing with a real surd or only an apparent one which, for the time being, escapes our ability to resolve. But whether real or apparent, we human beings cannot really "face" surds with just human resources. We must either resolve them, however inadequately, or retreat from them, or go crazy. If we are blessed, we will be able to react as Paul did when faced with his great surd in Romans 9—11: "Oh the depths of the riches and wisdom and knowledge of God. . . ." Paul knows that he must, somehow, make sense of the apparent contradiction between God's faithfulness and Israel's non-conversion. But in the end at least, he realizes that he cannot. The situation remains for him a surd which he can "face" only by appealing to a higher instance, by committing himself in faith to God's transcendence.

[handwritten footnote: ✱ retreat from them = Freud retreated to reductionism]

To indulge in a possibly illuminating aside, it is revealing to read the opening sections of Nietzsche's *Also Sprach Zarathustra* in this light. The pages are filled with a wealth of biblical, especially New Testament imagery used with a remarkable degree of literary (and, one is tempted to say, spiritual) sensitivity. His imagination was filled with the Bible—apparently even more than with classical themes—but his will was committed to a program of liberation of reason from the bondage of religion (= fantasy or imagination?) or "unreason." His own reason was thus destructively torn between the call of his imaginative, pre-conscious *discrimen* and his will to carry out the program he was committed to.

These are examples of *cognitive impotence,* our inability to solve, on our own, the surd of our existence. The specific Christian reaction, when we have gone as far as we can with reason, is to commit ourselves to the folly of the cross. But we are also faced with the problem of *moral impotence.* Our incorporation into Christ dying and rising is real, not just symbolic or "forensic." In the language of the Greek Fathers, we are divinized. But then the surd: we don't act as if we are divinized, at least not usually. Thus analysis of experience puts a question mark beside the validity of the unquestionable principle of *agere sequitur esse/credere.* Once again it is Paul, in the closing doxologies of Romans 7 and 8, who shows us how to deal with the surd of moral impotence: "Who will deliver me from this body of death? ..." (Rom 7:24–25); "It is [or "Is it"?] Christ Jesus who died, yes, who was raised from the dead, who is at the right hand of God, who indeed intercedes for us. [?] Who shall separate us from the love of Christ? ..." (Rom 8:34–39).

Second, the Christocentricity of Christian ethics has an obvious relationship to the question of, or quest for, the historical Jesus. This is part of the unavoidable question of access. If Christ is the center, he must *really* be the center, and we must have *actual* access to him as the center of our Christian lives. There are two major modes of access which, of course, interpenetrate each other and therefore, in the ideal situation, would be integrated in the way we conceive of and live out our Christian-ethical lives.

There is, first, the personal, existential appropriation by way of entering into the life of Christ. This corresponds in large part, but not exclusively, to the "mystical mode" (see above 58–61). And the concrete matrix or context of this personal appropriation is, of course, life in the family, community, and Church.

There is, secondly, cognitional appropriation by means of historical knowledge about Jesus. A few brief comments: We are sympathetic to the general position of J. Jeremias, but would probably qualify our approach more strongly in the critical direction than he does. There have indeed been notable hermeneutic advances made since the time Jeremias wrote. We, in fact, associate ourselves very strongly with that growing consensus among students of history and hermeneutics which judges fully objective history in the sense of the nineteenth century to be impossible. What one can know of the historical Jesus does not of itself provide an adequate cognitive base for Christian ethical knowledge and action. One has to fall back on "Christian biblical revelation" in the broader sense in which we understand it, which thus also includes Church tradition. We are back within the hermeneutical circle and must learn to live with the situation.

But what shall we do about the quest itself for the historical Jesus? The answer is decided largely on the meta-ethical levels of epistemology and ecclesiology. The answers run all the way from "full speed ahead" with all possible methods and means in order to establish critically the historical foundation of Christian life and faith, to a complete rejection of the search as impossible and doomed to failure and/or as an improper activity for a Christian person of faith or one enlightened by existentialism. If one thinks that the only raison d'être of the historical-critical method is to bring us to the historical Jesus or to the "canon within the canon," one inevitably will be disappointed in the method. Our position in the matter amounts to recognition of historical studies about Jesus as a valid and important function of biblical studies. However it is not so much because we hope to gain extensive and certain knowledge about the historical Jesus, but because we can thereby deepen and enrich

our understanding of the New Testament portrayal of Jesus.
In addition, when the search for the historical Jesus is
carried out by a *vigorous* application of the tools of the
historical-critical method, then the search itself can become a helpful "control" or "conscience" against the dangers of eisegesis. A great deal of work obviously remains to
be done on this topic.

Third, Christ as model and examplar, and the use of the
Bible for character-formation.[2] The interconnection of these
themes with the historical Jesus question is obvious. For if it
is the Bible that shows us the God-human relationship in
action, then the Bible is the privileged medium of our access
to Jesus, *the* mediator. But biblical studies alone cannot
provide this access to an adequate degree, or for all people,
and we are again back in Church tradition and the hermeneutical circle, or, as we will explain below (114–138, esp.
116) in the "bypass" mode of doing Christian biblical ethics.

Looking on Christ as the exemplar of our moral lives
has roots which go back at least to Paul. "Be imitators of me
as I am of Christ" (1 Cor 11:1). In patristic soteriology
Christ's active exemplarity was seen as one of the modes of
his saving action. The following of Christ has always been a
central Christian theme, but it has not always rested on the
same theological and ecclesiological foundations. To ven-
ture into some oversimplifying categorization, it seems that
those who make Christ as exemplar the focus of their ethical systems or who suggest that character formation is
where biblical materials can and ought to exercise their
greatest impact on Christian ethics (e.g., Hauerwas, Birch
and Rasmussen) are usually members of the Protestant tradition of Christianity. This tradition characteristically does
little with, or even rejects, another Christological soteriolog-
ical model strongly witnessed especially among the Greek
Fathers: Christ as divinizer. If then we have been divinized,
that is the way we should act. But we don't seem to act that
way, as we have just mentioned, and we must try to make
something of this contradiction, paradox, or surd.

To break off at this point in order to move on, we need
only to remark that the rather extensive agreement as to the
fact of the Christocentricity of Christian ethics covers a
broad spectrum of different and at times strongly conflicting theological positions.

(handwritten margin notes) ③ you can't erase 2000 years of living. Nor can you ignore the need to constantly renew your interpretation of scripture

3. THE NORMATIVITY OF THE BIBLE FOR CHRISTIAN ETHICS

To affirm the Christocentricity of Christian ethics is to affirm that Christ is the ultimate norm of Christian ethics. Since it is from and through the Bible and Christian biblical revelation, as we have broadly defined it, that one gains knowledge of and access to Christ, the Bible is obviously in a privileged position with regard to Christ, the ultimate norm of Christian ethics. Thus, with regard to the normativity of the Bible, we begin with an affirmation that is broad enough to win the initial assent of almost any Christian ethicist: *The Bible is at least inceptively normative for Christian ethics.* No Christian ethicist would categorically deny this, although some (e.g., those representing a fundamentalist, theonomic moral positivism) would want to make a much stronger statement than this, and others (e.g., those representing a strongly rational, natural-law or autonomic ethic) would probably want to hedge this statement with strong qualifications. As should be clear from the preceding pages, we intend to go far beyond such a minimalist affirmation. But it makes for a good starting point. Our immediate task in this section will be to explain what is meant by "norm" and other related ethical terms and concepts.

However, in this one minimalist and apparently innocuous affirmation, we are already involved in serious methodological difficulties. For, to a significant extent, exegetes and ethicists neither speak the same language nor operate in the same conceptual world. More often than not, exegetes and ethicists simply talk past each other.

The most obvious problem is language. Some of the words commonly used are: *norm, principle, rule, value, heteronomic, theonomic, autonomic, ontonomy, autarchy, moral positivism, deontological, teleological, objective, subjective, eudaimonism, utilitarianism, hedonism, parenesis, normative ethics, commandment, ethos, behavior, law, Gospel, obedience, freedom, faith, reason, judgment, conscience, commands, directives, exhortations, obligation, indicative, imperative, narrative, paradigm, model,* etc.

One cannot discuss the normativity of the Bible without using at least some of these terms. But practically all of them are laden with a history, and behind many of them lie the presuppositions of whole philosophical or theological systems. In our attempt to build bridges to other disciplines, it would be foolish and even counter-productive not to be at least somewhat aware of the language used and insights achieved by some ethicists in their discussion of what the norms of Christian ethics are. What follows is a selection of what seems to be the more important of these for our project.

NORM

A typical dictionary definition of norm is:

1. an authoritative standard: *model.* 2. a principle of right action binding upon members of a group and serving to guide, control, or regulate proper and acceptable behavior. 3. *average:* as a: a set standard of development or achievement usu. derived from the average or median achievement of a large group. b: a pattern or trait taken to be typical in the behavior of a social group. c: of, relating to, or pre- scribing norms.[3]

No. 2 defines what is now called a *directing* or (*imperating norm,* i.e., which has some consequences regarding obliga- tions in practical behavior (used to be called "*norma nor- mans*—norming norm"). No. 3 defines what is now called a *theoretical* norm, i.e., which applies only in a specific area and without consideration of its practical consequences (used to be called a "descriptive" norm).[4] Ramsey points out, in what is by now a commonplace of theological criticism, that the difference between a theoretical and a practical type of norm is often overlooked when pyschologists and sociologists speak of "normal behavior."

One could suggest that (at least some) biblical theolo- gians should apply this distinction more vigorously to the Bible itself. For example, the way some use Scripture for arguments against women's ordination is often an instance of confusion between theoretical (descriptive) and practical norms. Of course, the study of the theoretical (descriptive) norms of morality present in the Bible is a specific task of the exegete. But the study (and derivation) of directing/imperating (norming) norms of morality from the Bible is a task not only for the exegete but for many others as well.

Some specifically theological attempts to define norm: "In philosophy and theology, one speaks of norms as principles, phenomena, values or situations which are recognized as definitive or authoritative in relation to a system, attitude or behavior."[5] "Norm signifies the *rule* or the *measure* to or against which a specific reality (in ethics: human action in so far as it is morally good or evil) is to be compared."[6]

It seems to be worth noting that these *theological* definitions of norm are less specific and forceful regarding the obligatory or binding character of norm than is the dictionary definition. The dictionary, reflecting more clearly the general, popular understanding of norm, affirms more directly its binding, guiding, controlling and regulating character. But when the ethicist or exegete begins to reflect critically, definitions of norm tend to emerge which are less rigidly binding or regulative. For example, the use of "law" in such concepts as natural law, positive law, divine law, law of Christ, and Gospel and law is anything but univocal. Further terminological or conceptual confusion can arise when we speak of Jesus Christ as norm, or as *the* norm.

VALUE

Bernard Häring points out that, whether expressed in positive or negative form ("speak truthfully" or "don't lie"), a norm refers back to a *value* which is much richer than what the verbal form of a norm can ever express.[7]

> *It is the value that is normative.* The value is the really important object of the moral act. In its value-in-itself and in its value-grounding relationship to the human being, the value writes the rule for him/her, i.e., the unchanging measure (the norm). . . . *A norm which is not based on a value and does not direct one to a worthwhile (werthaft) action has no moral binding force.*[8]

This distinction between "norm" as a rule and guide for concrete moral action or behavior and "value" as the more ultimate principle behind the norm (i.e., *value* as ultimate and therefore more absolute norm) is an important one for our task. Some, for example, are willing to recognize the Bible as the (or a) proper source for the *values* on which the practical norms of Christian morality are based, but not as the proper source for the practical norms in themselves. An example of this is A.K. Ruf's thesis:

> *Moral norms for action are not as such contained in revelation; they are rather constructs of the practical reason in so far as the practical reason— in perceiving reality and in being responsible to reality—is the seat of moral decision.*[9]

Ruf claims contemporary exegesis as support for this thesis, and also points out that it also implies, in the use of the word "norm," a distinction usually made in traditional moral theology which used "norm" in an undifferentiated fashion for all moral directives. Drawing upon the conceptual tools of social psychology and sociology, "norm" is understood as an imperative statement which, in its content, admits of no possibility of modification or variation. A "norm" is thus to be distinguished from *"action imperatives"* or *action principles* which do admit of possibilities of modification and variation. For example, the former Church law of abstinence was a "norm"; its content admitted of no modification or variation. On the other hand, the Christian "law of love" is not a norm in this sense, but rather a *principle;* it admits (by its nature) of considerable modification and variation in just how it is to be fulfilled. In the formulation of such principles of action, the indirect ethical statements of revelation are of special importance, i.e., those affirmations which, in the context of the theology of creation and redemption, provide interpretations of human beings and their world and mediate to them an experience of reality which can become the basis of an action (or behavior) adequate to reality.[10] The convergence of this with what we have above described as the discrimen (57, 62) is obvious.

It is clear, then, that an ethicist who denies the presence

of moral norms in revelation is by no means necessarily
denying the normativity of the Bible for Christian ethics;
for that same ethicist may also insist that the Bible, while
containing no moral norms in the sense just defined, is
indeed the central and primary source for ethical *action-
imperatives* or *action principles* such as the *law of love* or
the *Kingdom of God.* Helmut Merklein's discussion of the
Kingdom of God as an action-principle *(Handlungsprinzip)*
is a fine example of this type of exegetical-ethical argumentation.[11]

HETERONOMY (HETERONOMIC, HETERONOMOUS)

The basic meaning of this term (increasingly used by
Catholic as well as Protestant and philosophical ethicists) is
determined by Kant's condemnation "as 'heteronomous' (as
opposed to 'autonomous') any system which tries to derive
ethics from anything but the nature of the rational will as
such."[12] Contemporary ethicists often use the term, without
necessarily affirming or denying allegiance to the Kantian
system, to refer to any norm, rule or source of moral knowledge or moral action which comes from outside the human
person.

AUTONOMY (AUTONOMIC, AUTONOMOUS)

The contemporary use of this term is also determined
by Kant who, in his attempt to "root morality in practical
reason independent of external influences and constraints,"
made autonomy the central principle.

> Autonomy means the power of self-determination
> and freedom from alien domination and constraint.
> Autonomy stands opposed to heteronomy or subjec-
> tion to the determination of another. A distinction
> may be drawn between the autonomy *of* ethics and
> autonomy *in* ethics. With regard to the latter, the
> focus is upon the individual self and its capacity for
> self-determination; autonomy in ethics means free-
> dom and the power to bind the self by a law which
> the self promulgates. By the autonomy of ethics is

meant the doctrine that the moral dimension of human life has a form and structure of its own that is independent of religion, of custom and convention and indeed of any other sphere of life or form of authority. The autonomy of ethics has frequently meant the separation of ethics from religion, but there are other factors—mores and customs, psychological and cultural determinism—from which ethics is also to be free if it is to retain its autonomy. . . .

In recent decades the autonomy of ethics has been a central issue both in religious and in ethical thought. Those who are skeptical about the validity of religion in an age of science argue for the complete independence of ethics from religion in the belief that the good is not dependent on God and that values can be preserved even if a religious interpretation of morality is no longer tenable. On the other side, the proponents of the religious view claim that ethics can never be entirely independent of religion because religion supplies the insights from which moral ideals are framed and without the grace of God the moral self has insufficient power to perform its duty.[13]

These are the two classical and, when taken in their strict sense, mutually exclusive positions on the norm of morality. The ultimate norm of morality is either outside of the human person *(heteronomy)* or within the human person *(autonomy)*. Rational ethics, especially when dependent on Kant, has, of course, insisted on autonomy. Christian ethics, holding that God (the will of God/divine revelation) is the ultimate norm of morality, has insisted on heteronomy. This is sometimes called *theonomic moral positivism.* In its biblical form, it insists that the *Bible alone* is the norm of morality. In its "authority-form," it insists that official Church or community teaching is the ultimate practical norm of morality.

A recent very significant development is the extent to which contemporary Christian ethicists, including Catholics, opt for the autonomy model. Among them are most of the leading figures of contemporary German Catholic moral theology: Bruno Schüller,[14] Alfons Auer,[15] and Franz Böckle.[16] They have succeeded in introducing (integrating, if you agree with them) Kantian concepts of autonomy into contemporary Catholic moral thinking.[17] When autonomy and heteronomy are understood in their classical, mutually exclusive sense, it is indeed hard to see how a Christian ethicist can opt for autonomy. But much of the mutual exclusivity of the old positions has in fact broken down. As Böckle asserts, "Dependence on God and human autonomy are not mutually exclusive." "The dualism of autonomy and heteronomy is truly overcome only where heteronomy itself guarantees autonomy, where God's Spirit lays claim to the human person and himself guarantees it freedom: in a theonomic human autonomy."[18] It does not seem to be merely eisegesis to see this insight as at least suggested in the prophetic words of Jeremiah 31, esp. vv. 31–34, and of Ezekiel 34.[19] Thus, regardless of the extent to which theologians might agree that the basic Christian moral position is that of a (heteronomic) *theonomic human autonomy,* as Böckle suggests, and regardless of how this might be understood, they can hardly afford to ignore the growing theological and conceptual consensus being achieved by contemporary Catholic moral theology on this point.

AUTARCHY

Autarchy is the perversion of autonomy. It is, in general, a belief in the limitless moral power of the human alone, the utopian conviction of the ability to overcome alienation and conquer evil in the world by one's own power alone.[20] Thus, it is possible to argue that autonomy, as understood by *some* ethicists, is reducible to autarchy. But, in the light of recent developments in Christian ethics, it would be an unjust oversimplification to claim that autonomy as such equals or is reducible to autarchy.

ONTONOMY

Ontonomy is sometimes used in ethical discussions, usually to describe an ethical position which consciously attempts to derive ethics from ontology, i.e., from the reality of divine and human existence. It can signify the attempt to develop the fundamental principles of morality from the ontological principle: *agere sequitur esse*—action is consequent upon being. It is, in itself, an indeterminate concept which needs to be filled out with specific theological and anthropological positions. Generally, the term tends to be used by those whose philosophical and theological positions approximate those of Aristotelian-Thomistic Scholasticism and a moderately realistic epistemology.

OBJECTIVE—SUBJECTIVE

This pair of terms can also carry a great variety of meanings. Particularly careful attention to the context in which they occur is needed. One must in particular beware of the uncritical presumption that "objective" = good, true, corresponding to real facts and situations, and that "subjective" = bad, erroneous, arbitrary, and not corresponding to real facts and situations. "Objective" is sometimes associated with heteronomy, and "subjective" with autonomy—often in the superficial judgmental sense just mentioned. These two terms can, however, refer to the very important distinction between ("objective" as) the *morally correct,* i.e., an action good in itself and/or leading to good ends, and ("subjective" as) the *morally good,* i.e., an action performed according to a good intention.

TELEOLOGICAL—DEONTOLOGICAL

Together with heteronomy-autonomy, this is perhaps the most commonly used pair of concepts in contemporary fundamental ethical discussion. They too refer to well-known, clearly identifiable "classical" ethical positions. According to the *teleological* theory, the rightness or wrongness of an action is "always determined by its tendency to produce certain consequences which are intrinsically good or bad," while the *deontological* theory argues: "Such and such a kind of action would always be right (or wrong) in such and such circumstances, *no matter what its consequences might be.*"[21] At this point we are at the center of the ethical discussion regarding the foundation of moral norms.

TELEOLOGICAL—TELEOLOGY—CONSEQUENTIALSM

From *telos* (= goal/finis), teleology characterizes that theory which states that *all* actions must be judged *exclusively* by their consequences. As Böckle points out, a growing number of Catholic moral theologians are convinced that moral norms on the inter-human level can be grounded only upon a consideration of all foreseeable consequences of an action.[22] (The major reason for this seems to be little more than the obvious realization that an ethic grounded in love cannot afford to prescind from the effect an act may have on other human beings.)

> Their main proof lies in the fact that the goods and values proposed to our action are exclusively conditioned, *created* and thus *limited* goods and values. Hence the moral judgment concerning an action can be carried out only under the consideration of this limitation as well as the weighing of possibly competing goods. The human person is indeed unconditionally bound by the absolute ground of what is moral; but, as a contingent being in a contingent world, he can bring to realization the absolute "good" to which he is called only in relation to, and in, the "goods" which as contingent goods or values are really "relative" values and as such can never be put forth a priori as the greatest value which in no way could be brought into tension with a higher value. With respect to the *bona,* only the question of the good to be preferred remains thus possible; and that means that every concrete categorical decision *must*—in order to avoid falsely absolutizing the contingent—ultimately rest on a preferential choice in which we must decide according to priorities of goods and values.[23]

Objections to this position come mostly from the fear that it would lead to the relativization of all norms, and from the insistence that basic human goods may never be directly violated, or from those who hold in principle to an absolute deontological position.[24]

EUDAIMONISM, UTILITARIANISM, HEDONISM

These three concepts/terms are related to teleology and often ordered under it. *Eudaimonism* (the ultimate end of man/woman is happiness, fulfillment, beatitude—and human actions are to be judged according to their relationship to this end) can describe the ethical systems of Plato, Aristotle and Aquinas. The term is not particularly laden with negative connotations; its history, in fact, makes it quite respectable. *Utilitarianism,* however, seems to be too heavily laden with the morally negative connotations of hedonism for it to be used without qualification as a respectable counter-position to the formalistic, deontological position of Kant (see below). Ethicists like Paulsen, Rashdall, G.E. Moore, Brentano, and Knaus have preferred terms like "non-hedonistic utilitarianism" or "ideal utilitarianism" in order to avoid the negative connotations of hedonism. Regarding the term *hedonism* itself, there seems to be no serious effort among moralists to "rehabilitate" it.[25]

DEONTOLOGICAL, DEONTOLOGY

Deontology (*to deon* = obligation, *not* de + ontology) literally means the "science of duty." It is most commonly used to signify that theory which maintains that *not all* actions are morally determined exclusively by their consequences. This theory thus does not exclude that many actions must be judged teleologically. It denies, however, that this is generally the case. Its representatives are convinced that there are actions which, independent of any possible circumstances, are morally wrong in themselves, regardless of what consequences might also be connected with them. Among these they include, for example, lying and excluding generation from the sex act. Beyond this, they hold that there are also actions which, at least under certain conditions, and independent of their consequences, are always and without exception forbidden. Among these would be considered, e.g., the killing of an innocent person.[26]

It is to be noted that numerous arguments commonly characterized as deontological are ultimately reducible to teleology, and that behind deontology, in the strict sense, lies necessarily a specific understanding of the natural order such as has been traditional in Roman Catholic theology.[27]

Deontological ethics is sometimes called *formalistic* ethics, especially as referring to the Kantian position that absolutely nothing outside human reason—i.e., no exterior or ulterior motives or causes—can be constitutive of the true norm of morality.[28] Only the *formal* grounding of the goodness of an action, i.e., that it is performed according to the *categorical imperative: "Act only according to those (subjective) maxims through which you at the same time could wish that they should become a general law,"* is constitutive of the true norm of morality.

Regarding teleology—deontology, Schüller finds three distinguishable positions in Anglo-American ethics:

1. The moral correctness of all actions is determined *exclusively* by its consequences.

2. The moral correctness of all actions is *always also,* but *not always only,* determined by its consequences.

3. There are at least some actions whose moral correctness is in no way determined by their consequences.

Position 1 is called *teleological* or *utilitarian;* positions 2 and 3 are called *deontological.* Schüller remarks that Catholic theologians may regret that positions 2 and 3 are grouped together under the same name. This is not much of a problem in the mainstream of Anglo-American ethics where position 3 is hardly represented by anyone; it is, however, still represented among Catholic moral theologians. It is due time, remarks Schüller, that Catholic moral theology should discuss its relationship to positions 1 and 2, asking particularly how each of them might relate to a Christian ethic of love.[29] We might comment further that, since the Christian ethic of love is nothing if it is not a biblical ethic, the exegete obviously has an essential role to play in this discussion.

PARENESIS

Parenesis is "commonly used as a technical term to refer to all general exhortations (in the Bible) of an ethical or practical nature."[30] Although a "technical term," it is often a very general one, frequently used to refer to any text containing material of a moral, exhortatory or practical nature. It its strict sense, however, *parenesis* is restricted to material of a general *exhortatory* nature, as opposed to a strictly binding command or law. This strict sense of parenesis is what Schüller has in mind when he contrasts *parenesis* with *normative ethics.* It is Schüller's thesis that where law is joined to Gospel, parenesis takes place; that parenesis, when it appeals to the Gospel, does not stop expressing itself in true imperatives, but does so by referring to the judgment to come; that where in the Old Testament and New Testament moral demands are presented in connection with the Gospel and the judgment to come, parenesis and not normative ethics is what takes place; that parenesis in itself does not give new ethical insights, but the power of bringing into practice; that parenesis occurs also in fables, parables, similitudes and stories; and that biblical ethics is, by far for the most part, parenesis. This helps explain why exegetes can write fine, extensive works on New Testament ethics without ever feeling the need to formulate explicitly the peculiar (specific, characteristic) status quaestionis and problematic of a normative ethic.[31]

This insight of Schüller is a profoundly challenging one for the Christian theologian and exegete. But is it valid? In answering this question, exegesis obviously has an essential role to play. It is significant that, in the years since it has been abroad (well over a decade in Germany), there has been no serious critical attempt to oppose it on its own ground. Schüller presents the central point of his thesis as follows:

The theologian whom the Bible renders familiar primarily with exhortations frequently does not seem to find it easy to come to grips with normative ethics. For example, he may come upon the two rival theories regarding the source of ethical norms—the teleological and the deontological—and form the judgment: "Paul is acquainted ... with 'teleological' motivation (future judgment and retribution) just as he also argues 'deontologically' from the implications of membership in the body of Christ" (J. Ratzinger). But to use the future judgment as an "argument" is to engage in judgment-based exhortation and not to deal with normative ethics. The *lex praemians* [law that rewards] and the *lex poenalis* [law that punishes] presuppose the *lex moralis (praecipiens vel prohibens)* [moral law that commands or prohibits] to be already known. Only when it is already established that a certain type of action is morally reprehensible can one meaningfully urge that "anyone who acts thus will not inherit the Kingdom of heaven." Furthermore, one is a member of Christ in virtue of the Gospel. To "argue" from the implications of membership in Christ means therefore to exhort by appealing to the Gospel.

All this makes it clear that in determining the specific characteristics of a Christian ethics it would be profitable to distinguish between exhortation and normative ethics.[32]

The wide-ranging implications of this thesis, should it stand, are obvious. For one thing, it effectively dismisses as a false question most of the (sometimes quite agonizing) attempts to distinguish between authoritative (i.e., binding) kerygma and non-authoritative (i.e., non-binding) parenesis in the Bible. It also highlights the dangers of seeing biblical ethics too much in terms of law rather than of Gospel.

GENESIS AND TRUTH-VALUE OF MORAL INSIGHTS

In a further distinction of great clarifying importance, Schüller insists that a distinction must be made between the *genesis* and the *truth-value* of a moral insight.[33] Failure to observe this distinction, especially in comparing Christian with non-Christian, or faith with non-faith ethics, can lead to some egregious oversimplications. In Schüller's words:

> It seems nonetheless to be often the case that theologians concerned with system building intend to compare Christian ethics *as such* with natural ethics *as such*. They proceed by presenting as natural ethics the ethics of one or other philosopher: the ethics of Epictetus or Kant or Scheler or Bloch; or frequently they are content with very sketchy references to the history of philosophy or with references to whatever ethics is currently popular. In doing so, the theologians seem to think that genuine philosophical ethics is to be identified with the ethics which the "others," i.e., non-Christians, cultivate.

> It is clear that such a procedure leads inevitably to a distorted (and unfair) comparison. For example, in the resultant comparison the *one* Christian ethics, inherently true and certain, is set over against the seemingly bewildering multiplicity of philosophical opinions from Plato down to the modern positivists and analytical philosophers. The superiority of a Christian ethics that is presented in *this* manner is really to be explained simply by logical sleight-of-hand. After all, one need only take "Christian ethics" in a historic-genetic sense, and one would have no great difficulty in producing a picture of it that is no less bewildering than the picture of philosophical ethics understood in a historico-genetic sense.

> If we correlate Christian ethics with faith and natural ethics with reason, the same defect shows up in the way in which faith *(fides)* and reason *(ratio)* are often compared. People take "faith" in a normative sense, so that "faith" is equivalent to "true faith." This identification is rendered all the easier inasmuch as the language of theology "faith" very often means "truth of faith" *(fides quae creditur)*. The term "reason," on the other hand, is understood in a genetic sense, so that one may without inconsisten-

cy attribute to reason every manner of self-deception and error. Once again, this identification is made easier because when people speak of "reason" they are usually thinking of a faculty or *power* of knowing. Now it is immediately evident that, given these assumptions, faith must exercise toward reason the functions of a critical guardian, since truth exposes errors as such.

But it takes no great ingenuity to conceive the relation between faith and reason in such a way that they automatically exchange their roles. One need only use the word "faith" in a genetic sense so that it includes erroneous beliefs and superstitions. Then one takes "reason" in a normative sense so that only "true reason" (= "reason that knows the truth") is meant. At this point reason becomes the critical guard in relation to faith. Then what a theologian claims is a mystery of faith may prove in fact to be a logical absurdity.

Therefore, if we want to compare faith and reason from a gnoseological point of view, we must compare true knowledge through faith with true knowledge through reason, or truths of faith with truths of reason. Then the relation between the two turns out to be that *fides supponit rationem et transcendit eam* [faith presupposes reason and goes beyond it].

Similarly, the comparison should be made between the demands of morality as Jesus lived and preached them and the demands of morality as these present themselves in the form of truths grasped by reason. Since the Christian believes in Jesus Christ, he is certain that Jesus perfectly fulfilled the requirements of morality in his life and authentically interpreted them in his preaching. Consequently, the Christian has every reason for relying unconditionally on Jesus as an infallible authority in matters of morality. But it by no means follows from this that the demands of morality as lived and interpreted by Jesus take us beyond the realm of knowledge accessible to reason. From the theological viewpoint the requirements of morality, insofar as they are accessible in principle to natural reason, are commandments of the Creator. If we keep this in mind it is not clear how anyone can show that Jesus did not intend simply to revalidate the commandments of the Creator against possible misunderstandings.

But even if we prescind from this point, the question of whether and to what extent the requirements of morality as lived and interpreted by Jesus are accessible to rational insight must be answered in principle by undertaking the task of making the moral message of Jesus intelligible in terms of reason. Even as a Christian theologian the student must at this point engage in philosophizing. It cannot be objected that since the Christian already believes, he is unfitted for such philosophizing, that he will be inclined to claim as a truth of reason what in the last analysis he owes solely to his Christian faith. Such a tendency to rationalism does occur. But the opposite tendency, to fideism, also occurs among theologians: that is, the tendency to restrict the possibilities of reason as much as possible, in order to extend the sphere of faith that much the more. To the fideist philosophical skepticism and philosophical positivism are the most endearing of all the historical forms philosophy has taken. Yet how else is anyone to err who attempts to define gnoseologically the realms of faith and reason except by falling into either rationalism or fideism? But if the Christian is to be ill-fitted for philosophizing simply because he can err, then everyone else is equally unfit for philosophizing because everyone else too is capable of erring.

Whether the person who systematically studies philosophical ethics is a Christian or a non-Christian is relevant only to the genesis and not to the truth-value of his ethics.[34]

From this it should be clear how essential it is, when talking about *faith and reason,* to distinguish carefully between the *normative sense* (i.e., truth-content) of faith and reason, and the *genetic sense* (i.e., the process of coming to know the truth) of faith and reason. Similarly, when speaking of *"faith-decision,"* one must be clear whether one is speaking of *faith as obedience* (which relates to the normative sense of faith), or of *faith as a way of knowing* (which relates to the genetic sense).

4. THE DISTINCTIVENESS OF CHRISTIAN ETHICS

Is there a distinctive Christian ethics? This is one of the most central, most fascinating and, as one surveys the situation, more unanswerable of questions. Fortunately, C.E. Curran and R.A. McCormick's *Readings in Moral Theology No. 2: The Distinctiveness of Christian Ethics* (New York/Ramsey: Paulist, 1980) makes readily accessible to us the major issues in the present state of the discussion among Catholic ethicists. The articles in this collection were written between 1970 and 1979. From the earliest, by Joseph Fuchs, S.J. in 1970, to the latest, by Richard McCormick, S.J. in 1979, one can, at least in general, detect an obvious development in the quality and sophistication of the argument. It is an impressive example of a community of scholars mutually helping and influencing each other. One cannot now ask this question with the same naiveté as one could ten or fifteen years ago.

Charles Curran, "Is There a Catholic and/or Christian Ethic?," pp. 60–89 (1974), deftly locates the question in the context of recent Christian, especially Roman Catholic theology and ecclesiology, and comes to his well-known position that, in its material content, there is nothing specifically distinctive about Christian/Catholic ethics that essentially or fundamentally sets it apart from other serious ethical systems. Bruno Schüller, S.J., "The Debate on the Specific Character of Christian Ethics: Some Remarks," pp. 207–233 (1976), approaches the issue with such speculative depth and analytic sharpness as to set an agenda for a whole generation of fundamental moral theologians and exegetes (cf. the preceding section of this book). Schüller is the acknowledged leader in the discussion. It is largely due to him (we have in mind his numerous other publications as well) that the negative answers now seem to be stronger than the positive ones. Richard McCormick, S.J., "Does Religious Faith Add to Ethical Perception?" pp. 156–173 (1979), sums up a great deal of the discussion and shows us some of the consequences, contributions and pitfalls associated with different parts of it. Thus, in terms of usefulness, this article probably stands at the head of the list.

The present state of what is obviously an unfinished discussion can be characterized as a general convergence of opinion that at least *most* Christian ethics is not distinctively Christian in any exclusive sense. But thinking Christians, aware of the uniqueness of Christ, the reality of Christian biblical revelation, and the Christian Church and community which mediates these "goods" to them, generally react with a strong, even visceral aversion to a negative answer to the question of whether or not there is a distinctive Christian ethics. It would be mistaken simply to write this off as the prejudicial effect of their particular religio-cultural background, but it would also be a mistake simply to affirm the positive and then enter into a shouting match over it.

First, some terminological and conceptual clarifications:

NATURE AND GRACE

If there is confusion here, clarity and progress in the discussion are impossible. James Walter focuses the issue when he says:

The real problem seems to lie with the issue of whether one believes there is only one moral order or two. Those who maintain that there is only one moral order (an engraced ground of ethics) tend to agree that there is no distinctiveness and/or specificity to Christian ethics at the level of dispositions, intentions, actions, principles and norms. On the other hand, those who tend to maintain that there are two orders operative in man's moral life, one based upon creation and the other based upon redemption, tend to believe that there is indeed distinctiveness and/or specificity on the level of dispositions, intentions, etc. (James Walter, "Christian Ethics: Distinctive and Specific?" pp. 90–110 [1975] 94–95).

Since contemporary Catholic theology is generally characterized by a dismantling of the strong or absolute distinctions between the natural and supernatural orders which formerly held sway, and by the belief that all human beings are actually called by God to self-transcending love—whether or not they call this the "supernatural existential" as Rahner does—it is easy to see why Catholic ethicists and theologians are tending more and more to deny the distinctiveness of Christian ethics.

The strong negative reaction of many Catholics to this perceived "betrayal from within" can be explained in large measure as due to a failure to recognize the difference between approaching the question of distinctiveness from within the classical world-view of essence or from the horizon of contemporary historical consciousness. From the classical world-view, the question "Does the essence 'Christian morality' contain individual actions and/or intentions that are not included in the essence 'human morality'?" requires an obvious "no." But from the horizon of historical consciousness (or when, like Gustafson or Hauerwas, one attempts a phenomenology of Christian existence in the light of a belief in Jesus Christ), the obvious answer is "yes, there are many" (cf. Norbert Rigali, S.J., "Christ and Morality" pp. 111–120 [1978] 111–13).

GROUND OF ETHICS, ETHICS, MORALS

Different authors may use different terms, but the realities are approximately the same.

Ground of ethics refers to the transcendental level of human existence, the human being's capacity and possibility to be free, and conscious of self, and thus to become a moral subject.

Ethics is a theoretical task, several steps removed from

the actual conduct of human beings, "the reality of a set of principles and judgments which one *thematically* uses in determining one's moral action" (Walter 94).

Morals refers to the actual conduct of men and women. Obviously, one's answers to the questions of distinctiveness will be different depending on which of these levels one has in mind. But note that many authors do not distinguish between ethics and morals (Walter 93–94).

McCormick brings this kind of distinction between levels a bit further when he distinguishes between:

1. An *essential* ethic: norms regarded as applicable to all persons, because rooted in the dignity of the human person.

2. An *existential* ethic: "the choice of a good that the individual should realize, the experience of an absolute ethical demand addressed to the individual."

3. *Essential Christian* ethics: the ethical decisions a Christian must make precisely as belonging to a community to which the non-Christian does not belong; moral demands made upon the Christian *as Christian* (e.g., to regard others as brothers and sisters in Christ, etc.).

4. *Existential Christian* ethics: the concrete or specific ethical decisions that the Christian *as individual* must make (McCormick 157–58).

DISTINCTIVE AND SPECIFIC

These words are often used interchangeably, but there is an important distinction in meaning here which it would be very helpful to apply to the debate at all times: i.e., whether one is speaking of an *exclusive* quality or only of a *generally characteristic* quality. It is not a question of terminological authoritarianism, but of trying to keep genuinely different things unconfused. Walter (p. 101) suggests the following:

Specific: exclusivity; something special or peculiar only to the reality in question.

Distinctive: not (or not necessarily) exclusive; a
                   characteristic quality or set of relations
                   which are typically associated with a
                   given reality.

MATERIAL AND FORMAL

Material/materially is used to refer to the subject matter, contents or actions of ethics/morality, focusing thus on
the *morals* part of the distinctions just made between
ground of ethics, ethics, and morals.

Formal/formally is used to refer to the more fundamental approach, theory, presuppositions, etc., that one brings to
ethics/morals, focusing thus on the *ground of being* and of
the distinctions between morals, ethics and ground of ethics. Most contributions to the discussion begin by distinguishing, whether or not they do so in these precise terms,
between material and formal distinctiveness/specificity.

INTENTIONALITY, DISCRIMEN

We have already spoken of the *discrimen,* that pre-
discursive and largely imaginative construal of the mode
and reality of God's presence and action in the world which
grounds Christian theology and life (above 57, 62). Many
ethicists refer to this reality with the word *"intentionality."*

"Motivation" is also used. This is obviously what Mc-
Cormick has in mind when he begins his discussion of the
origins of moral judgments:

> The first thing to be said is that moral convictions
> do not originate from rational analyses and argu-
> ments. Let me take slavery as an example. We do
> not hold that slavery is humanly demeaning and
> immoral chiefly because we have argued to this
> rationally. Rather, first our sensitivities are shar-
> pened to the meaning and value of human persons
> and certainly religious faith can play an important
> part in the sharpening. As Böckle notes, it can influ-
> ence our insights. We then *experience* the out-of-
> jointness, inequality and injustice of slavery. We

then *judge* it to be wrong. At this point we develop "arguments" to criticize, modify, and above all communicate this judgment. Reflective analysis is an attempt to reinforce rationally, communicably, and from other sources what we grasp at a different level. Discursive reflection does not *discover* the right and good, but only *analyzes* it. The good that reason seems to discover is the good that was already hidden in the original intuition (McCormick 164).

"a priori"

Notice the similarity of this to the way many Americans came to experience the out-of-jointedness etc. of the Vietnam War, and *then* judged it to be wrong and undertook to develop arguments against it.

Enrico Chiavacci, toward the end of his 1978 article "The Grounding for the Moral Norm in Contemporary Theological Reflection," pp. 270–304 (after McCormick's perhaps the second most "useful" article in the collection), distinguishes three basic "movements" made at the level of establishing the norm of Christian conduct. He writes:

It is easy now to shed some light on the equivocation found in the expression "the Christian specificity" regarding the matter of normative ethics which

a. moves from the acceptance of faith in God who is charity (the God of our Lord Jesus Christ),

b. proceeds by searching for actions which better respond categorically to such a fundamental experience, and

c. in so doing moves within an ecclesial moral experience, in the light of biblical parenesis.

We must note, however, that elements (a) and (b) for reasons which are by now known are not exclusives of Christianity. Although they are specifics of Christianity in the sense that a Christian ethics cannot have any other grounding or process, they are not exclusives in that the calling and operative

presence of the Holy Spirit on one side, and the
capacity to reason on the other are also not exclusive. Element (c) instead is exclusive of Christianity, but it is not decisive in the normative process. It
never automatically justifies the norm, but helps
and aids in finding it (Chiavacci 299–300).

These final distinctions of Chiavacci, when added to
what we have already mentioned, enable us to bring some
kind of synthesizing order into the discussion. Element (c),
the movement "within an ecclesial moral experience, in the
light of biblical parenesis" is indeed exclusive of Christianity. But to say that it is not decisive in the normative process
because it never automatically justifies the norm, but helps
and aids in finding it, and then to stop there as Chiavacci
does, is misleading. It leaves one with the impression that
the hermeneutical center of a mature, integral Christian
life, one's individual and community experience of "passing
over" with and in Christ, is irrelevant.
    Now much of our argument here is terminological, for
Chiavacci apparently has in mind cognitional appropriation of the norms for the material content of morality. But
we are interested in more than that: we want not only to
know but also to be able to do the good. This, for a Christian,
is done only by a personal appropriation of biblical revelation, an appropriation which is not just cognitive, but also
volitional and affective and, as a consequence, also effective. The mature Christian does not move through elements
(a) and (b) except as a person who is *de facto* also moving
within element (c). Thus, although element (c), the only
element which is exclusive of Christianity, is not in one
sense *(per se)* "decisive in the normative process," it is in
another sense really the whole story. For element (c), one's
"ecclesial moral experience in the light of biblical parenesis" is the very womb, matrix and context of a Christian
person's *discrimen* or *intentionality.* Or, in terms of the
schematic outline we will present below of the process of
doing Christian biblical ethics (Figure 1 p. 117), element (c)
corresponds to the absolutely indispensable intermediate
step between "Christian biblical revelation" and "the art of
Christian biblical ethics."
    Another way of expressing this is the way McCormick

presents James Bresnahan's summary of Karl Rahner's thought on the problem:

> Since Christian ethics is the objectification in Jesus Christ of what every man experiences of himself in his subjectivity, "it does not and cannot add to human ethical self-understanding as such any material content that is, in principle, 'strange' or 'foreign' to man as he exists and experiences himself in this world." However, a person within the Christian community has access to a privileged articulation, in objective form, of this experience of subjectivity. Precisely because the resources of Scripture, dogma, and Christian life are the fullest available "objectifications" of the common human experience, "the articulation of man's image of his moral good that is possible within historical Christian communities remains privileged in its access to enlarged perspectives on man" (McCormick 162).

Is there then a Christian ethics, distinctive and/or specific? Depending on how one understands the various issues, almost any answer is possible. However, the question still needs a great deal of conceptual clarification and terminological consistency before the functional specialty of dialectic can effectively do its work. In the meantime, exegetes have their contribution to make to the discussion in studying the biblical evidence and the nature and functioning of Christian biblical revelation.

5. BIBLICAL COMMANDS AND PARENESIS. LITERARY FORM AND *SITZ IM LEBEN*

We will treat this material in four sections: (1) the literal meaning of the text; (2) form criticism and the *Sitz im Leben;* (3) the distinction between parenesis and normative/authoritative ethic; (4) imperatives in the context of story. Each of these four themes has already been at least alluded to in this work.

(1) When we say that the primary task of the exegete is to search out the *literal meaning of the text,* whether we define this as the meaning intended by the original human authors, or as the meaning a text had when it left the pen of its human authors/redactors, we are talking about a much more complicated task than at first meets the eye. For example, Genesis 2:24, the "command" to monogamy, was probably initially a gnomic statement inserted into the Eden scene; it probably was not intended as legislation. But by New Testament times it was understood as binding, though not always with the same precise meaning. What is the ultimate literal meaning (or who is the human author) when Paul is obviously just borrowing from stereotyped lists of moral do's and don'ts common to his day? How can one distinguish between more and less important prescriptions? How can one distinguish hyperbolic exhortation from halakah (law) and haggadah (exhortation) in the Matthaean sermon where they all seem to exist side by side? Further, just what is the literal meaning itself, and what ultimately is its significance in those instances where the exegete can move behind the Gospel text, toward the level of the historical Jesus, and there find aspects of meaning not identical with those presented by the biblical text itself? And, finally, how do we react to, or what sense do we make of, the position that it is the "logicity" of the text or its "biblical meaning," i.e., the way in which the Church in its life, liturgy and theology comes to understand the Bible, and not (or much more than, or just as much as) the meaning intended by its human authors that is all-important? (On the different meanings of a biblical text, see above 23–32).

(2) To help make sense of a biblical text in terms of command and/or parenesis, practically all the historical-critical tools (see above 17–23) can, in various ways, be used. The most important of these for our purposes is *form criticism* and the concern of the form critic for the *Sitz im Leben* (situation in life) of the passage in question. A law text will contain prescriptions or commands; proverbs and parables are obvious carriers of parenetic or exhortatory material; dominical sayings could contain either. However the determination of the literary form is just the beginning;

for that which is imperative in literary form may actually be just parenetic or exhortatory in purpose (i.e., in the mind of the human author). To discern with some degree of accuracy what one is dealing with requires careful attention to the context. This means as clear a knowledge as possible of the *Sitz im Leben.*

This term was originally used by the early form critics to refer to the situation in the life of the community which gave rise to, or provide the context of, the individual Gospel pericope (miracle story, parable, proverb, etc.) being studied. The assumption here is that those particular situations in the lives of the primitive communities which gave rise to particular Gospel passages are essential to a proper understanding of the literal meaning (= meaning intended by the human authors, or the meaning the text had when it left the hands of its human authors or redactors).

This helpful insight was subsequently extended by applying the term *situation in life* to refer to the situation in the life of (the historical) Jesus which gave rise to the text, and also to the situation in the life of the Gospel to refer to the final redaction-critical context of the passage in question. This increased the potential usefulness of the term, but also its potential for confusion; for it is not always immediately obvious in the way some scholars use the term *Sitz im Leben* whether the reference is to the primary meaning of "situation in the life of the community" or to some other "situation." Obviously, as much information and understanding as one can bring to bear on a text from the point of view of these three "situations in life" is an important step toward disclosing its literal meaning and its relation to command and/or parenesis. Actually, the reality is far more complex than this, for, as Schuele points out (below 204), it is now possible to distinguish as many as seven different situations in life. And, in addition, the term is sometimes, by extension, used to refer to contexts beyond the strictly biblical, such as post-apostolic, patristic, medieval, reformation, etc., right up to the present.

In addition to the *Sitz im Leben,* biblical scholars in recent years have been paying increasing attention to literary context. This is not merely special attention to what we have just referred to as the "situation in the life of the

Gospel"—often synonymous with *redaction criticism*—but also includes what we have referred to as *structural, literary* and *rhetorical criticism* (see above 21).

(3) As is by now obvious, the distinction between parenesis or exhortation and normative ethic or command is key. But one of the first things that one encounters in attempting to make such a distinction is an extraordinary variety of terms, concepts and underlying presuppositions. The terms are often used in contrasting pairs such as authoritative kerygma versus non-authoritative parenesis, juridic versus gnomic, etc. Let us begin at least by attempting to list the terms signifying commandment and normativity in one column and exhortation or parenesis and counsel in another.

normative ethic/ commandment	*parenesis/exhortation*
halakah	haggadah
juridic	gnomic, wisdom
law	grace, Gospel
order	freedom
imperative	indicative
	parabolic
	exhortative
commandment	counsel, call, vocation
authoritative kerygma	non-authoritative parenesis
binding	optional
absolute	relative or conditioned
norm, normativity	principle, action-principle
material norm	formal norm
rule, virtue-lists, *Haustafeln*	value
	example, model
	observation, comment

This is, of course, only an approximate list. There is no suggestion of univocity from the mere listing of the terms, and their categorization (in one column or the other) is often only approximate. It is quite possible, for instance, that what we have put in one column might, from a different point of view, be put in the other. However, just the presentation of a list like this graphically illustrates the complexity of this topic even on just the terminological level.

Now although the new covenant seems to put more emphasis on freedom and calling than on law and commandment, it is also fairly obvious that the early Chuch had no hang-ups about rules. Laws and regulations were at the heart and soul of early Christianity. This is true not just of Jewish Christianity's resonance with Matthew 5:17–20, but also of the apostle of freedom from the law. The Pauline and deutero-Pauline epistles abound with rules and regulations of all kinds. These vary from ordinances which Paul specifically proclaims as "from the Lord"—obvious examples of what he understands to be authoritative, binding kerygma, to recommendations which he characterizes as just his own personal advice in practical matters, to a mere handing on of the given mores of society in stereotyped form (virtue-lists or *Haustafeln*). Sometimes the distinctions between these are fairly obvious; at other times they are not. For example, much of Paul's thought could be described as a rapid series of irregular oscillations between, on the one hand, a profound appreciation (in indicative mode) of the reality of Christian being *in Christ* and exalted statements of the conduct or way of life consistent with that reality, and, on the other hand, relatively trivial rules and regulations designed simply to maintain order in the community. Just where one is in the pendulum swing is not always easy to determine. In other words, it is not always easy to determine when one is dealing with a true and absolute imperative, or with something which, although imperative in form, is really only exhortatory in meaning, or related only to a particular situation.

Is there any reliable way of telling the difference? Context is the obvious answer, but that requires great knowledge of and sensitivity to the biblical text, of the kind that even exegetes often do not claim for themselves. Is there any more practical or applicable rule of thumb? Bruno Schüller, as we have indicated above (85–86), proposes one such helpful rule of thumb. He states that wherever in the Old Testament and New Testament moral demands are presented in connection with the Gospel and the judgment to come, it is parenesis and not normative ethics that is taking place. In other words, when a Christian is being told: "If you do this you will be saved (judged approvingly), and if you don't you will suffer for it in the judgment to come," the logic of that situation requires that the Christian already knows what is right and wrong. What is going on there, even if expressed in imperative form, is not the imparting of a binding norm—that is already there and accepted—but exhortation and empowerment to live according to that norm. It is parenesis, not normative ethic; it is aimed at overcoming moral impotence, not cognitive impotence.

It is hard to underestimate the force and implications of this insight. It cuts under and through the presuppositions of much of the sometimes quite anxious search for a sure means of distinguishing the normative and binding from the merely parenetic. It provides a clear base for arguing that the function of the Bible in Christian biblical ethics is predominantly parenetic, not normative, and that the Bible is not the place where contemporary Christians should go looking for rules and regulations (material norms), but the place where they should look for revelatory insight into one's "stance" or into the "ground of ethic" or one's "essential Christian ethics" (see above 92–93). The Bible thus contains and brings to us the (story of the) indicative which grounds every Christian imperative and exhortation; the Bible contains and mediates to us the formal norms, the values, principles and action-principles, in other words the "images" on which we base our morals as Christians.

Two further distinctions: (1) The opposite or alternative to the non-normativity spoken of in this disucssion (when the Gospel puts ethical demands in the context of the judgment to come) is *not* "non-binding" or "optional" or any kind of "autarchy," but rather the call, the appeal, to recognize what one is *en Christō* and to live accordingly (cf. Rom 12:1–2). It is an invitation to self-transcending love; it is the "law" of love that guides life in Christ. (2) "Normativity" in this discussion seems to refer directly not so much to aspects of binding and obligation as to aspects of *knowing* that to which one is bound. Thus the assertion "not normative ethics but parenesis" is saying that one is not being instructed as to what is right and wrong, binding or non-binding, but rather is being exhorted and empowered to live up to that to which one is called.

(4) From this we can see how helpful it is to see Christian imperative and Christian parenetic in the context of our individual and communal Christian story, as has been and will be pointed out or alluded to numerous times in the course of this study (e.g., above 54–62 and below 131–137, 156–169).

6. BIBLICAL PARADOX

James A. Fischer, C.M.

Every moral decision involves a tension. Within an Aristotelian-Thomistic framework, every moral decision is a case of double effect. Good alone can be willed; the choice is always between two goods, at least as seen by the subject. It may be objected that scientific ethics cannot deal with subjective decisions, but only with objective ones. Some accommodation is made toward subjective elements by introducing "circumstances" as a factor, either excusing or intensifying. However complex these circumstances may be, the ethicist attempts to make objective judgments about them. Yet this very objectivity itself introduces a tension. There are no objective moral acts; they exist only in books, not in people. For an act to be moral, it must be subjective. An ethicist writing about euthanasia may be guilty of the crime of bad writing but not of murder.

The mode of communication of a moral imperative is crucial. It may be made in either scientific or literary language. Scientific language is object-centered. When a doctor says myocardial infarction, he is speaking an impersonal language of science. Nothing is said of the doctor's or the patient's feelings. If one speaks of "the passion of the broken heart," the language is literary and conveys feelings by means of images.

The literary forms of the Bible are those of literature, not of science. It is one of the main theses of this book that the root element in the ethical language of the Bible is story (see, e.g., 54–62, 131–137, 156–169). Then the stories of people's customs get summarized in proverbs, parenesis and instruction. Finally, the Bible deals with commentary on law. It is commentary; the legal forms are used simply as the basis for insights and are most often taken from pre-existing law forms. In all of these literary forms, the Bible is speaking from experience, not theory; it is dealing with actual lives with a story from just beneath the surface even when it is not up front. It deals in images, contrasts, irony, paradox, etc. These are experiences of life, not principles. The ethical implications must be approached through the literary forms in which the biblical authors expressed themselves.

The first literary form which we consider is that of paradox. Paradox, of course, is the literary artist's way of expressing tension. It is not, at its best, a literary trick or conscious technique; it is a reflection of life. We make decisions on the basis of images more than on the basis of logic. This fact seems to lie behind the prediscursive origin of moral judgments that Richard McCormick writes of.[35] The images are in conflict. In story form we have Qoheleth's parable of the wise man who saved the city (Qoh 9:13–15). And everyone forgot the wise man. Here the wisdom writer's image of the respected wise man clashes with the actuality. It also validates the basic premise of the book that all things are vanity and the implicit premise that the most important thing is to write of vanity. The only apology to be made here is for expressing these ideas in abstract language instead of locating them in the vivid story-telling form in which the Bible presented them.

In fact, all Christian decision-making is presented as a conflict. It may be a conflict between Christians (e.g., how were the Corinthians to exercise *koinōnia* by casting out the incestuous man? cf. 1 Cor 5:9–13), or it may be a conflict within the Christian (e.g., the tensions imposed by the love commandment).

The function of literary paradox is to lead the reader into a consideration of mystery, not into the blank wall of contradiction. Paradox, of course, has been a respected tool of scientific theology from Augustine to Luther to Heidegger (to mention only a few names). Bonaventure and Nicholas of Cusa developed the *coincidentia oppositorum*. Similar methodologies have been used in philosophy (e.g., Hegel), in mathematics (e.g., Pythagoras), and in psychotherapy (e.g., Watzlawick).

Perhaps the most immediately illustrative is that of Watzlawick. For example, if a schizophrenic patient has been conditioned to take the love commandment literally, he may indeed be caught in a "double bind." In any Christian concept of love there must be a free offering. Yet the subject is commanded under obedience to love freely. In abnormal reasoning there is no escape from this dilemma, and the patient expresses the bind by acting out and communicating both horns of the dilemma; he/she is both compulsively loving and compulsively free. Normal human beings seek some logical escape by compromise or by discovering some fallacy in the argument. More often than not such explanations discover a *via media.* But the literary artist insists on both horns of the dilemma being accepted in order to find a higher logic or insight.

For example, in the paradox "He who would save his life will lose it" we are confronted with two powerful images. One is the safety image embodying the fundamental drive to preserve life at all costs. The other is the risk-taking image which we know by experience often leads to success. The paradox is non-religious in itself and is usually resolved by *prudent* risk-taking. In the biblical uses a religious meaning is introduced either by the context or by additions to the saying: "Whoever would preserve his life will lose it, but whoever loses his life for my sake and the Gospel's will preserve it" (Mark 8:35). The context (an instruction on the paradox of carrying the cross) and the additional words shift the logic of action from self-accomplishment to faith in Jesus, a superhuman cause. The paradox lifts the problem from one of conventional logic to a consideration of mysterious causality. The paradoxical injunction does not function precisely as a command to do thus and so, but as an insight into the true focal point of decision on the basis of faith whatever one does.

Paul abounds in such paradoxical parenesis. For God's folly is wiser than men, and his weakness more powerful than man" (1 Cor 1:25). On a logical basis, this statement is self-defeating. If God is foolish or weak, he is not God. One may try to escape logically by saying that the sentence means that God appears foolish and weak. That is probably true, but that is not what Paul wrote. Within the context of decision-making about the style of Gospel preaching, the

saying is an invitation to probe the deeper causality of how
the Gospel works. One may use all human means of effective preaching and expect success. In this case, according to
Paul, the preaching is in vain whether it succeeds or not. If
one sees divine power operating, then even the most meager
human means may succeed, as experience indicates. The
function of the saying is not to prescribe immutable and
precise ways of preaching—only in the Corinthian situation
can that be applied—but to penetrate what is behind the
action. Such, incidentially, has been the *sensus fidelium*
about the interpretation of the passage. The Gospel can be
preached by intense professionalism or by utter simplicity.
In neither case can one expect that the method will produce
results.

Watzlawick in his therapeutic use of paradox observes
that patients are caught in a "no-end" game. They have
defined for themselves some double-binding situation
which makes it impossible for them to escape from the
rules they have made. A managing wife and an alcoholic
husband have set up for themselves a set of rules in which
each needs the other's weakness. "I couldn't stand my wife
if she didn't drive me to drink" countered by "If I didn't take
care of that man he would fall apart." The therapeutic
procedure introduces a third party (therapist) who pushes
both parties to a greater *reductio ad absurdum* of their
logical game. For some reason this final absurdity of logic
may enable them to break out of the game. A different and
yet paradigmatically similar procedure is noted in Alcoholics Anonymous—a Higher Power must intervene when life
has become unmanageable. In some similar way, normal
living brings us to absurdity, as in the saying that life is
irrational. The paradox pushes both ends of the absurd
dilemma to an extreme and so provides an escape from
logic as usually understood. "For when I am weak, then I
am strong" (2 Cor 12:10). It is at this moment of paradox that
an insight into a different dynamic leading to decision can
be embraced. As appears in the schema of Christian decision-making used in this book, it is only at the decisive
moment of shaping action on the basis of faith that a moral
act finally becomes ethical in the full Christian sense.

The literary form of paradox carries personal experience from the author to the reader. The final function is the

search for a person. Persons are perceived as paradoxes. No rigid framework of logic unifies our personalities; however "simple" a person may appear, we know the individual as a complexus of disparate qualities, drives, abilities, weaknesses, strengths, etc. On a psychological model, there is no such thing as maturity of fullness; various maturities are more or less developed, various capacities are more or less fulfilled; a tension exists between what is and what we suspect can be. Such is God, a person in biblical literature. God is not the monolithic One, but the uncharted Many; there is no one biblical picture of God but a whole portrait gallery. God is Creator and Destroyer, Lover and Judge, Father and Son, Warrior and Husband, male and female, hidden and close, etc. Eventually all religious ethics depends on a concept of God. In biblical literature God is a paradox. He can only be sought as a person. He integrates in the only way that a person is integrated, by combining disparates. Biblical ethics, a portrayal of human search for God, functions in the same way. Chesterton once remarked that paradox is a knot and only this knot can tie together the loose strands of human existence. Precise ethical decisions are difficult to make from a biblical basis, but on the other hand, in revelatory insight into persons, the Bible is rich.

7. LAW AND WISDOM

James A. Fischer, C.M.

The biblical background of Christian ethics is often fitted into a pre-existing logical framework of theology. Thus in the natural law-divine positive law schema, biblical texts are attached to various divisions of schematized, scientific outlines. The same is true for other philosophical approaches to ethical frameworks. The biblical texts usually do not fit well because they are atomized apart from their context. More fundamentally, literary writing is forced into the form of scientific language. Even then the systematizing does not work well. Some natural law dictates, if that system is used, get distorted. Lying and deception is an on again-off again biblical vice. Murder and violence seem to have no consistent evaluation. Ceremonial laws, which seem to be divine-positive in origin, are changed without any clear criterion as to how far the change extends. Mixed cases are puzzling; divorce seems at one time to be only a civil matter and then again a deeply theological dictum; at one time it is approved and at another time denounced. The assimilation of biblical materials into other systems does not seem to work much better.

Two factors need attention: codification and literary quality of imperatives. Codification is considered here first. To fit into any schematized ethics the biblical material must first be systematized in itself. However, there seems to be no way of doing this. The Ten Commandments would seem to be the most fruitful area for codification. In logical systems almost all ethical matters are attached in some way to the ten sayings—at least, that is the way our ethics textbooks and popularizations proceed. Yet the Ten Commandments do not really function as a code either in the Old Testament or in the New. If they are a code, it is odd that the code is cited only twice in the Old Testament (Exod 20:1–17; Deut 5:6–12) and never as a complete list in the New. The various laws in Exodus, Leviticus, Numbers and Deuteronomy cannot be said to be governed by the code or arranged according to it. The J and the E tradition seem to know nothing or very little of this codification: The New Testament only rarely cites any of the Commandments, and when it does, a sampling from the fourth to the eighth sayings is given. Surely the Ten Commandments, at least as code, do not rule New Testament morality.

Perhaps the most codified section of the Old Testament is the so-called "Code of Holiness" in Leviticus 17—25. Yet even a cursory glance at the material will indicate that it is not really codified by topics or principles. It is somewhat unified by an underlying thought of holiness, but not by a scientific outline. Almost all of its individual sayings, simply as decisions, can be paralleled in other ancient law codes and customs; where the lacunae occur, we may suppose that we lack documentary evidence. The sayings are modified by assimilation into Israelite religion; for example, the civil rights legislation is without the class-consciousness of Hammurabic law. But there is nothing to suppose that an organizing principle of logic underlay the modification.

Neither does the New Testament manifest a codification. The "new law" in Matthew 5 is actually a jumble of commentary on assorted Ten Commandments, annexed legislation and misstatements of traditional parenesis. The *Haustafeln*[36] and virtue-lists in the Epistles seem to be the only other organized code-like sections. However, the codification of the *Haustafeln* and the virtue-vice lists seems to predate the incorporation into the Epistles. In effect, the New Testament seems singularly devoid of codified law.

If codification is essential to scientific law study, then there must be a complete system of legislation, judiciary and enforcement. In civil legislation the making of laws cannot stand by itself; there must be courts and policemen and specific penalties. It is rare that these elements come together in the Bible. In Deuteronomic legislation there are penalties aplenty, often of the most severe type. But something is lacking. "If a man has a stubborn and unruly son who will not listen to his father or mother, and will not obey them even though they chastise him, his father and mother shall have him apprehended and brought out to the elders at the gate of his home city, where they shall say to those city elders, 'This son of ours is a stubborn and unruly fellow who will not listen to us; he is a glutton and a drunkard.' Then all his fellow citizens shall stone him to death" (Deut 21:18–21). To accept this literally as a legal process defies credibility.

Nor is an appeal to moral law more satisfactory. Good and evil must be balanced by their outcomes in some way, either by achievement of an end or as the fulfillment of duty either by teleology or deontology to use the ethicist's terms. But this runs into difficulty also because of the literary form. For a story-teller the *telos* (end, goal) is the story; the villain achieves his necessary end as much as the hero. Adam and Eve are necessary characters; they are creatures of their author and they achieve his end, whether it is the proper ontological end or not. If the story-telling technique infects all ethical matters in the Bible, then this is a most important consideration. It is noteworthy that even the most injunctive codifications (insofar as they exist at all) are deeply immersed in a narrative. The Ten Commandments without the Exodus setting are not the point of the discourse.

If moral law is revealed as moral by a system of rewards and punishments, then we might have a principle under which actions could be categorized. That there is evidence for such a retribution theology in the Bible is undeniable. That it is consistent or all-embracing is unprovable. In fact, it is derided at times:

> Love from hatred man cannot tell; both appear equally vain in that there is the same lot for all, for the just and the wicked, for the good and the bad, for the clean and the unclean, for him who offers sacrifice and him who does not. As it is for the good man, so it is for the sinner; as it is for him who swears rashly, so it is for him who fears an oath. Among all the things that happen under the sun, this is the worst, that things turn out the same for all (Qoh 9:1–3).

No scholar has been able to make a consistent theory out of earthly retribution, and as to heaven and hell, we know too little from biblical literature to make much of them. All we can say is that we have faith that God will right all evils, we do not know how.

The other major problem concerns the literary form of imperative. In a scientific system an imperative arises from a principle or a specific injunction which can be applied to a subordinate case. It implies at least some univocal meaning for imperative. Such is not the case in literary language. The imperative mood (and its substitute forms) is imprecise in any language. Its use in legal texts seems to depend more on sayings of a wisdom origin than on strict legal definition. Rifat Soncino[37] has studied such expressions both in the Old Testament and in Mesopotamian literature and has concluded that the motivation is more clearly attached to wisdom teaching than to legal principle. He is, of course, attracted to Gerstenberger's analysis that Deuteronomic legislation is dependent on clan wisdom rather than the other way around.

The same can be adduced for the New Testament. 1 Corinthians 7 may serve as an example; the passage discusses numerous ethical problems addressed to Paul. The chapter contains thirty-six imperatives. Even in so precise a language as Greek, these are not all equally imperative. As a matter of fact, only six of them are clearly injunctive; the others range from wishes to advice. How the injunctions are intended to function is also complex. As is well known, the Pauline approach comes down to the "in Christ" statement or some equivalent. Whether this is teleological or deonto-logical may be argued; it is not obviously either.

The argument being pursued here is not that there are no strict imperatives in the Bible or that they cannot be embraced within some larger entity. The argument is that there is no apparent or provable system. If biblical language is to be incorporated into the scientific language of science, then there must be some decoding mechanism which can be used consistently. It is the lack of consistency which baffles the translator who must go from one type of language to another. What may seem to validate a systematic approach in one instance may not do so in another seemingly equivalent passage. Some other approach must be sought if the Bible is to shed light on contemporary ethical problems.

We turn to the more positive hypothesis that a wisdom tradition underlies the legal tradition. The hypothesis is based on the use of similar words and expressions in both traditions. Which came first cannot be proved, although the New Testament evidence especially in Paul is strong that the injunctive sayings are dependent on wisdom sources. Gerstenberger's reconstruction of clan wisdom as the basis of legal texts is suppositional. We have no way at present of proving by source criticism that clan wisdom antedated legal texts; we cannot even prove that it existed. But it does explain the subsequent facts better than other theories.

An examination of some of the crucial legal texts indicates that they are always situated in a narrative context. Thus the decalogue texts are always associated with the constitutive Exodus narrative. This is what made a people. There has always been an argument as to whether the first Commandment is a Commandment or an historical declaration. Certainly the rest of the code depends on the assertion of what kind of God the chosen people worshiped. In the Code of Holiness (Leviticus 17—25) the recurrent phrase

"For I am the Lord" gives a framework of insight into the laws. The laws themselves are drawn from the common body of law. They might have marked off this societal group as different, but they are not different enough to have constituted them a distinct people. The historical matrix is indeed the constitutive element; the interpretation given to the picture of God constitutes the people in this particular way. God is a potential, someone that the people can be like. The matrix interprets the people as his people, in a "one of us" sense.

The tradition of the decalogue interprets it as interpretative rather than injunctive. *Torah* was esteemed as a set of stories and potentialities which were to be meditated upon. The Septuagint popularized the concept of *decalogue*—ten "words" with an emphasis on the revelatory character of word. The rabbinic methods of interpretation, convoluted as they may be, tended to be mystical in their humanism; legalism was as much a distortion to the Jew as to the Christian. The Johannine Prologue emphasizes Jesus as the Word, the ultimate revelation of what a human being could be. The wisdom tradition would explain much better what was being sought in legal texts than an ethical system or a legal tradition as such.

This approach may, indeed, be extended to all legal enactments. If one asks: What is the function of law? the most evident answer is to preserve order in society. This may be expanded and expounded upon, but it is sufficient for our consideration to leave it there. If one asks: What order? the answer throws one back to a theoretical order in the universe or to a consideration of the people involved in the laws. The first, of course, leads to a philosophical construct of some sort. The second leads to the revelation of the character of people. The despot, the timid leader, the confused, the charismatic, the Machiavellian, the simple, etc. are revealed by the laws they make. So also they reveal what they think of the people for whom they make the laws. Since people are not entirely sheep or slaves in any social system, the laws also reveal what people think of themselves and what they will allow to be imposed on them. Laws are revelatory. Such is *Torah*.

Now if this is accepted as a working hypothesis, what

does this add to ethical discussion? Let us say that both a Christian and an atheist refrain from violence. Let us say that both agree that such a law is necessary for the benefit of the other people in society. Let us say that on logical grounds both use the same arguments. What distinguishes the Christian from the atheist? One may say motivation. What is motivation? Is it a subjective element added to objective pragmatic truth? Is it a separate moral problem in itself? If the Christian is a pacifist out of cowardice, is that a moral act to be considered apart from the conclusion to be a pacifist? Is this additional element to be considered part of the moral act under discussion or is it an accessory, like a silencer on a pistol?

The biblical approach from wisdom would persuade that what is often called motivation is constitutive of the moral quality of the acts of the chosen people. The disciplinary and logical value of moral acts within society remains. An expression taken from Paul symbolizes this function of law: "the tutor stage" (cf. Gal 4:1–2). In this stage the primary function of moral law is the decision to perform right acts, and the function of the teacher, whether parent or ethicist, is to clarify which acts are right. But the Christian has come of mature age, free of the law, able to act on the imperative of being like God. Interpretation of who God is as a person and what one can be as a person becomes paramount. This is the function of wisdom.

The preceding paragraphs have attempted to sketch the argument that it is not law or precise moral imperatives which are central to the biblical approach to ethics, but the wise man's search for understanding. No claim is made that this approach has been proved by apodictic argument and no claim is entered that it solves all the problems. It is an hypothesis. It may be strengthened by further verbal and legal investigation; that in turn may be aided by discoveries in other sciences such as archaeology. It cannot at present be proved that legal texts developed from clan wisdom or even that narrative, proverb and legal text are united in some sort of *continuum.* It can be said that there is evidence pointing in the direction we have indicated. The more pragmatic validation shall come as the hypothesis is applied to various texts. If the results are worth the effort, one can accept that there is some truth in the hypothesis. The articles in Part Two of this book are, in various ways, attempts to do just that.

8. THE SCIENCE AND THE ART OF CHRISTIAN BIBLICAL ETHICS

(This section stems from extensive discussions among Daly, Fischer, Keegan and Tambasco, and is, for the most part, a systematized account of those discussions. The final draft was written by Daly in March 1983.)

As we work our way towards a more adequate *method for doing Christian biblical ethics* (see above 7–10), we are increasingly agreed that for ethics to be truly Christian in the fullest sense, the Bible, more specifically *Christian biblical revelation, must be integrally involved in its very process.*

In this statement we are carefully distinguishing between "the Bible" (see above 13–14), "biblical studies" (what exegetes and biblical scholars do), and "Christian biblical revelation" as we have defined it above (14, 46) and will further explain below. This implies that biblical scholars do not necessarily ever get around to doing biblical theology or ethics, and that when they do it is not necessarily good theology or good ethics. It also recognizes, quite obviously, that not all Christians who are doing ethics are even attempting, let alone succeeding, to integrate the Bible into their work to the extent we have been proposing in this study. In fact, the logic of what we are doing seems to be pushing us to the conclusion that the only ones who can do Christian biblical ethics are those who are at home not just in biblical studies but in practically all the other theological sciences as well, to say nothing of literature and the social sciences, and in addition to this are also spiritually sensitive to the life of faith and the workings of grace in the individual and community. But even remote approximations of such holy polymaths are not to be found in great number among us, nor is it likely, with the increasing specialization which characterizes all areas of human knowledge, that the number will increase. Nevertheless, Christians have in the past, are now, and will presumably continue in the future to engage in ethical reflection and make ethical decisions. Not all of these reflections and decisions are "good," but some of them are; indeed some of them seem to correspond impressively to at least the ultimate substance of what we are attempting to define as Christian biblical ethics. As a phenomenon, there is nothing new here; it is nothing more than the way we are experiencing the classical tensions between knowledge and virtue reflected on in such a variety of ways in the Greek philosophers as well as in the Bible. In the course of this study we have found it helpful to conceive of these tensions in terms of the relationships between Christian biblical ethics as a *science* and as an *art*.

Taking "science and art" as an image for what we are doing can be helpful. All the techniques of graphic presentation: color, light, form, perspective, etc., are elements of painting that can be scientifically studied and practiced. Yet mastery of them does not guarantee that one can produce truly beautiful paintings. Conversely, persons with no technical training in these things (e.g., the primitives) have produced truly beautiful art. This is not because there is no relationship between the "scientific rules" of graphic production and a true work of art, but because the true artist, with or without sophisticated technique, is guided by an instinct, a feeling, an integrating vision of how things fit together—or do not fit together—and will find some way to express this effectively. Artists can greatly enhance their natural artistic talent by learning and mastering the rules and techniques of their art. They can also allow their talent, if it, or they, are not strong, to become smothered by rules and techniques. So too, all the technique in the world might indeed produce something superficially pleasing, but never something truly beautiful; while careful learning and application of the rules can enable a modest talent to produce something far more beautiful than would otherwise be the case. Great art, of course, usually results from the marriage of great talent with great technique.

Thus, in our distinguishing between the Bible, biblical studies and Christian biblical revelation, we are not thinking in terms of opposition but of complementarity and inter-relationship. Other terms such as "Christian Life," "Christian Theology" and "Christian Ethics" come into play as well. We have tried to express some of these interrelationships graphically in Figure 1. In this figure we express "Christian Biblical Revelation" as the starting point, and "The Art of Christian Biblical Ethics" as the fulfillment of a process, here presented in the ideal, which we call "Doing Christian Biblical Ethics." In this ideal process, "Christian Biblical Revelation," as we have carefully defined it (above 14, 46), flows into "Christian Life" which in turn flows into "Christian Theology." At this point, as we have already indicated, "Christian Biblical Revelation" + "Christian Life," with or without the further reflected stage of "Christian Theology," may flow more or less directly into the final stage of "The Art of Christian Biblical Ethics," *bypassing* the more technical or scientific phases of "Biblical Studies," "Christian Ethics," and "The Science of Christian Biblical Ethics." Since most Christians have no significant access to the scientific phases of the process, this *bypassing mode* approximates the way the vast majority of Christians make moral decisions or engage (if at all) in ethical reflection.

But in the ideal realization of the process, "Christian Biblical Revelation" + "Christian Life" + "Christian Theology" flows into and through both "Biblical Studies" and "Christian Ethics," and thence into "The Science of Christian Biblical Ethics," which is then applied or brought to fulfillment in "The Art of Christian Biblical Ethics." What this schema also tries to bring out is that "Christian Biblical Revelation" and with (or after) it "Christian Life" both permeate and are integral to the whole process. "Christian Theology" is or is not integral to the process depending on how one defines it. Maximally defined, "Christian Theology" as a scholarly discipline is bypassed by that great majority of Christians who practice "The Art of Christian Biblical Ethics" without benefit of technical theological knowledge. But in the minimal sense that no true Christian life is

FIGURE 1

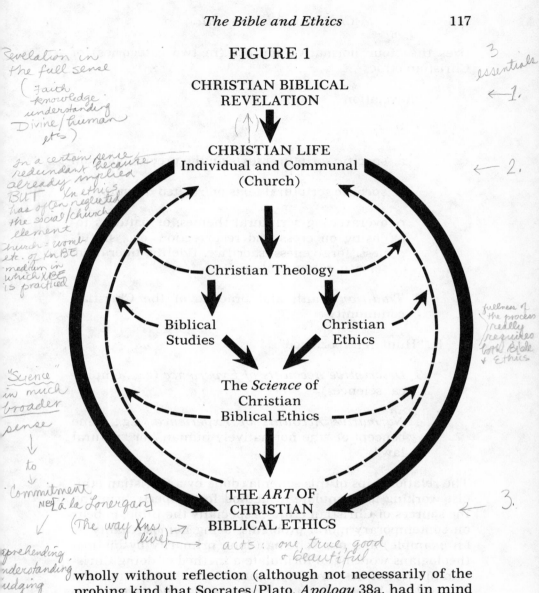

Revelation in the full sense
(faith
knowledge
understanding
Divine/human
etc)

In a certain sense redundant because already implied BUT In ethics has often neglected the social/church element church = womb etc. of Xn BE medium in which XBE is practiced

3 essentials
←1.

← 2.

fullness of the process really requires both Bible + Ethics

"Science" in much broader sense
↓
to
↓
Commitment
NB [á la Lonergan]
(The way Xns live)

apprehending, understanding, judging, deciding

← 3.

acts: one, true, good + beautiful

CHRISTIAN BIBLICAL REVELATION

CHRISTIAN LIFE
Individual and Communal
(Church)

Christian Theology

Biblical Studies

Christian Ethics

The *Science* of Christian Biblical Ethics

THE *ART* OF CHRISTIAN BIBLICAL ETHICS

wholly without reflection (although not necessarily of the probing kind that Socrates/Plato, *Apology* 38a, had in mind when proclaiming that the unreflected life is not worth living), "Christian Theology" is also integral to the process.

One helpful service provided by this graphic is the order and flexibility it can offer to the important question of the sources of Christian ethics and their prioritizing. We find helpful the way Lisa Sowle Cahill defines and schema-

art = the gift which is beyond final analysis

tizes the "four normative sources (in two categories) of Christian ethics."[38]

A. "Revelation"

   1. Scripture

      a. specific scriptural texts on the precise question

      b. specific scriptural texts on related questions

      c. overarching scriptural themes, or patterns focusing on cross and resurrection, e.g., sinfulness, forgiveness, sacrifice, fidelity, liberation, service, reconciliation

   2. Tradition (faith and practice of the Christian community)

B. "Human Experience"

   3. Descriptive Accounts of Experience (e.g., empirical sciences)

   4. Normative Accounts of Experience (e.g., some concept of "the normatively human," or "natural law")

The relationships of this schema (done by a Christian ethicist working to formulate a method for properly bringing the sources of Christian ethics, especially the Bible, to bear on contemporary moral problems, using homosexuality as an example) and our schema (done primarily by biblical theologians working to formulate a method of doing Christian biblical ethics) are fascinating. But before getting into this task, or leaving it for our readers, we should pause to expound more fully the elements of our schema. (The most immediate obvious relationship of Cahill's schema to ours is that of part to whole. Our schema attempts to show how the ordinary Christian as well as the theologian, exegete and ethicist does Christian biblical ethics.)

First, and most obviously, "Christian Biblical Revelation" is both foundational to and pervasive in the whole process. We repeat here the descriptive definition given earlier in this book (14, 46):

> "Christian Biblical Revelation" is the written re-
> cord and faith-recollection of particular entrances
> of the divine into the realm of the human as record-
> ed by the Jewish and Christian faith communities
> which experienced them and continue to live by
> them. Thus, "Christian Biblical Revelation" is that
> written history and recollected experience, not only
> as it has been recorded in the Bible, but also as it is
> *now* being appropriated (continuing revelation) in
> the human and religious experience, knowledge
> and understanding of those living in a Christian
> faith community, i.e., in people attempting to live
> according to the reality and consequences of these
> divine entrances into the realm of the human.

This definition tries to give due place to the distinction between biblical revelation as "descending revelation" and the human response to or reception of it, or between biblical revelation itself ("objective") and its subsequent ("subjec-tive") appropriation. But modern hermeneutics warns us against assuming a dichotomy between these two aspects of the definition. Thus no definition of biblical revelation which allows us to prescind from the question of our *access* to it can be considered adequate. Biblical revelation is not merely something that happened *then,* got completed or "bottled" at the end of the apostolic age, and comes to us now only in its "bottled" form. One of the characteristics of Figure 1 is that it attempts to show that there is not an exclusively logical, linear or temporal process from "Chris-tian Biblical Revelation" to "The Art of Christian Biblical Ethics." It attempts to illustrate the pervasive circularity of the process. For "Christian Biblical Revelation" has not only taken place, it is in reality still taking place in and through both individual and communal experience of some or all of the other things indicated in Figure 1.

As for the rest of the elements in Figure 1, "Christian Life" is the individual and communal experience of implic-itly or consciously living under the sign of "Christian Biblical Revelation." It is the "place" where, as we shall see below, "ecclesial moral experience in the light of biblical parenesis"[39] takes place. "Christian Theology" is the reflection (whether systematic/academic or general/popular) on this "Christian Biblical Revelation" as actualized in "Christian Life." "Biblical Studies" refers to the specific activities or functions of biblical scholars. "Christian Ethics" refers correspondingly to the specialized activities of Christian ethicians or moral theologians. "The Science of Christian Biblical Ethics" is the "science" or the "method" of doing Christian biblical ethics which results from the confluence of "Biblical Studies" and "Christian Ethics" in the context suggested by the schema of Figure 1. "The Art of Christian Biblical Ethics" is the actual application or putting into practice of "The Science of Christian Biblical Ethics." As the diagram suggests, the *"science"* of Christian biblical ethics comes most immediately from the confluence of "Biblical Studies" and "Christian Ethics." The *"art"* of Christian biblical ethics, however, comes most immediately (and in all cases at least minimally) from the confluence of "Christian Life" and "Christian Theology." In the ideal realization of the process, "The Art of Christian Biblical Ethics" is fundamentally and pervasively influenced by "The Science of Christian Biblical Ethics," but in actual practice this is bypassed far more often than not in Christian moral decision-making and action. Thus, in all instances, "The Art of Christian Biblical Ethics" stands under the sign and pervasive influence of "Christian Biblical Revelation" and "Christian Life."

Hence, three of the seven "elements" or "phases" of doing Christian biblical ethics as depicted in Figure 1 are absolutely essential. That is, if one wanted to reduce the schema to its simplest form, and still have something that would make sense in at least some instances, the three essential elements would be "Christian Biblical Revelation," "Christian Life" and "The Art of Christian Biblical Ethics." Strictly speaking, since the role of the community is at least implicitly contained in our broad definition of "Christian Biblical Revelation," "Christian Life" could also be scratched from the schema. However, such a further simplification of the schema would run the risk of neglecting to emphasize the all-important *role of the community* ✕

✕ This "role of community" concept needs to be clarified. Ethics in Germany's 1930s "community" were quite confused. What *is* the voice of the "Comnty"?

in Christian biblical ethics. It is also under the rubric of "Christian Life" and its inevitable community aspect that we locate most of what is meant by the terms "image," "value," *"discrimen"* and "character." These are precisely the elements which most prevent us from forgetting that, in doing Christian biblical ethics (as indeed in doing any ethics), we are inevitably and inescapably involved in a hermeneutic circle.

It is a very complex hermeneutical circle, and made more so by the fact that different people have greatly different ideas about whether it exists at all, and how extensively it exists or needs to be reckoned with, and what its nature and function is. What one means or understands by image, value, *discrimen,* character and community can vary almost endlessly. Numerous places in this study point out that it is only *through* such realities that contemporary Christians, whether they are conscious of going through them or not, engage in ethical reflection or make moral decisions. This, however, is just the first level of complexity. What we tend to forget is that all of these terms and realities have meanings and nuances which are different, sometimes quite different, from those of the New Testament (which itself contains multiple levels of reality, formulation and composition from, e.g., the level of the historical Jesus to that of the final redaction of a Gospel (see above 99 and below 203–204).

The role of the historical Jesus in Christian biblical ethics is a case in point. Most Christians, if not led astray by a docetic conception of the incarnation, would love to know more about the earthly Jesus. And it may well be that critical scholars are far too negative on this point. But the realistic fact is that even when we consider the problem as optimistically as possible, we do not know a great deal in terms of detailed, concrete information. But the telling point is that even if we had extensive, detailed knowledge of the historical Jesus, we would still need the interpretative framework of the New Testament to make sense of this information, and we would still be receiving it necessarily, although no longer so exclusively, through our own individual and communal experience of Christian life (images, values, *discrimen,* etc.). The hermeneutic circle would be modified, but not essentially altered. In addition, the histori-

cal Jesus does not now exist, nor did he any longer exist in
the years when the New Testament was being formed and
written. The Jesus who exists now and existed then (in the
time of the New Testament formation) is the Jesus who did
indeed take flesh in concrete historical circumstances, but
who has since *passed over* to the Father and who, through
the ongoing community of faith he left behind, invites us
and empowers us to enter into the process of passing over
with him to the Father. This process or *transitus* is what
Christian biblical ethics is about. If we take this seriously, if
we believe this, then we must not only be willing to speak of
the "science" and the "art" but also of the "spirituality" or
"practical mysticism" of Christian biblical ethics (recall
what we wrote above about the "mystical mode" 58–61).

Let us now look more closely at the role of "Christian
Life" (or Christian community) in this process. First, let us
repeat even more clearly and forcefully our conviction that
"Christian life" or the experience of Christian community
is absolutely essential to the process of doing Christian biblical ethics. This holds not just in the ideal realization of the
process, but actually and in every instance of human ethical
reflection and decision-making. For all moral decision-
making is based on an imaginative construct (or *discrimen*)
of what the world and the human community (or communities) are and how they work. In other words, the process we
are attempting to describe and analyze by way of Figure 1
will have basically the same structure no matter what the
religious belief or philosophical Weltanschauung of the
persons involved. We cannot pause here to provide the theoretical grounding for this assertion except to point out that
it would rely on the same kind of analyses Lonergan has
used to formulate the basic processes of human understanding and the basic functional specialties of theology.

E. Chiavacci, in explaining the difference between
what is "specific" and what is "exclusive" in Christianity,
finds in the process of Christian ethical reflection three
elements or stages which can help clarify our position. The
process, he says:

  a. moves from the acceptance of faith in a God who
     is charity (the God of our Lord Jesus Christ),

b. proceeds by searching for actions which better respond categorically to such fundamental experience, and

c. in so doing moves within an ecclesial moral experience, in the light of biblical parenesis.

We must note, however, that elements (a) and (b) for reasons which are by now known are not exclusives of Christianity. Although they are specifics of Christianity in the sense that a Christian ethics cannot have any other grounding or process, they are not exclusives in that the calling and operative presence of the Holy Spirit on one side, and the capacity to reason on the other, are also not exclusive. Element (c) instead is exclusive of Christianity (Chiavacci 299–300).

It is helpful to compare these three "elements" with the elements of our schema for doing Christian biblical ethics (Figure 1), for when we do this we find that the *order* of the process is not so much (a) to (b) to (c), as it is (a) to (c) to (b). Moreover, (c), ecclesial and moral experience in the light of biblical parenesis, not only influences and determines (b), but also colors and influences (a). Or, to put it in a way that highlights its hermeneutical circularity: one's ecclesial experience (c) provides the womb and matrix of one's acceptance of faith, (a), and these together provide the full context and grounding for the searching for actions (b), which better correspond to this fundamental experience (a) with (c), which leads to (b), etc.

In addition it is important to note that although (a) and (b) are not *exclusively* Christian acts, i.e., others than Christians can experience and perform them), they are indeed *specifically* Christian acts (i.e., one cannot have Christian biblical ethics without them). And, in the process of doing Christian biblical ethics, they are also graced acts, or faith acts. In other words, the tantalizing question for which no consensual answer seems attainable—"Where in the process of Christian biblical ethics does Christian faith or grace itself enter in?"—turns out to be a misleading question. If it is indeed Christian ethics, then grace, and faith at least implicitly, are there from the beginning of the process. *Theoretically,* one can conceive of the process beginning with "Biblical Studies" and "Christian Ethics" which then come together to form "The Science of Christian Biblical Ethics" from which one can then go on to practice "The Art of Christian Biblical Ethics"—and think of faith entering the process somewhere between the "science" and the "art." But *practically,* or in reality, it doesn't happen that way. There are no "Biblical Studies," there is no "Christian Ethics" without "Christian Biblical Revelation," "Christian Life and Community" and "Christian Theology" (or their equivalent, should one prefer to follow other schemata than the one outlined in Figure 1). And these elements of the process, as we have been pointing out, are grace-laden and faith-laden realities. There is no clear point at which one can say that a good act becomes a faith act or graced act. The extreme dichotomizing which characterized the distinction or separation between nature and grace in the Catholic theology of several decades ago has been, at least on the theological level, largely overcome. If an act is good, Catholic theologians now tend to see it as graced from its inception; or if it was not good and has become good, the "point" of its becoming graced will be identified with the point or process of conversion that has taken place.

But we must return again to "Christian Life" and see more clearly how indispensable and central a role it plays in the process of all Christian biblical ethics, both in its ideal realization (Figure 1) and in its more common, simpler realizations which bypass most of the middle, scholarly elements in the process we have outlined. A few pages ago we spoke of "Christian Life" as:

> The individual and communal experience of implicitly or consciously living under the sign of "Christian Biblical Revelation." It is the "place" where . . . "ecclesial moral experience in the light of biblical parenesis" takes place.

With the scholar, theologian or philosopher, this can involve a highly complex understanding of oneself and one's community and of the interrelationship of these in terms of past, present and future, or origin, realization and destination. But with everyone, scholar or not, Christian or not, this involves at least an imaginatively construed, pre-discursive awareness (*discrimen*) of who and what one is, of whether and how God is present and active in the world. Thus, what we say about doing Christian biblical ethics will not differ much in fundamental structure and process from any human being "doing" ethics.

The central or pivotal "moment" in the process is when images and values come into contact with each other and with a person's or community's *discrimen.* Automatically, instinctively, one compares and contrasts. This goes on, at least on the pre-conscious level, as long as the contact lasts. When this process becomes conscious, one steps into the realm of ethical reflection and, in a Christian context, has the opportunity or challenge to move through the middle phases of Figure 1 to arrive at "The Art of Christian Biblical Ethics." When the images and values which come into contact are not in tension with each other, or with the images and values implicitly or virtually behind a proposed action or mode of living, there usually results little or no *conscious* moral activity. One simply goes ahead and does or continues to do the things one has been doing, or continues to live the way one has been living without much thinking about it, without consciously making a moral decision. Such actions or ways of living may be good, bad, or mixed. The mere absence of tension says, of itself, nothing about the moral rightness or wrongness of a particular image or *discrimen,* or of a particular action or way of life. For example:

1. *A good image or value in contact with a proposed non-conflicting (i.e., good) act.* Persons with a self-image of being considerate, sensitive, and committed to help others in need as far as possible (values which can only have been communicated by family and community) will "automatically," "instinctively," reach out to help a fellow human being in need. They will not even give this much thought unless the action of helping would be particularly costly or dangerous. Even then, heroic actions of assistance are

and personal prayer life

why is this omitted?

sometimes done "almost without thinking" when the self-image as a self-sacrificing, helping person is particularly strong.

2. *A bad image or value in contact with a proposed non-conflicting (i.e., bad) act.* Some racist and sexist attitudes, for example, are simply ingrained in the imagination and consciousness of some individuals by the cultural milieu into which they were born and have lived. They can have an image of themselves which is de facto sinful (racist or sexist) and thus peacefully, without tension, without ever making a conscious moral decision, perform racist or sexist actions which correspond to their (unconsciously) sinful self-image.

3. *A good image or value in contact with a proposed conflicting (i.e., bad) act.* The gradual disillusionment of millions of Americans with the Vietnam War in the late 1960's and early 1970's is a helpful example. Most Americans who originally supported the war but later turned against it probably did not get involved at all in applying the just war theory and concluding therefrom that the war could not, or could no longer, be justified (as the American Catholic bishops did in 1971). What seemed to happen in most cases is that more and more people came to "feel" or "sense" that the war they saw on television night after night didn't fit in with their (basically good) image of themselves as human beings, as Americans, as Christians. Many moved from supporting to opposing the war on an "instinctive" level, so to speak, without ever getting much, or at all, involved in conscious decision-making.

4. *A bad image or value in contrast with a proposed conflicting (i.e., good) act.* Persons with, for example, an extreme hedonist view of reality are likely to look on other persons as objects or means of their own personal gratification. For the most part, they will be able to interpret the actions of men and women around them in the light of their hedonistic views—

until that moment when they themselves may be fortunate enough to be touched by altruistic, self-giving love. Such an event will not fit into their image of themselves and their world. They will be challenged to return love. In effect, and even though they may not be conscious of it, they will be deciding whether or not to change their *discrimen* enough to make room for authentic love in it.

Even in their oversimplification, these examples help us to see a little more clearly what goes on in the ethical process. When the images are not in tension, the community and the culture that is behind it "carries" the moral action, whether it is good, bad, or, as in most cases, mixed, in a kind of unreflected, peaceful state. Until or unless there is challenge from a conflicting image or value, the moral process, as we have been describing it, does not become activated. Where there is consonance between images that are good, we tend to call the situation naturally good. However, it may be a potentially weak situation for not having been tested. It is also misleading to think of it as "naturally" good, for this overlooks the roles of faith and grace in establishing and maintaining that situation.

One can summarize the dynamics of the process as follows: (1) If one has a good image of oneself and community, good moral action consists in attempting to articulate and live by conclusions and actions which are authentically consistent with that image. (2) If one has a bad or deficient image of oneself and community, good moral action consists in attempting to be sensitive to images and values which challenge the badness and deficiency of one's image. (Of course one is not comparing an image to an action but to the images behind or implicit in an action.) In the full, ideal process of doing Christian biblical ethics, one attempts to resolve images in tension by means of "The Science of Christian Biblical Ethics." The non-theologian does this in a less formal way by somehow making the images "fit." *Somehow or other, whether for good or for ill, the tension is removed or covered over.*

Human beings and communities do not live comfortably with unresolved tensions. If we cannot arrive at authentic resolutions, we will invent or adopt inauthentic resolutions that only appear to resolve the tensions but, at least, give us a situation we can live with. But then we take these resolutions and, whether they are in harmony with an integrally appropriated "Christian Biblical Revelation" or in tension with it, whether they are adequate or inadequate, authentic or inauthentic, we tend to absolutize them and, as the Pharisees did with the Law, build a wall around them.

Thus, the *discrimen* or imaginative, pre-discursive construal of one's individual and community reality is the overridingly dominant element in human morality as well as Christian ethics. In our schema (Figure 1) it corresponds to the point where "Christian Biblical Revelation" flows into "Christian Life." But as we have seen, a *discrimen* (one's overall imaginative construal of reality) is almost inevitably partial, one-sided, incomplete, and at times wrong. At best, we are dealing mostly with only partial appropriations of the whole reality. (The one-sidedness of most of the nineteenth century lives of Jesus, and some of their twentieth century counterparts, are fine examples of this.) In addition, *discrimina,* images and values tend to become absolutized, and they change, if at all, very, very slowly.

From this, one can conclude that a primary and indispensable task of the ethician is to *clarify images*. When this is done within a particular tradition or community (church) which enjoys a reasonably integral and authentic appropriation of "Christian Biblical Revelation," this clarification of images usually takes place "peacefully" under the sign of that community's *discrimen.* The ethicist or moral theologian will "clarify" the basic values and images of the community mostly by way of exposition and application to the community's situation, and within that context articulate and apply principles and rules. The pastor, counselor and spiritual director then apply this practical Christian wisdom to the needs of individual and community. In most cases, Christian biblical ethics "takes place," is "done" within this community context. One assumes that the discrimen of one's community is true and adequate, and attempts to live by its realities and implications. There is also something comfortingly "absolute" in this, for, as church, every community is, however partially, a realization of the body of Christ on earth. Most Christians are more than enough challenged by the images and practical consequences of the images of being a child of God, a member of the body of Christ, a follower and imitator of Christ, etc.

However, on a deeper level, it is also the task of the Christian theologian to attempt to "clarify" the *fundamental* values and images, the fundamental *discrimina* by which we live, and not only to clarify them but also to question and challenge them. But because of the protective walls we build around our *discrimen,* questioning and challenging on this level, and the concomitant change and development this causes, comes about only with great difficulty, slowly, and not without great pain and tension. This can be seen from numerous events and developments of the past decades in the Roman Catholic Church as the image of a fortress Church preoccupied with apologetics was challenged by the image of a Church more open to the world. When one does not move to this deeper level of challenge, theological and moral problems can be "solved" with relative ease and with a comforting degree of authoritative certainty. One has only to determine whether the challenging image, teaching or conclusion is consistent with the rules and conclusions that come from the community's *discrimen* and hierarchy of images. If there are differences, they are to be ironed out according to the *discrimen* and images of the community, or rejected as false. If one is ready and willing to try to resolve such differences, even if only on the level of a new practical application of a traditional fundamental *discrimen* which itself nevertheless remains sacred and untouched, one is often looked upon as being particularly liberal or open-minded.

Fundamental changes in a discrimen do indeed take place. Many conversions are instances of such. (We are not thinking of the merely apparent or "cosmetic" conversion in which there is no fundamental change but only an adjustment of one's external allegiances to make them more visibly authentic, i.e., more in line with the *discrimen* and images by which one has already been living.) Such changes are usually slow and painful. They may in reality be quite common in the sense that they are taking place "quietly" and internally in the lives of people and communities all around us. In fact, the process by which the old and the sick, the wise and the holy come to contemplate the prospect of death is probably just such a fundamental change. But whether frequent or not, such changes do not take place before our comprehending eyes very frequently, and in any case they are so involved with those depths of personal being where the incalculable grace of God is at work that they are not easily subject to analysis. Indeed some scholars feel that once one has uncovered or "clarified" one's fundamental *discrimen,* one can go no farther. Kelsey's exposition of this position (see above 57–58) seems to be the best known at the moment in the context of our topic. But C. Hefling has shown how a careful use of dialectic, as proposed by Lonergan, enables us to distinguish between more or less authentic *discrimina.*[40]

However, recognizing that a discrimen is more or less adequate is one thing. But *what is the process*? How does one go about changing from a less adequate to a more adequate image or *discrimen*? Change in reaction to a "frontal" challenge is almost impossible. This requires an almost impossible, superhuman degree of psychological and spiritual heroism. For, as part of our efforts to live up to the demanding consequences of our fundamental Christian images and values, we tend to absolutize them, give them more authority and validity than they actually have or merit. This is not too bad until they need to be challenged by more adequate or more authentic images. To do this "frontally" is equivalent to asking people to let go of everything that gives them security and self-identity. The Gospels portray Jesus as one who was not afraid to challenge people or institutions frontally, but they also portray him as one who continually tried to convert internally and indirectly, so to speak, by image and parable. This latter method, although often neglected and undervalued, is every bit as important for the preaching of the Kingdom of God as the direct, indicative, and confrontational declaration or proclamation of the way things are supposed to be in the Kingdom of God. This is as true for the contemporary preaching and proclamation of the Kingdom as it was in the time of Jesus.

For through the imaginative media of expression, ideas,

attitudes and values enter slowly and gently, and often deeply, through the preconscious and subconscious. They work internally, building and strengthening values and images that are good, challenging and confronting values and images that are bad or deficient. This goes on in a hidden way, within, until a conscious "moment" of conversion, deeper commitment, or decision is reached. We tend to think of this "moment"—which may in fact be an extended period of time—as the point at which the conversion takes place. But, in fact, the conversion has been taking place within all along. The point of conversion only marks the point of conscious realization of what has been taking place.

yea !

EXCURSUS: *
WHERE HAVE ALL THE STORIES GONE?[41]

The point of this excursus centers around several observations on the role of story and imagination in Christian life. First, and most obviously, Christian biblical revelation is unimaginable apart from story. In the Old Testament, almost everything is clothed in and carried by a story line, a story line which is a complex intertwining, gathering and amalgamation, and sometimes just simple juxtaposition of many stories and subplots. Even highly detailed collections of legal prescriptions, as in Leviticus and Numbers, are clothed in a story line. The same continues in the New Testament: the evangelists and the communities which formed the Gospels created a new narrative form "Gospel" with which to proclaim the central message of the New Testament: the story of Jesus. And down through the ages, as this "good news" was preached and handed on, this has taken place predominantly in story form. First and foremost, the story of Jesus was told and retold, eventually taking four similar yet distinct shapes in Mark, Matthew, Luke and John. Luke's Acts of the Apostles is a continuation of the story of Jesus in the new community he

* Excursus: (Latin) to make an excursion

founded. All the other books of the New Testament
which are not in story form presume and build on at
least general knowledge of this story. And within a
few centuries, the imaginative, story-telling patterns with which Christianity identified itself and
by which it strengthened itself and its members
internally and propagated itself externally were
quite clearly established. Everything centered
around the biblical story with its many stories, culminating in the story of the birth, life, teaching,
works, death and resurrection of Jesus. But in addition, a rich variety of story-telling activity quickly
grew up in the Church. The Lukan Acts (which
really seems to go with the Lukan Gospel as the
second half of the one whole) was only the beginning. Rich and sometimes fantastic gardens of apocryphal and pseudepigraphical literature sprang up
everywhere, trying to meet the obvious need of the
people to "fill out" the Bible stories with narrative
detail and strengthen the community's imaginative
construct of itself. Tatian's *Diatessaron,* composed
shortly after the middle of the second century, was
the first known attempt to harmonize the Gospels
into a consistent, non-conflicting story line. (Some
Christians are still attempting to do this, and even
scholars who are aware of the dangers of harmonizing and the significance of redactional differences
will, when they come to preach the Word to the
people, often fall back on a kind of harmonizing
story line as a means of carrying their message.)
Acts of the martyrs, histories of the Church, and
lives of the saints flourished in one form or another
all across the Church. They became the means by
which the Church explained to itself and others
who and what it was. This, of course, corresponds to
a fundamental human phenomenon which is as
operable today as it was in biblical times. For this is
the way peoples and cultures everywhere experience and express themselves. And for our age and
culture, even though we can describe ourselves with
a daunting series of post-phrases (post-enlighten-

ment, post-rational, post-romantic, post-religious, post-Christian, etc.), we still live and breathe from our stories. But now they are called by names such as Kojak, Barnaby Jones, Quincy, Star Wars, The Waltons, Roots, E.T., Gandhi, etc. These are the stories which now possess and captivate us, tell us who we are or are not, fill our imaginations with images and values in relation to which we can, if we are fortunate enough to have some basic story which identifies the root of our being and expresses our basic self-identity, clarify our own values and grow in Christ.

The "if" in this last sentence carries a lot of meaning. We must not underestimate the power of grace and the ability of the Word of God to enter and influence lives in ways we least expect. However, realism and experience tell us that unless we are already at least implicitly aware of a story with which we identify and which gives fundamental moral meaning to our lives, we cannot count on much success in shaping one that is both consistent and enduring from the confusing diet of stories available in the modern media. But if one has been made part of the Christian story, i.e., through family, community and church, one can even find help in or in reaction to the stories with which our modern world expresses its hopes and fears and joys.

In recent years there has been a significant, and in one sense ominous, change in the way "story" has come to be used less and less in the Roman Catholic community. This is what prompted our question: "Where have all the stories gone?" A few decades ago, Roman Catholic identity was bred and fostered in a very extensive way by the telling of stories. These stories sometimes had a strong ethnic coloring which emphasized who one was as an Irish-American Catholic, or Italian-American, or Polish or French or German-American Catholic, etc. But most of all, they were stories that emphasized what it meant to be a Catholic, in contrast, very often, to what it meant to be a Protestant, or something else. The stories were bits of history, lives of saints, jokes, parables, biographical and autobiographical anecdotes, things which were true, or imaginative embellishments, or wholly fictitious. They are what gave life and context and excitement and fulfillment to a religious way of life otherwise confined by rigorous rules and the rote learning of a carefully formulated question-and-answer catechism of which one was not encouraged or expected to ask challenging questions.

American Catholic religious life has, in the view of many, "come of age" in the past few decades. Rote learning of the catechism is hardly ever seen as a blessed end in itself, especially if at the expense of an understanding of the Christian life. Much has been demythologized, not only in the Bible but also in our respective ethnic and Catholic histories. A good sermon, or preached retreat, or popular mission (if you can still find one) will hardly anymore be a more or less skilled weaving together of the stories which tell us who and what we are; they are much more likely to consist of a careful exposition of the meaning of Scripture, a more or less sound psychological analysis of the experience of human and Christian life, etc. These developments, of course, are not bad; one can only welcome the openness, the lessening of narrow prejudice and the waning of an apologetic ghetto mentality which has accompanied them. But with these developments has also come the danger of losing something very important; for we no longer have the old certainties and enthusiasms by which we knew who we were, where we belonged, and what was right and what was wrong in this world. In other words, all these stories were the effective medium—and they were indeed a very effective medium—by which Catholics learned, shared with each other, and strength-

ened the *discrimen*, the imaginative construal of
reality which gave their lives order and purpose.

Another way of putting this is to note that four or
five decades ago the lives of American Catholics
were filled with stories which shaped the values
and images by which they lived. Many of these were
stories they shared with the rest of the country,
stories designed to entertain, or instruct, or edify in
a generally human and religious way, stories which
served the purposes of cultural, national and patri-
otic identity. But a significant number of these stories were also specifically "Catholic" stories, with
or without ethnic coloring. These were the stories
one heard in sermons, retreats, Communion break-
fasts, missions, novenas, catechism class, and even
in streets, bars and clubs—wherever Catholics met
and conversed with each other. These stories are
mostly gone now. Most of the religious situations
and practices which provided the context in which
they lived have receded or disappeared from Catholic life. But the actual life of a modern Catholic is
still as filled with stories as it ever was. Only now,
these stories are almost wholly secular. Most of
them come to us through television.

Thus, most of the Catholic "story time" that used to
fill and form the imaginative *discrimen* of a Catholic has been secularized. In addition, much of what
has remained has been demythologized in a highly
scientific or scholarly way. There has been too little
imaginative *re*mythologization and too much reduction to a rational or analytic level that has no
chance of firing the imagination and motivating
lives the way a story can. This, of course, is not the
whole picture of modern Catholic life. There are
many "new" things (in the Gospel sense of "newness") that give hope for the present and future,
things like the rediscovery of Scripture and the discovery of the graces and joys that come from a more
consciously shared Christian community life. The

old *discrimen,* like Humpty Dumpty, can never be put back together again, nor should it. But if we are ever going to have a new Catholic *discrimen* (or several; for more than one, or at least a more complex one, may be needed to do justice to the ecumenical and pluralistic realities of the new age), it seems that we will somehow have to recover for the Catholic mind and imagination something of the "story time" that we have ceded to our secular culture.

To bring this excursus back to our schema (Figure 1) on the process of doing Christian biblical ethics, the "waning of story" (as long as our story does not completely disappear) which we have been describing will indeed have an important effect on, but will probably not substantially threaten, what we have described as the ideal realization of the process. This cannot be said, however, for the great majority who do Christian biblical ethics in what we have described as the *bypass mode,* i.e., moving from "Christian Biblical Revelation" and "Christian Life" more or less directly to "The Art of Christian Biblical Ethics," bypassing the technical theological steps in between. In this bypassing mode, the Christian is moving fairly directly, pre-discursively, or at least without much conscious reflection, from the level of *discrimen* and image to that of practical life and action. But for the Christians who are bypassing the technical theological steps, the "waning of story" becomes critical, for story is the best and also most indispensable means of forming their *discrimen* and images. Thus, the *discrimen* of the non-theologian today is likely to be less clear and less strong than it was in non-theologians of the past. On the other hand, the opening up and flourishing of the theological sciences affords the theologian and scholar at least the opportunity to make up for the loss of story. Thus the chasm between theologian and non-theologian grows wider. They no longer share to the same degree in the same story life of the Church which used to provide an impressive degree of unity on the levels of imagination and feeling—the levels on which most of us, including scholars, live most of the time.

To conclude this discussion of the science and the art of doing Christian biblical ethics, let us again look to the one who is the center, the Alpha and the Omega of Christian life: Jesus Christ. We are talking about the risen, glorious Christ, the mystical Christ who is present through power, grace and sacrament to his whole body, the Church, and to the individual. Catholics tend to say that Christ is present, or is becoming present, to the individual *through* the sacramentality of the Church. Protestants tend to say that Christ is present, or is becoming present, to the individual *in* the Church, underemphasizing, according to the Catholic view, the sacramental-mediational role of the Church. Logically, this leads the Protestant to emphasize the personal, individualistic aspects of Christian morality, and the Catholic to emphasize the ecclesial and societal aspects. When one puts the whole picture together, this difference is fairly broadly realized. But when one comes down to details and practical situations, reality becomes vastly more complex, and, in some cases at least, apparently inconsistent. For example, the Catholic Church has often been associated with a privatized, individualistic morality, and somewhat less with community and social morality. And in modern American history, some of the Protestant Churches have been much more involved in issues of public and social morality such as civil rights and social justice than have the Catholic Churches. Such differences from what one would expect from the fundamental *discrimina* of "Protestant" and "Catholic" shows how wary one must be of generalization, oversimplifcation or deductive thinking in such matters. Thus the fact that in recent years it has been predominantly Protestant theologians who have developed the notion and role of "character" in Christian ethics is not surprising.[42] But this means neither that character and individuality are particularly "Protestant," nor that Church and community are particularly "Catholic." Both belong to the fullness of "Christian Life" which flows from an integrally and authentically appropriated "Christian Biblical Revelation."

In the last analysis, "The Art of Christian Biblical Ethics" represents not only the culminating point of Christian ethics but also of all Christian life in this world. The "art" refers specifically to the active coming to perfection of the highest of God's creatures in this world: the human being. Only the relatively few, the scholars and the theologians, know the technical rules and can, at least when they pool their skills, analyze the steps and processes of this art. But all Christians are themselves the subject matter or "medium" of this art, and all are called to practice it. Ultimately, it is all part of God's ineffable, beautiful plan before which Paul could only cry in awe: "Oh the depths of the riches and wisdom and knowledge of God!" (Rom 11:33). But the key point in the human contribution to this greatest of art works—and this applies to the peasant as well as the scholar, to the individual as well as to the community—is what Paul mentions a few verses later at the pivotal point of Romans: the proving (i.e., testing, feeling, sensing, working out, doing) what is the will of God:

> And so I beseech you, my brethren, by the very bowels of God's mercy, to present your bodies as a sacrifice which is living, holy and pleasing to God: your spiritual worship. And do not be conformed to the values and images of this age, but be transformed with a new vision of reality (*tē anakainōsei tou noos*) so that you may prove (*dokimazein*—i.e., test, feel, sense, work out, do) what is the will of God, what is good and pleasing and perfect (Rom 12:1–2; cf. also 5:4).

The Letter to the Philippians gives us a somewhat more powerful, somewhat more confident expression of this same central reality of Christian living:

> And this is my prayer, that your love may grow ever more and more in knowledge and every moral sense (*pasē aisthēsei*) so that you may have the right sense (*dokimazein*) for the things that really matter (*ta diapheronta*) and be pure and blameless for the day of Christ, filled with the fruits of righteousness which come through Jesus Christ, to the glory and praise of God (Phil 2:9–11).

9. FIRST AND THIRD WORLD ETHICS

Anthony J. Tambasco

The principal focus of this section is to examine what third world liberation theology can offer to first world Christian ethics by way of methodology in its use of the Bible for ethics. It is important to realize at the outset that we are concerned primarily with methodology and not with specific ethical content. Some of the particular ethical conclusions of individual liberation theologians may be debated. However, the general methodology employed by most of the liberation theologians offers fruitful insight that seems of important value to Christian ethics. Some of this methodology simply carries out in a more dramatic and perhaps more radical way the approaches suggested in the first world as new insights into the Bible's relationship to Christian ethics. We have ample area for fruitful dialogue, much of it even with what has preceded this section in this book. Our aim now is to point out the specific areas for dialogue.

Before entering into specific points of discussion we need to state the chief hermeneutical principles upon which we wish to draw from the methodology of liberation theology. Simply stated there is one main principle, namely, that our interpretation of Scripture entails a hermeneutic circle: it is influenced by the continuing changes in our present-day reality and it addresses these same realities. This main principle can be elaborated into further points of methodology, which will become clear as we further specify the hermeneutic circle at this point and as we bring this method into dialogue with first world insights in the following paragraphs.

Juan Luis Segundo, who explicitly treats of the methodology of liberation theology, clarifies the meaning of the hermeneutic circle. He says there are two preconditions for an authentic reading of the Bible. We can, in fact, call them the major ingredients of the biblical hermeneutic. The first of these preconditions and ingredients is a deep and rich analysis of one's real life situation and the suspicions it would cast on the adequacy of previous judgments concerning life. The second precondition and major ingredient is the willingness and ingenuity to constantly reinterpret the Bible in the light of the present life situation and analysis.

As Segundo develops these two preconditions for the hermeneutic circle, he evolves to four final elements for that circle:

Suspicion

> These two preconditions mean that there must in turn be four decisive factors in our circle. *Firstly* there is our way of experiencing reality, which leads us to ideological suspicion. *Secondly* there is the application of our ideological suspicion to the whole ideological superstructure in general and to theology in particular. *Thirdly* there comes a new way of experiencing theological reality that leads us to exegetical suspicion, that is, to the suspicion that the prevailing interpretation of the Bible has not taken important pieces of data into account. *Fourthly* we have our new hermeneutic, that is, our new way of interpreting the fountainhead of our faith (i.e., Scripture) with the new elements at our disposal.[43]

reinterpretation

Another specific main point of methodology for liberation theology comes to the fore when we detail the first two elements of the hermeneutic circle. The first two steps can actually be combined, for the first step can only be carried out in combination with the second. For a coherent and meaningful perception of one's life situation the experience of reality must be submitted to some category of analysis which already defines that experience. It is step two which organizes the experience in such a way that it casts suspicion on previous ideas and judgments about life. Now the particular contribution of liberation theology is the insight that social analysis provides the perspective and the tools for analyzing the life experience. Social analysis brings the proper set of questions which then challenge exegesis to a new self-understanding and yield a new interpretation of Scripture.

Of course, what makes liberation theology's social analysis a particular method for biblical hermeneutics is the

Mosaic/Sinai tradition:
① oppression
② exodus
③ the new law
④ wilderness
⑤ promised land

fact that it is a particular kind of social analysis. It is the perspective of the poor, the disenfranchised, the marginated peoples of the world, especially the third world. They have a view of reality, a sociology, which most often is not given voice. Liberation theology claims to speak for them and from their view of life. When it does it draws forth new insights from the text because it brings new questions to begin with.

There are dangers of distortion of method and dangers of eisegesis in the biblical hermeneutics of liberation theology.[44] One must beware of not imposing viewpoints on the poor in the effort to draw desired conclusions. One must recognize that even the poor do not have exclusive insights into Scripture and that therefore their social analysis must be balanced by other viewpoints. Nevertheless, even with these caveats, liberation theology seems to make a solid point on methodology and offers a number of insights that challenge first world thinking on the use of the Bible for ethics. We can look now at one or two issues addressed by this volume to see more specifically where liberation theology may offer fruitful dialogue.

The first challenge of liberation theology is to the historical-critical method of exegesis. We have already said that we must distinguish various definitions and uses of this method. It remains a legitimate tool of research. It can also be distorted when taken as a Weltanschauung or total philosophical hermeneutic deemed self-sufficient for arriving at truth and considered able to achieve full objective truth. We have seen earlier in this book that the method comes freighted with presuppositions to which we add or which we change into our own (see above 23–32). Liberation theology offers fruitful insight into the nature of the presuppositions.

The social analysis of liberation theology, the view of reality as seen by the poor and marginated of society, reveals that an unconscious and very influential ideology underpins any rational thought process or any reflective study of biblical texts or traditions. This is not a new discovery. Bultmann observed long ago that there is a precomprehension which prepares our reading of the Bible. What is new and what is, perhaps, taught us by the poor is the realization that this precomprehension is influenced by our socio-political position and our economic class just as much as by our existential, emotional or psychological experience. As José Miguez Bonino puts it:

> What Bultmann has so convincingly argued concerning a preunderstanding, which every man brings to his interpretation of the text, must be deepened and made more concrete, not in the abstract philosophical analysis of existence but in the concrete conditions of men who belong to a certain time, people, and class, who are engaged in certain courses of action, even of Christian action, and who reflect and read the texts within and out of these conditions.[45]

In effect, even first world ethicists can derive new meaning from the biblical texts because they bring a new partner with them into dialogue with the Scriptures. The historical-critical method, even with its awareness of presuppositions, has to this point been generally contained by the cultural climate of Western, first world society. The partner in dialogue with the exegete or theologian has usually been the first world citizen, a product of science and technology, of a successful and well-ordered society, or at least of a society in which most of the people have economic and political possibilities which afford the luxury of debating individual rights and personalist philosophy. With such a partner the ethicist and exegete have sought from the Bible the answer to questions such as: "How can we believe in God in an age of science?" "How does God order his creation and give ethical responsibility to humanity?" Now, however, the partner in dialogue can be much more frequently the marginated and the poor of the third world. They press us to read the Bible to answer new questions: "How can we believe in God in a society that systematically seeks to crush us?" "How can we justify a faith and ethics that permits the depersonalization of millions of people?"

The exposition of hidden ideologies and the uncovering of presuppositions to broaden the context and usefulness of the historical-critical method may be helpful in making the Bible more influential, especially in Roman Catholic circles. The presuppositions of the reader of the text have been noted as obstacles to using the Bible effectively for ethics. Charles Curran has indicated, "Scriptures themselves even in moral matters are in need of interpretation. Whether implicitly or explicitly the theologian will bring his own presuppositions to his interpretations of biblical moral-ity."[46] Because biblical hermeneutics involves presuppositions in interpretation Curran would prefer to rely on reason and human experience for deriving norms. It seems that liberation theology may be helpful at this point in bringing out the positive side of the historical conditioned-ness of the reader of any biblical text.

Rather than by-passing the use of the Bible or rather than seeing it as ineffective because of interpreters' presup-positions, liberation theology proposes that we frankly ac-knowledge the presuppositions and then use them to interpret. After all, the ideologies which evolve out of life commitments and experiences are unavoidable. The task is to make them conscious and self-reflective rather than to seek objective insights elsewhere. Such reflection may al-low the exposure of short-sighted ideologies and may allow the counter-influence of balancing and corrective ideolo-gies. The ultimate goal of ethics as for any other area of theology is the healthy balancing of ideologies to arrive at the fullest insight into reality. This process must apply to the reading of the Bible as well in order to derive its fullest meaning (recall our discussion above 139–141).

Such methodology may gain more use of the Bible for Christian ethics and may be more helpful than Curran's suggestion (based on what he perceives the situation to be rather than on what he would like it to be) that the presup-positions behind biblical interpretation render the Bible less useful for ethical norms. After all, Curran's alternatives are not any better, and should themselves be submitted to the social analysis and criticism of liberation theology. Cur-ran relies more heavily on reason and natural law. Howev-er, are not these also historically conditioned? Curran himself admits that classical natural law viewpoints were built out of static, somewhat immobile social structures. Liberation theology seems only to go a bit farther in the direction that Curran points already. It says that if every reflection is done with presuppositions, then reason is not any more advantageous than biblical interpretation for deriving moral norms. In fact, if we can uncover the presuppositions behind both reason and the biblical interpretation, we may enable them to speak to each other.

In any case, with a new self-consciousness and with a new set of questions proposed by liberation theology the use of even the historical-critical method will yield new insights into the ethical teaching of the Bible. Obviously, because the social analysis and life experience is coming from those who are economically and politically oppressed, the ethical teaching will reveal that the Bible says a great deal more about social justice than we have often reckoned.

We will not spend time at this point in elaborating the content of biblical exegesis that may come from the method proposed by liberation theology, since we are only interested right now in hermeneutical methodology. It will suffice to cite Robert McAfee Brown's examples which highlight how social analysis from the perspective of the poor can significantly affect the direction of historical-critical research and influence the kinds of conclusions one draws from the biblical text. Brown has randomly consulted several standard commentaries on passages which show Jesus making powerful statements against the status quo of those in political authority. Brown notes how a number of these commentaries betray the unconscious presuppositions of first world socio-political ideology which tends to soften strong statements that might upset first world structures. We cite two of his examples of commentaries on Luke 4:18–19 about the Spirit of the Lord being on Jesus to preach good news to the poor, release to captives and liberty to the oppressed, etc. From the Moffatt Bible Commentary:

> On Jesus' lips the "good news" has a purely religious import. . . . The term *the poor* is to be taken in its inward spiritual sense . . . and similarly the expressions *captive, blind, oppressed* indicate not primarily the downtrodden victims of material force, such as Rome's, but the victims of inward repressions, neuroses, and other spiritual ills due to misdirection and failure of life's energies and purposes.

From the *Interpreter's Bible:*

> The captivity referred to is evidently moral and
> spiritual. Thought is not moving now on the plane
> of opening the doors of physical jails, but rather of
> setting men free from the invisible but terribly real
> imprisonment into which their souls may fall.[47]

These observations would certainly not be the reading of
Luke done by the politically oppressed and marginated of
the third world. Liberation theology challenges the historical-critical method to recognize its presuppositions, and it
thus moves research in new directions which yield new
insights.

When we move beyond the historical-critical method,
liberation theology provides material for dialogue with the
first world in its search for how to relate the Bible to theology and ethics. We have tried to show that genuine Christian
theology and ethics involves the Bible throughout the entire
process of theological investigation (see above 114–138). Earlier in this book (42–45) we said that there are probably two
ideal positions for the relationship of the Bible to theology
or ethics. In both of them the Bible would be involved in the
investigation throughout the entire process, but it can be
involved either by being the source or by interacting on a
problem which originates elsewhere. The hermeneutic circle of liberation theology indicates that its preference would
be for the latter function of the Bible. It is not the biblical
data which functions as source, but the life situation and
the social analysis that ask the questions and give direction
to the reading of Scriptures and the traditions after them.

It may be at this point that liberation theology must be
challenged by first world hermeneutics which says that
sometimes the Bible is the source of the investigation; the
social analysis or any other data from theology or human
experience must be measured against the biblical data.
Nevertheless, if liberation theology is not held as the only
insight into hermeneutics, it yields material that needs to be
taken into account as the biblical methodology is elaborated. In any case, liberation theology would make a strong
point that the biblical data must be involved in the theologi-

cal investigation all along the way, even though it falls
more strongly into position 3/3 rather than 3/2 of the positions we outlined above 42–43).

Juan Luis Segundo makes this point explicitly by saying
that the hermeneutic circle requires the constant interplay
between social analysis and the biblical text. He observes:

> Now it is certainly true that one need not inevitably
> move from the third stage of the hermeneutic circle
> to the fourth stage we present here. One can cer-
> tainly move on to a new theology or a different
> tradition of "revelation." What seems odd to me is
> that any such new theology would continue to call
> itself "Christian," as they often do. The designation
> seems to make sense in such a case only as an
> indication of the point of departure.[48]

When we move to the question of how the biblical data
is to interact with the social analysis and the life experience
we find that again liberation theology may bring insights
which give an added dimension to what is already developing in first world hermeneutics and in what we have been
elaborating in this book. It is simply naive criticism and in
most cases unfounded criticism which says that liberation
theology moves uncritically from biblical text to present life
situation, as if the Bible could be made to contain all the
concepts for a present theology and ethics. J. Severino
Croatto addresses this issue directly when he says:

> Reading the signs of the times bears no similarity at
> all to any literal matching up of the Bible with some
> specific situation; to look for resemblance is to re-
> main on the exterior, superficial level. Authentic
> re-reading works from within. It links kerygma and
> situation along a semantic axis, disentangling an
> excess of meaning that is discovered to be such
> precisely because a *new* process or happening ap-
> pears "within," without having been on the author's
> horizon of understanding.[49]

One possible avenue for moving from Bible to theology
and ethics is that of story, as mentioned in previous sections

and further developed in the chapter to follow. It seems that liberation theology would support this direction and add its own particular dimensions. David Kelsey has developed this treatment of text as narrative rather than concept. Kelsey's work, *The Uses of Scripture in Recent Theology,* has been referred to already in a number of previous sections. We will repeat only what is helpful for our purposes here.

It will be recalled that Kelsey observes that Scripture is not so much a part of what the Church *is,* as what the Church *uses* to express its identity and to preserve its identity. The Scriptures function within the community. They *do* something. The authority of Scripture, then, is not a property of it. To give Scripture authority is to locate it in a certain way in the context of doing theology, i.e., in the process of the Church's coming to self-understanding. Since the Church can understand itself as community only in relation to God's activity, the decision about how to use the Scriptures for self-identity depends on how one construes God's presence in the community. Ultimately, then, the question is how God is using the Bible for his saving activity, for shaping Christian existence. How does the Bible effect God's presence?

This ultimate question for Kelsey leads to a prior imaginative judgment on the part of the theologian or ethicist as to how God's presence is to be construed and, therefore, how the Scriptures will be used to effect his presence. This prior imaginative judgment is, as we indicated above, thought by many to be ultimate. At this point Kelsey offers three different modes of presence of God and would therefore suggest three different uses for Scripture. We have taken the one which seems useful here for ethical inquiry and for dialogue with liberation theology. We have described it as the use of Scripture as narrative rather than as concepts. Kelsey maintains that God's presence can be perceived as a concrete activity, as the presence of an agent, in contrast to an ideational mode which is the perception of ideas and concepts about God.

In this view of God's presence, the stress in the Scriptures is put on the narrative element. The authority comes not from distilling concepts from the narrative, but consists in construing the narrative as identity descriptions. "Narrative can render a character. A skillful story-teller can make a character come alive simply by his narration of events, come alive in a way that no number of straight-forward propositional descriptions of the same personality could accomplish."[50]

It may be very well that this hermeneutical approach to the Bible fits particularly well for Christian ethics. James Gustafson has voiced his concern over trying to get concepts in the form of direct norms or principles from the Bible. There is a constant problem in determining which concepts are normative and which ways the concepts are to be applied today. Gustafson himself seems to move more comfortably in the direction of Scripture as "rendering an agent" or telling a story, much as Kelsey describes this use of Scripture for theology in general. Gustafson writes:

> The connections between God's lovingness and loving affections, while not easy to develop, perhaps in the Christian tradition are mediated principally through the narratives of the Gospel accounts of Jesus. . . . Indeed, if one is asked to indicate what he means by loving affections responsive to God's love, one is more likely to tell a story than to render a philosophical account. . . . The loving affections are evoked more powerfully by the narrative and parable than by more general commands.[51]

To return to liberation theology we may note that it moves in the direction of these suggestions by first world theologians and ethicists, while also contributing its own insights into social ethics and stressing that Bible as narrative will lead to issues of social justice as a more dominant theme than previously noted. That liberation theology would stress Bible as narrative seems indicated by the background of Latin American theology. Much of it comes originally out of the basic Christian communities and their reading of the text for prayerful discussion. Their application of the biblical text as one of liberation came more by the reading of the story of the exodus or the hearing of the parable of the last judgment than by searching for specific norms or ethical principles.

Juan Luis Segundo may have perhaps a more sophisticated way of describing the use of the Bible as narrative. He says that our task in using the Bible is "learning to learn." In this approach we first acknowledge that the biblical authors are historically conditioned, or, as Segundo words it in the specific contribution of liberation theology, all the biblical authors are tied down to their own particular ideologies. We are not able to separate the message from the ideology, but we are able to read the text on two levels. The first level, that of proto-learning, is that of deriving information as faith-content in the context of ideology. On this level information is simply added or subtracted. It is like a child being able to solve a problem that it was taught to solve, or to solve a problem that is a copy of the one taught.

There is however a second level of learning in which knowledge is multiplied. The child is soon able to solve problems that he or she has not studied. This is the level of deutero-learning. It is the application of the faith-content to the solution of new problems through new ideologies. The use of Scripture is, then, a total process. It is learning in and through ideologies how to create the ideologies needed to handle new and unforeseen situations in history. In our terminology, it is using the story of Scripture to tell our own story. It is learning to learn.[52]

Moving from general considerations of how the Bible relates to theology we can take up some of the issues which we discussed on the relationship of the Bible specifically to Christian ethics. One of these issues is that of the norma-tivity of the Bible for Christian ethics. In a previous section we noted that distinctions can be made between norms and values (above 75–78). We have also pointed out that a great number of ethicists believe that the real importance of the Bible is in naming values rather than in giving explicit principles or rules of conduct. Liberation theology would support this contention and would again bring its own distinctive insight into this role of the Bible. For one thing it reminds us that the interplay between the biblical text and our value system may go both ways in a kind of dialectic. Our historical conditionedness, our socio-political position and presuppositions, may accentuate some values more than others. That would affect the way in which we read the Bible to derive our values. We get what we look for.

Liberation theology would thus serve the useful purpose of widening our perspectives to derive fuller appreciation of the values that the Bible offers. In this regard liberation theology may correct what is a frequent criticism of teleological ethics which seeks to weigh values to determine the morality of actions. The criticism of such teleology, especially as it unfolds in Roman Catholic theory called modified consequentialism, is that it is too individualistic or self-centered in its methodology. Perhaps this method for doing ethics can still be effective, but with a stronger emphasis on social values that makes its weighing of values more comprehensive. Again Juan Luis Segundo makes a point about the weighing of values. He is hesitant to speak of values, e.g., in the form of human rights because the topic usually expresses the status quo or the interests of a North American personalist perspective with little concern for the economically oppressed as the victims of these "rights."[53] The values stressed under the heading of rights in this regard are often quite individualistic. Moreover, these are the values we would tend to derive from the Gospels, since these are the values we are looking for.

Jon Sobrino makes a point about the Bible naming values and does so in a way that relates to the Bible as story, as we have just discussed it. For one thing, Sobrino emphasizes a key point of value-centered ethics, namely, that it moves from an idealistic approach of describing abstract nature to a concrete approach which emphasizes persons. Sobrino writes:

> [The] shift in perspective [to the person of Jesus] is basic for any understanding of Christian morality because it indicates a shift from a line of action based on the universality of certain values (those of the kingdom) to a line of action based on a specific and particular reality (Jesus' own line of action).[54]

Moreover, value-centered ethics, precisely because it centers on persons, moves away from a static, hierarchical conception of social order and values to a pluralistic, historical and culturally conditioned world in which values are in genuine conflict. Ethics is primarily a question of weighing values. Precisely because of the contextual nature of weighing values the Bible is important because it presents the person of Jesus as story. One could derive generic values from the story as concepts or norms, but the real advantage of the story is the narrative element which shows Jesus not only naming values, but doing it contextually. "Jesus becomes normative for personal morality, not by proclaiming the validity of certain universal values but rather by historicizing them."[55] Thus, liberation theology shows us the Bible as naming values and indeed as moving these values beyond concerns of just individuals, yet it names these values above all as story. It shows Jesus naming values in specific configuration for time and place. There must be a deutero-learning process to find the normativity of the Bible for contemporary ethics. As Sobrino sums it up, "We can say that Jesus showed us the absolute dimensions of an historical path but he did not show us any path as being absolute in itself."[56]

Much of what we have developed in this section is but a starting point, a preliminary dialogue between first and third world ethics. We have sketched some lines of contact. It seems that liberation theology can speak to some of the research that we in the first world have developed in the challenges to the historical-critical method, in the very content which we derive from the Bible, in the efforts to relate the Bible to theology and ethics in general and in the struggle to find the normativity of the Bible for ethics in particular. We hope that this preliminary foray will stimulate further thought and discussion on these important issues for today.

Notes

1. For this formulation we are indebted to Lisa Sowle Cahill; cf. her "Moral Methodology: A Case Study," *Chicago Studies* 19 (1980) 171–87.

2. Cf. James Gustafson, *Christ and the Moral Life* (New York: Harper and Row, 1968) and Stanley Hauerwas, *A Community of Character* (University of Notre Dame, 1981).

3. *Webster's Seventh New Collegiate Dictionary* (Springfield: G. & C. Merriam, 1970) 575.

4. Cf. I.T. Ramsey, "Norm" in *RGG* (Tübingen: Mohr-Siebeck; 3rd ed., 1960) 1520–22.

5. Ramsey, "Norm" 1520.

6. A. Laun, "Norm und Normenfindung," *Lexikon der christlichen Moral* (ed. Karl Hörmann; Innsbruck/Munich: Tyrolia, 1976) 1197.

7. Bernhard Häring, *The Law of Christ.* Still quite helpful and insightful is Häring's treatment of norm and law, although not expressed in the technical language now current in the contemporary European and American discussion. Our remarks are based on the German edition: *Das Gesetz Christi* (3 vols.; 8th ed.; Munich/Vienna: Erich Wewel, 1967) 1.260–69.

8. Häring, *Das Gesetz Christi* 1.260.

9. A.K. Ruf, "Enstehung und Verbindlichkeit sittlicher Normen," *Normen in Konflikt. Grundfragen einer erneuerten Ethik* (ed. J. Sauer; Freiburg/Vienna: Herder, 1977) 83–101.

10. Ruf, "Enstehung . . ." 87–89.

11. Helmut Merklein, *Die Gottesherrschaft als Handlungsprinzip. Untersuchungen zur Ethik Jesu* (Forschungen zur Bibel 34; Würzburg: Echter, 1978).

12. A.C. Ewing, "Heteronomy," *Dictionary of Christian Ethics* (ed. J. Macquarrie; London: SCM, 1967) 148.

13. J.E. Smith, "Autonomy of Ethics," *Dictionary of Christian Ethics* (ed. J. Macquarrie; London, SCM, 1967) 25.

14. Bruno Schüller, "Die Bedeutung der Erfahrung für die Rechtfertigung sittlicher Verhaltensregeln," *Christlich Glauben und Handeln. Fragen einer fundamentalen Moraltheologie in der Diskussion* (eds. K. Demmer & B. Schüller; Düsseldorf: Patmos, 1977) 261–88; *Die Begründung sittlicher Urteile. Typen ethischer Argumentation in der katholischen Moraltheologie* (Düsseldorf: Patmos, 1973); "Typen der Begründung sittlicher Normen," *Concilium* 12, No. 12 (1976) 648–54; "Zur Diskussion über das Proprium einer christlichen Ethik," *Theologie und Philosophie* 51 (1976) 321–43, Eng. trans.: "The Debate on the Specific Character of Christian Ethics: Some Remarks." *Readings in Moral Theology No. 2: The Distinctiveness of Christian Ethics* (eds. C. E. Curran & R. A. McCormick, S.J.; New York/Ramsey: Paulist, 1980) 207–33; "Zur Problematik allgemein verbindlicher ethischer Grundsätze," *Theologie und Philosophie* 45 (1970) 1–23; "Zur Rede von der radikalen sittlichen Forderung," *Theologie und Philosophie* 46 (1971) 321–41.

15. Alfons Auer, "Die Autonomie des sittlichen nach Thomas von Aquin," *Christlich Glauben und Handeln* 31–54; "Die Bedeutung des christlichen bei der Normenfindung," *Normen in Konflikt* 29–54; "Das Christentum vor dem Dilemma: Freiheit zur Autonomie oder Freiheit zum Gehorsam," *Concilium* 13 No. 12 (1977) 643–47; "Das Vorverstaendnis des Sittlichen und seine Bedeutung fuer eine Theologische Ethik," *In Libertatem Vocati Es-*

tis: Miscellanea Bernhard Häring (Rome: Academia Alfonsiana, 1977) 219–44.

16. Franz Böckle, *Fundamentalmoral* (Munich: Kösel, 1977) passim, cf. index; "Glaube und Handeln," *Concilium* 12 No. 12 (1976) 641–47; "Der neuzeitliche Autonomieanspruch. Ein Beitrag zur Begriffserklärung," *In Libertatem Vocati Estis* 57–77.

17. Joseph de Finance, "Autonomie et théonomie," *Gregorianum* 56 (1975) 207–35; "La détermination de la norme morale," *Gregorianum* 57 (1976) 701–40; Dietmar Mieth, "Autonome Moral im christlichen Kontext," *Orientierung* 40 (1976) 31–34; Dalmazio Mongillo, "Theonomie als Autonomie des Menschen in Gott (Der Prolog von S.th. I—II, 90)," *Christlich Glauben und Handeln* 31–54; Joachim Piegsa, "Autonome Moral und Glaubensethik: Begrüundung der Autonomie aus dem Glauben," *Münchener Theologische Zeitschrift* 29 (1978) 20–35.

18. Böckle, *Fundamentalmoral* 19 and 158.

19. Cf. Hans Urs von Balthasar, "Nine Theses in Christian Ethics," *Readings in Moral Theology No. 2* 200.

20. Cf. Böckle, *Fundamentalmoral* 128.

21. Cf. C.D. Broad, *Five Types of Ethical Theory* (9th ed.; London: 1967) 206–07, as cited by Böckle, *Fundamentalmoral* 306. Böckle refers to Schüller as the leading contemporary "authority" in Catholic moral theology on this point. Cf. esp. B. Schüller, "Anmerkungen zu dem Begriffspaar 'teleologisch-deontologisch'," *Gregorianum* 57 (1976) 741–56.

22. A great deal of the theoretical grounding of this position among contemporary moralists can be found in Peter Knauer, "The Hermeneutic Function of the Principle of Double Effect," *Readings in Moral Theology No. 1: Moral Norms in the Catholic Tradition* (eds. C.E. Curran and R.A. McCormick, S.J.; New York/ Ramsey: Paulist, 1979) 1–40. This first appeared in English in *Natural Law Forum* 2 (1967). Knauer has recently updated this work in "Fundamentalethik: Teleologische als deontologische Normenbegründung," *Theologie und Philosophie* 55 (1980) 321–60.

23. Böckle, *Fundamentalmoral* 307.

24. Böckle, *Fundamentalmoral* 310.

25. Cf. Schüller, "Anmerkungen . . ." 744; 747.

26. Cf. Böckle, *Fundamentalmoral* 315.

27. Böckle, *Fundamentalmoral* 315–17.

28. Cf. Schüller, "Anmerkungen . . ." 745.

29. Cf. Schüller, "Anmerkungen . . ." 756.

30. D. Schroeder, "Parenesis" in *The Interpreter's Dictionary of the Bible. Supplementary Volume* (Nashville: Abingdon, 1976) 643.

31. Cf. Schüller, "The Specific Character . . ." *Readings in Moral Theology No. 2* 207–33.

32. Schüller, "The Specific Character . . ." 220.

33. Cf. Schüller, "The Specific Character . . ." 335–43.

34. Schüller, "The Specific Character . . ." 224–26.

35. See esp. the section on "Origins of Moral Judgments" in R. McCormick, "Does Religious Faith Add to Ethical Perception?" *Readings in Moral Theology No 2* 164–67. See also P. Watzlawick, *"Pragmatics of Human Communication, A Study of Interactional Patterns, Pathologies, and Paradoxes"* (Paul Watzlawick, Janet Helmick Beavin, Don D. Jackson; New York: W. W. Norton, 1967) 187ff.

36. *"Haustafeln* (exhortations addressed to the members of the *familia*) . . . formulate the duties of husbands and wives, parents and children, and masters and slaves (Col 3:18—4:1; Eph 5:21—6:9; cf. 1 Tim 2:8–15; Ti 2:1–10; 1 Pt 2:18—3:7). These exhortations represent the closest that Paul comes to a systematic formulation of social ethics; but they are limited to the domestic society and contain only generalities" (J. A. Fitzmyer, "Pauline Theology," *JBC* No. 79:162; II 827.

37. R. Soncino, *The Motive Clauses in Hebrew Law* (SBL Dissertation Series 45; Chico, California: Scholars Press, 1980).

38. Lisa Sowle Cahill, "Moral Methodology: A Case Study," *Chicago Studies* 19 (1980) 171–87, esp. 182–83. The purpose of comparing the two schemas is illustrative rather than evaluative, for Cahill (certainly less presumptuous than we) is not attempting to schematize all of Christian ethics. Commenting on our use of her schema in this study, she writes: "My thesis, I guess, is really pretty minimal: these are 'the sorts of' things to which the Christian ethicist must attend (183) in making an argument. But my language throughout remains on the tentative side—a lot of 'may's' and 'might's' (171). The little outline on pp. 182–83 is more an indicative statement about what the tradition has to say about homosexuality than an imperative one about how exactly all Christian moral reflection ought to proceed" (Letter 3/18/1983 to R. Daly).

39. E. Chiavacci, "The Grounding for the Moral Norm in Contemporary Theological Reflection," *Readings in Moral Theology No. 2*, p. 300.

40. C. Hefling, "Lonergan on Development: *The Way to Nicea* in Light of His More Recent Methodology" (diss., Boston College, 1982) 302–54.

41. Although composed independently of the work of Stanley Hauerwas, our comments here are obviously based on the same kind of fundamental insight into the role of story in Christian life which seems to inspire his work (see the following note).

42. I am thinking especially of Stanley Hauerwas and the works: *Truthfulness and Tragedy* (Notre Dame, 1977) and *A Com-*

munity of Character (Notre Dame, 1981), although it is difficult to think of Hauerwas as a particularly typical or representative Protestant (R. Daly).

43. Juan Luis Segundo, *The Liberation of Theology* (Maryknoll, New York: Orbis, 1976) 8.

44. For a fuller critique of the methodology of liberation theology, both positive and negative, see Anthony J. Tambasco, *The Bible for Ethics* (Washington, D.C.: University Press of America, 1981) esp. chap. 5.

45. José Miguez Bonino, *Doing Theology in a Revolutionary Situation* (Philadelphia: Fortress, 1975), 91–92.

46. Charles Curran, *Catholic Moral Theology in Dialogue* (Notre Dame: Fides, 1972) 43.

47. Both citations are in Robert McAfee Brown, *Theology in a New Key* (Philadelphia, Westminster, 1978) 82–83.

48. Segundo 38, footnote 55.

49. J. Severino Croatto, *Exodus, A Hermeneutics of Freedom* (Maryknoll, New York: Orbis, 1981) vi.

50. David Kelsey, *The Uses of Scripture in Recent Theology* (Philadelphia: Fortress, 1975) 39.

51. James Gustafson, *Can Ethics Be Christian?* (Chicago: University of Chicago, 1975), 72.

52. Segundo 118–22.

53. Juan Luis Segundo, "Derechos humanos, evangelización e ideologia," *Christus* 43 (November 1978) 33–34. The entire issue is on human rights.

54. Jon Sobrino, *Christology at the Crossroads* (Maryknoll, New York: Orbis, 1978) 118.

55. Sobrino 114.

56. Sobrino 131.

Chapter Four

STORY AND IMAGE

James A. Fischer, C.M.

1. HUMAN LIFE AS STORY

Herman, John Joseph, deceased on March 13, 1983 at St. Joseph's Hospital, fortified with the sacraments of the Church. Dearly beloved husband of Mary, father of Joseph, Fred, Cecilia and Ann. Member of the Knights of Columbus Council 1023. Executive Treasurer of Gaston and Co. Liturgy on Thursday, March 17, 10:00 A.M. at St. Mary's Church.

The notice is formalized and remote; one wonders what is the story behind it. We speak easily of life as a story and we expect it to reveal something. Yet there is a distinct difference between the facts of life and the story. The facts happen both externally and internally. Nobody controls them. There is no meaning or revelation in facts as such. We ourselves who live the life may put interpretations on the events as we go, but we realize that this is very tentative since we do not know how the story ends.

Story is different. It is different from the events of life in that a selection can be made by the story-teller and an interpretation can be put on them. Story is also different from mere chronicle such as a death notice which simply records facts. It is even different from history, although the difference is narrower. History does make a selection and does give an interpretation. The interpretation is made on

156

the basis of some logical nexus such as cause and effect, the connection of great movements, a special theme, etc. The aim of the history writer is truth of a particular kind—namely, the truth which comes from sifting facts and devising a theory which explains the facts.

Story may be factual or not; it does not matter. The events are not described primarily because they are factual, but because they are fitting. Story-telling is an art, not a science. Like any art it shapes content to fit form. The result is truth but of a different kind. The truth of art is in the beauty which results from capturing reality in a precise and fitting manner. This is not to say that story-telling as an art must be realistic; the imagination may capture realities which escape normal observation.

So also story differs from the concrete problems of life which ethicists discuss. Pinpointing some of the differences is important for defining narrative ethics especially of the biblical kind.

Story demands a unity. It seems simplistic to say that a story must have a beginning, a middle and an end. Yet the absence of any one of these elements will be a glaring defect in any story. So important is this factor that Aristotle not only demanded it in tragedy, but defined the terms:

> A beginning is that which does not itself follow anything by causal necessity, but after which something naturally is or comes to be. An end, on the contrary, is that which itself naturally follows some other thing, either by necessity, or as a rule, but has nothing following it. A middle is that which follows something as some other thing follows it. A well constructed plot, therefore, must neither begin nor end at haphazard, but conform to these principles.[1]

For the sake of study or of reading, we may isolate a sub-plot or a sub-story, but we cannot really interpret it without reference to the overriding plot of the whole. There is a tone, as Luis Alonso-Schökel calls it,[2] or a theme or general impression which the whole story makes and which must be considered in treating the sub-sections. Biblical stories, in particular, are part of an overarching plot which may run through whole books and which, in Catholic theories of inspiration, embraces the whole Bible and makes it *a* Word of God.

Secondly, stories may be told from various stances. If the story-teller involves himself or herself in the plot, the story is told in the first person. There are advantages to this. The story-teller legitimately knows the internal reactions of the principal witness. On the other hand, such an approach limits the story-teller to knowing only those things which one person would be likely to know. Stories may also be told from the third-person stance. In this case, the story-teller can claim a distance from the action in order to get a wider view. In fact, the story-teller may claim an omniscience in that the total outcome is known from the start.[3]

Any moral judgment in story-telling is secondary at best and is preferably left to the reader to form. The reader's judgment is primarily artistic—namely, was it a good story? The characters may have been repellent and the plot may have brought tears, as in tragedy, but if the story presented an authentic view of reality, it was good. Authors who need to explain the moral of a story are not in high demand.

Obviously there are many differences between the way in which a story-teller goes about spinning a tale and the way in which an ethicist describes the problem to be solved. The story-teller can select and create incidents at will; the ethicist must stick to the facts. Story demands unity of a most rigorous and overarching sort; the ethicist tries to eliminate the individuating circumstances as much as possible so that the problem or case may be applicable to a multiplicity of happenings. Story depends on a conflict of emotions; the ethicist tries to eliminate emotional considerations as much as possible. The story-teller either joins in the action from a first-person stance or assumes a quasi-omniscient attitude; the ethicist is confined to the third-person stance, but simply as an authority. The story-teller aims at an artistic form, the ethicist at a moral conclusion.

The difference goes deeper than these factors which are mostly matters of technique. Story-telling is an art; it has its canons of good taste and effectiveness as Aristotle indicated, but it is a creative act of the imagination. Ethics is a science; it erects its structure on ideas, not persons, and strives to create a system which can claim some objectivity and universality. Story-telling as an art aims to create something beautiful; if it succeeds, it engages us as readers to create our own analogies, among which may be moral judgments. Ethics as a science aims at ordered truth; if it succeeds, it gives us reasonable conclusions, and any aesthetic judgment which we can get from the form of writing is at least secondary.

Having established the distinction, the inevitable crossover must also be considered. Art and science are constantly crossing over even in the languages, literary and technical, in which they are expressed.[4] A good scientific theory has the beauty of simplicity; the art of clear exposition does play a part in the acceptance of theories. Good art does have precise canons which cannot be ignored subjectively either by the artist or by the critic. As in drawing, the line must be drawn precisely. So also the techniques do tend to overlap. The ethicist needs unity at least in his system as much as the story-teller needs to bring the tale to its completion and relate it to a world view. Both are striving for some multiplicity of application. The ethicist does not take an inhuman stance toward the subjects; indeed, in the first instance of confronting the problem, the ethicist may be talking personally to the person with the problem. For all of our desire for "objectivity" the ethicist is aware that great moral problems, such as abortion or war or sexism, are emotional problems and that the emotions need to be dealt with as much as the substance of the problem. The story-teller, on the other hand, may have a didactic purpose in mind. Exemplar stories are quite common and are a normal way of passing on the wisdom of previous ages to succeeding ones. Despite an omniscient third-person stance the story-teller realizes that the story involves the author if only as a representative of the community which accepts the story. The ethicist is aware that a "case" never actually exists; in real life it is embellished with a story. The story-teller knows that the story will never again be repeated in precisely the same way, but that there is an abiding truth to it. It is this cross-over which causes us many of the problems in relating story to ethics and especially of relating biblical story to Christian ethics. The adjectives themselves are cross-over points.

Human life, indeed, may be considered as a story. It has

events, plot, a clash of emotions, characters and an outcome. We may sample the trend of the story at any point by organizing it in an artistic way. That is a matter of interpretation. Since we do not know the end of the story or all the facts in which it is immersed, we are not sure of the final interpretation; hence room must be left for the reader as well as the author to put the judgment upon it. In Christian theology we call the final verdict the last judgment. No one knows what it is. We also speak of eschatology which simply means that we recognize the necessity for a story to have an ending. The kind of ending we posit is an act of faith. The Christian ethicist would also recognize that all systems and all practical conclusions fall under final judgment. Until the reality of the after-life intervenes, moral judgments will remain theories. Only then does life and story or life and ethical system come to full understanding.

2. THE BIBLE AS ETHICAL STORY

References have already been made to story as the archetypal milieu for moral observations in the Bible. The purpose of this chapter is to probe more deeply into this concept. It may be a helpful oversimplification to repeat that ethicists are interested in individual acts and literary authors in drama. The ethicist confronts a question such as, Is abortion wrong? Obviously, the question needs much fleshing out factually, and in individual instances the circumstances of the act must be considered. The ethicist tries to deal with this in a more or less circumscribed way lest the casuistry become endlessly shifting because of new facts and circumstances. The literary author, on the other hand, delights in the shifting circumstances since he or she is dealing with people.

Perhaps we can begin at the end. The ethicist asks: What is the solution? The story-teller asks: What is the ending of the story? The ethicist knows when the search ends; the biblical story-teller does not. Within the framework of salvation-story, no judgment is truly final; it is placed outside the framework of earthly life. Such a solution can appeal only to a person who believes. None of us knows the final judgment on Hitler or Mother Teresa. As literary artists the biblical story-tellers need to bring their tales to some conclusion however intermediate. So we speak of eschatological or apocalyptic elements, or of "realized eschatology," or sometimes we can point to nothing more than a conviction that there is order in the universe, perceived or not. These are only partial solutions.

To illustrate, one may consider the murder story. The ethicist would simply want to know whether the killing was justified or not. The story-teller wants to know how the murder happened. To isolate the act is to destroy the story. It is very difficult to tell a good murder story about a killing performed by someone who walked in off the street. For the story-teller, moral acts are a *continuum*, not isolated acts with however many attendant circumstances. Jezebel killed Naboth (1 Kgs 21:1–16). She was a pagan princess involved in that affair, but his murder must take into account the whole story of the conflict between Elijah and Jezebel. Nor does the story end with the death of Naboth; that is just the beginning. A satisfying vengeance comes when Jezebel is eaten by the dogs in the field of Jezreel. But that is not the end. The whole civil war of Jehu is triggered by the events, and despite the Deuteronomist's supposed retribution theology the story-teller leaves us wondering who was most guilty—Jezebel or Elijah or God. Now that is the story of a murder. So also with our individual lives—which is where we want to get as a function of biblical injunctions; they are stories of how we tried or rejected to become like God. The *hybris* makes the story scary, however prosaic the life may be. Just how much we should dare and how much we may not govern the drama. We do not fully know. But we do know that the story thus interpreted relies on faith, and presumably faith enters into each of the moral decisions which we make.

Since this matter is so important, a larger example may be helpful. In Numbers 11 the story is told of the marvelous feeding with quail during the Exodus. If it is considered as a moral case, it describes either gluttony or protest against God. Presumably the action is revealed as immoral by quick and drastic punishment. However, as a story the tale seems to be about something else.

First of all, we must define where the story begins and ends. The story belongs to the "murmuring tradition" which appears in several places in Exodus, Numbers and Deuteronomy. Numbers 11:1–3 begins with a brief account of a separate incident at Taberah. Numbers 11:4–34 is located at Kibroth-hattaavah. This passage is tied together by an inclusion formed around the word "greedy" in Numbers 11:4 and 34. Then Numbers 11:35 takes us on a journey to Hazeroth. So the story runs from Numbers 11:4 to 11:34.

However, this passage has two quite disparate scenes. Scene A tells of the murmuring over the lack of food (Num 11:4–15) and its punishment (Num 11:31–34). Scene B tells of the sending of the spirit upon the elders (Num 11:16–30). Source critics are uncertain as to the provenance of the text; in general, they detect a strong Yahwistic base with both pre-J traditions and later (possibly P) additions.[5] More definite conclusions are not possible, nor very helpful. The redacted and canonized text does make one story out of the two scenes, and we must proceed on the assumption that this was not done through clumsiness, but with deliberate intent.

Scene A is built around the catchword "lament" (cf. Num 11:4, 10, 13, 18, 20).[6] What the lament is about comes out through a dialogue technique. Two complaints are voiced:

People: "Would that we had meat for food!" (4–6)

Moses: "Why do you treat your servant so badly? (11–15)

The people are complaining about Moses; Moses is complaining about Yahweh. Hurling back at Yahweh the traditional image of father, Moses complains that Yahweh is treating him as if he were the father of the Israelites. Moreover, Moses complains that he is expected to do it alone. The speech ends with a mock dramatic plea to be struck dead rather than to continue thus. There is more than a little broad humor and irony in this speech which reveals an awkward side of Moses' character. At any rate, the problem has been escalated from a simple case of complaining about food by the people to a mild case of *hybris* by Moses who finds that playing God is too much. Of course, he does assume that he should have the job.

Scene B (Num 11:16–30) is a counterpoint to this story. It dovetails with the previous scene on the theme of divine assistance and it also uses the catchword "lament." Once again the dialogue technique is used.

Yahweh: "Assemble for me seventy of the elders" (16–17). The speech ends with a promise of giving some of the spirit that is on you "that they may share the burden of the people with you." Oddly, Yahweh seems to favor the *hybris* desire; he does not promise to take away the problem, but to spread out some of the godlike spirit on the elders.

Yahweh: "Sanctify yourselves for tomorrow when you shall have meat to eat"(18–20). The promise is not simply compassion; the people are to be given what they asked for "until it comes out of your very nostrils and becomes loathsome to you because you have rejected the Lord."

Moses: "Can enough sheep and cattle be slaughtered for them?" (21–22). Moses bluntly implies that God cannot do it.

Yahweh: "Is this beyond the Lord's reach?" (23). So God takes up the challenge as a competitor who can do better than Moses.

At this point a sub-plot develops. Joshua reports that not only are the sanctified elders prophesying, but that "Eldad and Medad are prophesying in the camp." He wants this stopped (27–28). Moses is now confronted with too many assistants and those beyond his control.

Moses: "Are you jealous? Would that all the people of the Lord were prophets" (29).

Moses recognizes in Joshua what he did not recognize in himself—namely, that he was presuming more control than he actually had.

So the answer to whether Moses can compete with God is given in this secondary conversation between Moses and Joshua. Once that is clear the story can go on. The prophesying of the elders accomplishes nothing practical toward the problem of providing meat; it simply attests to the power of God. What happens when the redactor returns to Scene A is a wondrous feeding with quail by God and an interpretation of some sickness which they suffered as a punishment for grumbling.

Such being the case, we may ask what was the moral problem being discussed. The greed for meat is simply an envelope story of secondary importance. The sickness and death is a punishment out of all proportion to the fault. Moses was the chief grumbler and was not punished at all. The indefinite "they" or "the people" are bit actors, and they bear the brunt.

The real problem is the *hybris*. Should Moses have tried to compete with God or not? The story doesn't solve that question. It says that God was the winner, but it doesn't say that Moses should not have tried. There is humor in the way the author fashions Moses' "poor me" speech (11–15) and his "you can't do it" objection (21–22). The author is not ridiculing his literary creation but expressing qualified admiration. We are left wondering, and even today we have not achieved a clear answer.

The purpose of this long explanation is simply to indicate that an ethicist's description of a moral problem is different from a story-teller's narrative. Biblical narrative cannot be cited as exemplar case without further ado. The next step will be to outline simply some of the techniques of story-telling within the enterprise of ethical inquiry, for, although different, it is not irrelevant.

Stories have plot and characters as has a moral case. The plot is a series of events which the author selects because they are related. Story is not simply record or evidence; the story element depends on a discernible logic of progression. In the simple example of a mystery story the problem is to bury the clues so that they do not seem to exist, but once revealed satisfy because they do explain the action. The plot may center around physical things or action, as is mostly the case in science fiction or westerns, or in psychological, mystical or feeling situations. However, the plot must be logical in some way; the *deus ex machina* solution never satisfies.[7]

Character is the other principal ingredient. Images must be created which move through the scenes. Some stories have scarcely any more character portrayal than the names of the *dramatis personae*. In other stories, the plot may be thin but the development of character makes the point. The best stories, of course, catch vividly drawn characters in some significant plot. It is probably the characterization which appeals to us most since we can identify or reject the characters on our self-images. Here, too, a logic prevails; the actions should flow out of the characterizations. This is the trans-temporal connective which has been previously alluded to; like the characters in a story, we also act normally out of images. The logic is not the abstract logic of right and wrong, but the logic of how well the actions fit the characters.[8]

Putting plot and characters together, we may make a simple division of story into hero-stories, tragedies and comedies.[9] Hero stories are basically straight-line plot stories in which the hero necessarily triumphs. The adversities may be great or small, but there must be some tension introduced by forces which threaten the hero. The triumph is inevitable, and one knows almost from the start that there will be a happy ending. Much of our TV fare is of this sort. The ending is not entirely conclusive and can be followed by another heroic episode. There are very few hero stories in the Bible, and they are almost all about God the Hero.

Tragedy, on the other hand, is a tale of necessary destruction. The principal actor is a hero; in classical Greek drama the tragic figure was usually a king. The hero has one flaw of character and that ultimately and decisively destroys him or her. In biblical lore there seem to be many tragedies and out of them we extract a retribution theology. Saul is utterly destroyed by seizing God's power; Judas must betray Christ and so commit suicide. The "must" is important. Tragedy involves us in a completely logical system in which the outcome cannot be avoided. Since the Bible is a total story into which the various stories must be fitted, we need to beware of labeling stories as tragedies too quickly.

Comedy has always been the hardest form to define and even harder to bring off successfully. The classical descriptions of comedy tended to think of it first as buffoonery. The standard comic character was not noble, but common. Indeed Dante apparently named his work *Divina Commedia* not because it was funny, but because it dealt with ordinary human beings and ordinary affairs. The *Divina* will be exploited below.

All humor depends on reverse logic, the divergent solution of which Schumacher speaks.[10] It associates things which are disparate but not unrelated. Disraeli's remark about Gladstone, "There but for the grace of God goes God" is illogical and yet in context precisely appropriate. So, too, is Paul's, "The foolishness of God is wiser than men." Moreover, the quality of comedy depends on the weightiness of the subject. We all have sayings about a limited number of basic jokes and the good ones are about death, sex and eating. Perhaps we should add taxes. At any rate, the better kind of comedy is no laughing matter in its substance. The best biblical stories from creation to resurrection are comedies. The outcome is not what we would expect, and it is this twist, often sudden, which reveals an appropriateness which we would otherwise have missed. I have called it a "reverse logic" for want of a better name. The early stories of Jesus, especially in the miracle narratives, are on the surface hero stories; the passion narrative in itself is a tragedy, but the total story is a comedy. It is most especially a comedy in the shorter ending of Mark where we are left with a final image of women standing forever in bewilderment and inaction.

Such a denouement does at least two things. It introduces a causality which is not normal and it makes us create the connective on our own. We may cry over a tragedy or cheer a hero, but the reaction is optional. If we don't laugh at a joke it is dead. Part of the genius of story is that it involves us in the action. We identify. In any good comedy we learn more about ourselves as we identify with the characters and then are suddenly revealed to ourselves. When we immerse comedies within a book which is confessedly the "word of God," then the revelation is not merely literary but theological. Our own appropriation of the "lesson" is not simply rational, but fiducial. In clearer terms, the Bible does not deal in rational ethics but in faith decisions.

Hans Urs von Balthasar has attempted to make something of a systematic approach to biblical theology in his *Theodramatik*.[11] In place of a static model of divine, immutable will he has substituted the construct of drama. God and man act out the drama on the stage of life. There is no script; that is made up as the play goes on. God takes the initiative by some action and then awaits our response. We may do what we want in our scene; when we have finished God at his time acts in response to what we have done. There are few absolutes for how either God or man should act. Previous experience may dictate something about what is prudent for us or what we may expect of God. But we are free and so is God. The human and divine story is revealed only in the living.

To summarize this chapter, a difference exists between the way in which the ethicist states the moral problem and reaches conclusions and the way in which the story-teller describes the human drama. For the biblical story-teller who is part of a revelatory tradition the operative elements in depicting moral decision within a story seem to be:

a. IMAGES ARE THE ARENA OF DECISION

The story-teller creates images out of fact or fiction and puts them into motion within a set of circumstances which must be considered *in globo* as reaching a climax. The quality of the story depends on how skillfully the images in action reflect normal human existence and hence how much we identify with them. Cultural differences as well as historical facts may distance the story from us, and the expertise of biblical scholars is needed to clarify such details. The history of the development of the story may also shed light on its meaning. Form criticism as well as all other technical aids should be welcomed to round out the total context, but these must be employed as tools, not explanations. The story comes first.

b. THE IMAGES ARE IN CONFLICT

The images may be of good and evil and then the sorting out of the characters and their moral decision is rather easy. But the images of God himself are certainly diverse—

perhaps introducing God as himself is itself a contested image. Warrior and Lover, Mother and Father, Virgin and Progenitor, etc., seem to be at war. When God appears in the human arena there is even more conflict, as Mircea Eliade has remarked about hierophanies in any mythology.[12] The human and the divine do not easily mix, at least as we experience them. It is the conflict which makes great literature possible; it is the conflict which makes it possible for us to relate to the images.

c. FOR THE BIBLICAL AUTHOR THE DECISION
   IS A FAITH DECISION

The images arise out of a faith tradition; the characters are people within or related to the chosen people, old or new; they are not secular figures. The dilemma (or worse) in which they are caught arises because of that milieu. The final result as inspired Scripture is to bring some insight into the significance of human actions. From beginning to end the whole process of story-telling has incorporated the faith element. The end of the story is not some rationally justifiable (or non-justifiable) outcome; it is the revelation of how God acts. Samson bringing down the pillars of the temple of Dagon needs no ethical justification or excusing; the climax is an act of faith on the part of Samson that God has restored his strength. The operating function for us is not in some parallel actions of self-destruction, but in the discernment of the need for faith whatever the individual decision may be. This is, of course, uncomfortable from the ethicist's viewpoint. It is, however, extremely important for each human being in a lived crisis situation. The responsibility belongs to the individual, and the only pragmatic test of rightness is how honest the agent is in responding to the demands of faith. ⨯

Notes

1. Aristotle's *Poetics,* VII; cf. S. H. Butcher, *Aristotle's Theory of Poetry and Fine Art* (New York: Dover, 1951).
2. Luis Alonso-Schökel, *The Inspired Word* (New York: Herder and Herder, 1972) 45–46.
3. Robert Alter, *The Art of Biblical Narrative* (New York:

⨯ Cantwell Smith's "faith is the most basic human quality"

Basic Books, 1981) 183–84; Cleanth Brooks, John Purser, Robert Warren, *An Approach to Literature* (Englewood Cliffs, N.J.: Prentice-Hall, 1975) 11–15.

4. Schökel, *Inspired Word* 151–72 has a very crucial discussion of the three levels of language.

5. Standard sources have been used for source and form criticism in this section.

6. Alter, *Art* 179–80 points out the importance of the *Leitwort.* So also many form critics use the same technique.

7. Brooks, *Approach* 7–8.

8. Brooks, *Approach* 9–10.

9. James Fischer, *How To Read the Bible* (Englewood Cliffs, N.J.: Prentice-Hall, 1981) 59–65. The description of tragedy is taken from Aristotle's *Poetics;* hero story is simply the converse. For comedy, cf. M. Conrad Hyers, *Holy Laughter* (New York: Seabury, 1969), 9–27 and 208–40; Edwin M. Good, *Irony in the Old Testament* (Philadelphia: Westminster, 1965).

10. Cf. the "Excursus on Schumacher" by Terence Keegan below 223–226.

11. Cf. Medard Kehl, "Hans Urs von Balthasar: A Portrait," *The von Balthasar Reader* (eds. Medard Kehl and Werner Löser; New York: Crossroad, 1982) 48–49. Also Ewert H. Cousins, *The Coincidence of Opposites in the Theology of Bonaventure* (Chicago: Franciscan Herald, 1978) 15–25.

12. Mircea Eliade, *Patterns in Comparative Religion* (New York: Sheed and Ward, 1958) 29.

Part Two

CHRISTIAN BIBLICAL ETHICS: SOME ATTEMPTS

INTRODUCTION

In the course of the development and composition of this work, various titles have been suggested for this second part. None of them, including the one finally chosen, are wholly satisfactory. Fairly early in its work, the task force resolved not only to talk about doing Christian biblical ethics ("method") but also, at the same time, to make some attempt at it ("content"). However, when the method subgroup of the task force began to prepare its work for publication, designating the first part of the book as "method" and the second part as "content" or "application" seemed unsatisfactory and perhaps even misleading. We want to avoid giving the impression that we first worked out a method and then applied it. For almost all the units in both parts of the book went through miltiple stages of discussion and composition extending over a period of several years. In addition, most of the units went through a penultimate stage of redaction in which the person initially or primarily responsible for that section rewrote it in the light of early versions of most of the material from the rest of the book. Finally, although we are convinced that the "method" we have begun to formulate is indeed the way we must go, we do not presume to claim that it is either definitive or comprehensive. It has, nevertheless, been our ambitious intention to try at least to begin to formulate such a definitive and comprehensive method. We hope that our readers and critics will share with us their judgment about whether we have taken constructive steps in that direction.

In contrast to the first part of this book in which an attempt was made to present the individual units in a logical progression and in relationship to each other, the units of this second part stand in relative independence of each other as individual works of exegesis and biblical theology. Their relationship is rather to the overall project of working

out a method for doing Christian biblical ethics. As an aid to
the reader and to facilitate discussion, we will begin by
outlining some of the actual steps of the method which is at
work in some of these units.

Early in his paper "Living Up to Matthew's Sermon on
the Mount," Schuele raises the question of the proper starting point. Should it be the text itself, Matthew 5—7, or
should it be the life situations from which our questions to
the text arise? Neither can be excluded, and some balance
between the two must be found. But Schuele answers the
question by reformulating it in terms of making the biblical
text itself the focal point of study in the sense that any valid
interpretation (or application, if you will) of the text must
always be an interpretation *of the text* itself. It is the biblical text that must be "the focal point and guidepoint of our
research" (200–203). From this, Schuele moves through a
brief survey of recent scholarship in order to help identify the
hermeneutical and methodological situation in which we
are attempting to study Matthew's Sermon. This in turn
enables us to ask how Matthew regards the question of
whether and how the Sermon is meant to be taken as a
guide for practical behavior by Christians today. Schuele
then summarizes in five points (206–207) what would appear to be Matthew's answer to this question. This, in turn,
enables him to formulate eight "practical guidelines for
Christian morality based on Matthew's Sermon" (207–209).
From this, one can see how essential the historical-critical
method is for studying what the text *meant* (the literal
sense), and how essential this method is for focusing and
basing one's interpretation on *the text*. But it is also clear
how we must move beyond the historical-critical method as
we study and analyze what the text means and how it functions or should function in Christian life today.

Topel's paper "The Christian Ethics of the Lukan Sermon" is organized in a somewhat similar fashion. Broadly
understood, the three tasks the exegete must perform are:
(1) grasp what the author of the text explicitly understood
and intended to express in his text; (2) make explicit that (or
those) understanding(s) only implied in the text (for only
thereby can the exegete verify one of his various hypotheses
about the explicit meaning of the text); (3) "complement
and correct that aspect of the text which reflects the *ex se*

unintelligible aspects of the author's experience" (51). Then, speaking more specifically in terms of the Lukan Sermon and in light of the method being developed in this book, Topel outlines three methodological steps: *(1) identify the various images and figures of speech* Luke uses to describe the Christian who is summoned to action by the Sermon; *(2) determine if any of these are particularly important* by reason of repeated Lukan usage or their place in the Sermon's structure; *(3) analyze these images in Luke's own work* to see what relationship between existence and ethical action they might provide (above 49–54; below 187–197).

Several of Fischer's papers in Part Two, especially "Politics and Biblical Ethics—Rom 13:1–7" (266–277) refines this developing methodology still further. Four steps are identified:

"STEPS"

(1) LOCATING THE IMAGES WITHIN WHICH THE PROBLEM IS EXPRESSED

The ethical problem must be located within the images which the biblical author used and then within the value-centered images which are the bearers of trans-temporal and trans-cultural meaning.

(2) IDENTIFYING THE CHALLENGE WHICH THE CONFLICTING IMAGES ESTABLISH

The images are multiple and lead to conflict. By "image" is meant (1) the literary images, (2) the psychological self-images, and (3) finally the ontological images, the "nature," or "character," or "root of being," or "value," or "vision." On the literary level the conflict most often appears as antithesis, paradox or irony; on the psychological level an attempt is made to discern something of the biblical author's internal struggle and to confront the decision-maker's own conflicting self-images.

(3) THE DYNAMISM IN THE CONFLICT EVENTUALLY CONCENTRATES ON A NECESSITY FOR AN ACT OF FAITH WHICH IN TURN LEADS TO GREATER UNDERSTANDING

On a literary level the antitheses, paradoxes and ironies of the biblical text are intended to lead to greater insight into the essential stance of the human being before God. Such techniques have always been used in biblical studies, but they are stressed more in recent study. At the psychological level the challenge emerges by defining as clearly as possible the *Sitz im Leben* of the biblical community which is confronted with a deeper understanding of accepted ways. "Law" of any sort is such an accepted way. However valuable and reasonable it may be, it represents a "tutor stage," to use Pauline terminology. The challenge is always to discover more of the true nature of the Christians before God as faced with an *ad hoc* decision which can only be made in faith.

(4) THIS ACT OF FAITH REVEALS THE PRESENCE OF GOD/CHRIST IN THE BIBLICAL AUTHOR AND BY CONTINUING REVELATION WITHIN THE HEARING CHRISTIAN

At the level of the text the literary analysis reveals that the author was not primarily involved in reaching a specific ethical decision, but in defining how the presence of God/Christ was seen in the "way" of community living. It is presumed that the Holy Spirit has acted and acts not only on the biblical author but on the believing Christian and on the Christian community. The distinctively Christian aspect of the decision-making process lies in the perception of the operation of faith at all stages in the process. The final test of rightness can be found only within acceptance by the Church. The individual Christian does not arrive at an ethical decision until faced with a situation in which an act of faith is the only final outcome. The individual Christian must recognize the partial nature of the process; the only criterion in this partial nature is perfect honesty with self.

A far more detailed presentation of these four methodological steps, as worked out by Fischer in the course of working with the task force, can be found below in the Appendix (289–295).

As is clearly shown by the structure and content of the two articles below which most consciously and thoroughly follow this method, "Politics and Biblical Ethics—Rom 13: 1–7" (266–277) and "Dissent within a Religious Community: Romans 9–11," (256–265), our methodological proposals are not in conflict or competition with the historical-critical method but are complementary to it. The historical-critical method is our best available means for investigating what the text *meant* (the literal sense). This method, however, cannot by itself bring us very far along the path of investigating the full biblical sense of a text, that is, what it *means* and *how it functions* in Christian life today. For to reach that goal, to see the Bible in the full, functioning reality of Christian biblical revelation, as we have been defining it in this book, and to see how the Bible can be and actually is an integral part of "doing Christian biblical ethics" (whether in the full, ideal realization of the process or in the much more common "bypass" mode we described above in the chapter on "The Science and the Art of Christian Biblical Ethics" 114–138), something like the hermeneutic and methodology we have been describing in this book is also necessary.

Chapter One

THE CHRISTIAN ETHICS OF THE LUKAN SERMON

(L. John Topel, S.J.)

Although relatively neglected by biblical scholars in comparison with the Matthaean Sermon on the Mount,[1] the Lukan Sermon's conciseness and narrower focus on ethical material might make it an especially fruitful field of investigation for the methods so far advanced in this book.

A. PAST RESEARCH ON THE LUKAN SERMON[2]

1. THE SOURCES OF THE LUKAN SERMON

This topic has preoccupied exegetes from patristic times. One can trace a movement from investigation of the history of Jesus' preaching career behind the sources, to interest in the earliest theology of the source (consistently identified as Q since 1838), and finally to interest in the evangelist's theology as one separates tradition from redaction. I find this work inconclusive, inasmuch as its two leading practitioners, Dupont and Schürmann, arrive at such strikingly diverse conclusions.[3] Therefore I prefer to emphasize *Kompositionskritik*, reading both source material and redactional variations as part of the conscious theolo-

179

gy of the evangelist until aporiae force a contrary conclusion.[4]

2. THE STRUCTURE OF THE LUKAN SERMON

Most Lukan commentators recognize a break between 6:38 and 6:39, and arrive at a threefold division:[5]

1. a prophetic section (6:20–26), in which Jesus indicates the virtues of the subjects of the Kingdom of God;

2. *a gnomic or parenetic section* (6:27–38), in which Jesus exhorts his disciples to his distinctive ethics;

3. *a parabolic section* (6:39–49), in which Jesus seals the Sermon with figurative language calling for action.

But there is considerable difference over where a putative second section (which all identify as containing Jesus' love command) ends, whether in v. 35, 36 or 38. This is important to our interests, because the theme of divine sonship in vv. 35c, 36 is central to an *agere sequitur esse* principle at least implicit in much ethical theory. With what parts of the Sermon this sonship is construed will determine the nature and normativity of Jesus' commands. We come, then, to the body of this section: How have exegetes understood the nature and normativity of Jesus' ethical teachings in the Lukan Sermon?

3. THE NATURE OF THE LUKAN SERMON'S ETHICS

Despite the paradoxical and challenging content, few commentators seem to go beyond an exegesis of the various verses in order to come to grips with the Sermon's ethics as a radical whole, although a glimpse into what might be called Lukan ethics can sometimes be teased from what is said about vv. 27–38 (for most commentators[6] seem to accept love of enemies, literally understood, as the basic principle of Jesus' ethics) or about the more generalizing verses (27, 31, 36).[7] Some see a connection between the Beatitudes and love of enemy, but only *suggest* a connection, such as openness to the Kingdom or filial relationship to God in faith and a converted heart, which might explain the radical nature of vv. 27–36.[8] Others, perhaps trying to distinguish the Christian's conduct from the autonomous moral striving of (stoic) ethical principle, intimate some new God-given power which enables us to respond to the Sermon.[9]

H. Kahlefeld, in the only full-scale monograph on the Lukan Sermon, is more explicit. He notes the need to see the Sermon in the context of all the Lord's teaching, especially on the imminent inbreaking of the Kingdom of God and the *metanoia* it requires, grounding the paradoxical and humanly foolish commands on God's fidelity, and from that coming to an authentic understanding and positive (hence "unlimited") formulation of the golden rule as summary of the section on love of enemies.[10] Over against "ethics" as a human performance, Jesus' preaching is seen as the unfolding of the will of God which goes beyond the created in order to touch the person (Kahlefeld 82–86). This brings us to a fundamental problem of Sermon exegesis: whether or not the will of God in the positive formulation of the golden rule is beyond the created order. Kahlefeld (82–86) thinks that it is; it is not clear that Grundmann agrees.

W. Grundmann seems in fact to be more penetrating than others on the roots of this ethic, which he discusses under two aspects. (1) *Its origin and nature* he uncovers in his comment on 6:27–30:

> The command to love enemies is the command for the beatified. They are placed in a new relation to God. This new relation to God becomes the ground of a new relationship to mankind, and the new relationship to mankind corresponds to the new relationship to God (p. 147).

Thus *lieben (agapan)* = *Dasein für*. Luke's further development in 6:28–30 makes clear that Christians are transformed in their whole human personalities: in their emotions, love replaces hate; in their words, blessing replaces curses; in their deeds, prayer replaces mistreatment. These examples demonstrate not casuistic directions, but a fundamentally different *sein* (existence) out of which a

Christian acts: it is a *Dasein für den anderen vor Gott* (pp. 147f.). (2) Its *purpose* he uncovers in commenting on v. 31: the positive formulation of the golden rule leads to love and community (since that is what humans want from one another), while the negative formulation remains in the realm of (juridical) rights. It is this positive conception, together with the love of neighbor command, which enables the Christian to overcome evil with good (cf. Rom 12:21), which is the purpose of the Sermon. But, like most exegetes, Grundmann is somewhat vague on what really constitutes the new *Dasein*. He seems to see it more in terms of eschatological hope.[11] There are some, however, who take 6:36, "Be merciful, even as your Father is merciful," as a more present reality which affects the Christian's ethical conduct.[12]

H. Schürmann takes the argument a step further, speaking of the ground of Christian ethic in our sonship from the Father. While the sonship of v. 35c is that of eschatological reward, yet, because of the position of 6:36 between vv. 27–35 and 37f, the *sonship is also a present reality* which enables the Christian not to judge others. As Rigaux puts it, by grace, the gift of the Father, the ultimate foundation of the Christian's new conduct is divine filiation which leads to the imitation of the Father (*Témoignage* 170). The next step, which seems to have been taken by non-exegetes, is to speak of participation in the personal life of Christ and entering into loving communion with him as the hallmarks of Christian existence. The extreme position is that of E.W. Hirst, who argued that only in the principle of unity in the body of Christ can one make sense of the principle, "From everyone according to his ability and to everyone according to his needs" which he finds the implication of the positive form of the golden rule.[13]

However at this point exegetes must ask whether such union in existence with the Son is really present, explicitly or implicitly, in the words of Jesus, as they were carried in the oral tradition, or as they are addressed by Luke to a community which had for some years been celebrating communion with Christ in the breaking of the bread.

Modern research has discussed two further questions on the Lukan Sermon: (1) Is this really an ethics? (2) Does the ethic constitute a social ethic?

For Jack Sanders, *Ethics in the New Testament* (Philadelphia: Fortress, 1975) there is no ethical system anywhere in the New Testament. Sanders takes *ethics* in its common and philosophical use as a *system* of moral principles and values from which one can argue to a determinate conclusion in affairs of practical life. In this sense I would agree that there is no *ethics* in the Lukan Sermon. However, I would also insist that what Jesus gives us in this Sermon is more than an *ethos*, a complex of fundamental moral values governing or distinctive of the Christian culture or community. (Such an *ethos* is mostly derived from and reducible to a *Geist* that pervades or animates a people.) What Jesus gives us is something between these two, which, for want of a better term, I am provisionally going to call an *ethic*.

William Manson (68–70), resisting the tendency to speak of the love of enemies command as too idealistic, sees it as "rooted in the nature of love" and as a call "to realize the divine potentiality of human nature." This is congruent with Grundmann's rooting the Sermon's ethic in human nature. Such grounding of Jesus' commands offers the possibility and likelihood of an implied ethics in Jesus' Sermon. But again it is a non-exegete, E.F. Tittle (60–78), who carries the argument to its greatest length, affirming non-violence as a basis for an ethic, and the golden rule as a real principle of a revolutionary ethic. This moves us toward the second question: Does the ethic indeed constitute a social ethics which can ground a social program?[14] B.W. Bacon unfolds the implications of this question:

> But neither Jesus nor the evangelist can have meant to represent God as absolutely non-resistant to evil. The Source teaches simply that the current tit-for-tat ethics, good for good, evil for evil, is *not enough*. The "righteousness of God" must exceed. It *goes beyond* the lex talionis. God not only resists evil, but (in Pauline phrase) "*overcomes* it with good." This goodness is to be limited by only one consider-

ation—its effectiveness. When it tends to encourage evil instead of overcoming it, it ceases to be imitation of God. Long-suffering, non-resistance are indeed to be carried to an extreme like that of the long-suffering Father. But when resistance is better adapted to overcoming evil than non-resistance, the divine example should be followed in this respect also.[15]

But again the questions: Is this in fact Luke's interpretation? Can it be vindicated in the Sermon itself, or does it come by argument from (i.e., moving beyond) the Sermon itself or from other parts of Luke-Acts?[16] When one surveys the literature, one can find at least some consensus that the Lukan Sermon does constitute a social *ethic* (i.e., as just explained, more than an ethos and less than an ethics).[17]

SUMMARY

From this survey it appears that there is no attempt to work out systematically the ethic of the Lukan Sermon. I would ascribe this lack to the traditional exegetical reluctance to obtrude a systematic viewpoint on a text which theologizes in a more narrative or symbolic mode of discourse. Still, we have noted elements which seem to imply or cry out for a system which makes deeper sense of the ethics. In particular, these have been some of the areas of discussion and agreement preparatory to such a theology of the Sermon's ethic:

1. There is a connection between the virtues of the Beatitudes and the conduct expected of a disciple. The authors speak mostly of these virtues as effects of the acceptance of the Kingdom of God, but there is no unanimity about the mode of presence of this Kingdom (nor how these virtues relate to the Christian *Being*).

2. The love of enemies command is universally accepted as the essence of Jesus' ethic in the Lukan Sermon (although why this should be, and how such a com-

mand relates to the golden rule, is not adequately treated).

3. This love is somehow driven by the Christian's being (or hopeful anticipation of being) a child of God (6:35c–36). (But we still need discussion about how this sonship might relate to the Christian *Being* in Luke's explicit or implicit thought.)

4. We need more discussion of whether Jesus' doctrine in the Lukan Sermon amounts to an ethic(s). The first step might be a determination of the meaning of *ethic* and *ethics*, and perhaps to develop such definitions from the kinds of decisions and actions that Jesus' injunctions can directly or mediately govern.

5. Finally, if there is an ethics in the Sermon, we must discuss whether this is a social ethics which could underlie a practical theology or ground a social program.

B. FUTURE DIRECTIONS OF RESEARCH

The first step in advancing the method of New Testament ethics is *removens prohibens*. I have spoken immediately above of the exegetical reluctance to obtrude any systematic understanding on a text expressed in aesthetic and symbolic thought patterns.

The roots of this reluctance seem twofold. First there was a reaction against the common practice in the history of Christian exegesis of imposing philosophical systems on the text to discern its spiritual meaning (e.g., the Stoic and Platonist categories from Justin and Origen to the high Middle Ages) or logical structure (e.g., the Aristotelian logical and metaphysical categories of Aquinas). From the Reformation to the twentieth century there was also the imposition of dogmatic categories (proof

texting) by Christian polemicists. The reaction is-
sued in this century in an unbridgeable chasm between biblical and dogmatic/systematic theologies.
Second, as long as hermeneutical method was conceived on the "subject-object" model of mathematics and physical sciences, the biblical interpreter in
reaction stressed the narrative and figurative qualities of his text. As theoreticians from Heidegger to
Gadamer to Ricoeur have reconceived hermeneutics on the model of whole human dialogue they
have been able to see and treat the mutual complementarity of symbolism and theoretic expression in
the interpretative process. This has attacked our
problem at both of the above-mentioned roots. Indeed, so theoretical a thinker as Bernard Lonergan
points out that to interpret a difficult text (even an
abstract one in the history of ideas) one must understand the author's thought-world and cast of mind,
particularly as these are held in the author's common sense (the area of primal intentional fields
where reality is described by imagination, emotion,
and aesthetic apprehension); cf. his *Method in Theology* (New York: Herder, 1972) 160f.

Still, contemporary interpretation theory indicates that
there is some inchoately systematic understanding of experience implicit in any symbolic expression of human experience.

R.E. Palmer, *Hermeneutics* (Evanston: Northwest-
ern U., 1969) is a rehearsal of the development of
hermeneutical theory from Schleiermacher to Gadamer in order to develop a more adequate hermeneutics for *literary criticism*. Beginning from
Heidegger's notion of Being coming to expression in
language, Palmer insists in many ways on the necessity of uncovering the world view implicit in a
literary text: ". . . the underlying sense of reality is a
key to understanding." "The *metaphysics* (definition of reality) and *ontology* (character of being-in-
the-world) in a work are foundational to an
interpretation which makes a meaningful under-

standing possible." ". . . an explicitation of the world view implicit in the language itself, and then in the use of the language in a literary work, is a fundamental challenge for literary interpretation" (pp. 30f.; emphases mine). Already in 1951 Heidegger had pointed out the necessity of going beyond the explicit meaning of a text to what it does not say, in *Kant and the Problem of Metaphysics* (ET J. S. Churchill; Bloomington: Indiana U., 1962), 206. Palmer indicates how this is a step into the realm of being in *Hermeneutics,* 234. Loretta Dornisch's fine summary of Ricoeur's theory of symbolic knowledge explains the necessity of this "going beyond" in two ways: (1) "More meaning is experienced than can be articulated or comprehended. Feelings are elicited. Man feels that he is addressed by an Other. He experiences synthesis which will not submit to analysis." (2) ". . . the symbolic experience will be three-dimensional: cosmic, psychic, and poetic . . . cosmic because it *ontologically* links him with a relational universe." Cf. "Symbolic Systems and the Interpretation of Scripture: An Introduction to the Work of Paul Ricoeur," *Semeia* 4 (1975), 1–19, esp. 14–16 (emphasis mine).

Now the interpreter cannot grasp this ontological interrelatedness which provides a synthesis underlying the text without dealing with the author's implicit metaphysics (by definition that science which deals with ontological relationships). This means that the exegete is not only invited, but even *required,* to probe beneath Luke's explicit formulations for the more systematic understandings of Christian existence which give unity and coherence to his artistic expression of Christian life. The rest of this chapter will try to sketch out how this might be done, first by suggesting a method, and then by attempting to approach the Lukan Sermon along these lines.

1. A METHOD OF INTERPRETATION

It is, however, one thing to affirm that one must uncover the author's world-view underlying a literary text and

another to say how this can be done authentically.[18] In the
final part of Part One, Chapter Two, Section Four: "Some
Methodological and Hermeneutical Observations," pp.
49–54 above, I have outlined an interpretation theory which
attends to the deeper unities of a writer's thought in his
artistic pre-conscious. There also I suggested a method of
getting at those "metaphysical depths"—by an analysis of
the images and symbols used in a text. Further, I indicated
that other New Testament authors clearly had pointed in
their images to ontological relationships to God and Christ
which grounded the Christian's ethical conduct. We now
turn to Luke's Sermon to see if his images there point to
existential grounds of the Sermon's ethic.

2. THE EXISTENTIAL GROUNDS OF THE ETHIC
OF THE LUKAN SERMON

(a) Images of the Christian in the Sermon

In spite of the "realism" of the Lukan Beatitudes, [19] the
makarism, as a wisdom form, becomes quite paradoxical
when it carries the full weight of the good news.[20] Here in
the Lukan Sermon the Beatitudes, as they are yoked with
virtues and conditions no one actively seeks (poverty, hunger, mourning, opprobrium and persecution), assume full
paradoxical significance. The oxymoron is at its sharpest in
"Blessed you who wail" (6:21c). The figure of speech does
not directly describe a new existential status of the hearer
of the Word, but it does signal at the outset of the Sermon
that Jesus' message cannot be taken like any merely humanly reasoned ethical system. We must look for more than
human grounds and powers for the Christian's conduct.

The section on the love commandment, 6:27–35 (–36)
(–38) (see our discussion of the divisions of this unit below
211–219), contains only one figure to describe Christians
who act on the Word: *kai esesthe hyioi hypsistou ... kathōs
ho patēr hymōn oiktirmōn estin* (and you will be sons of the
Most High ... even as your Father is merciful) (6:35c ... 36).
Notice that it is expressly in their ethical conduct by which
they exceed the reasoned virtue of the sinners[21] (they are to
love their enemies and do good to them, and lend without

hope of reward, 6:32–35) that the Christians reap a great reward (6:35b) and will be *sons of* the Most High (6:35c), who is of service to the graceless and the evil ones (6:35d). This characteristic of sonship is then taken as ground for the subsequent command to be compassionate as their Father is compassionate (6:36). Thus, as Schürmann observed, the sonship is a present characteristic which enables new action in the present world according to divine actions and virtues.

V. 38 contains the striking figure of the shopkeeper who presses the grain down into his measuring cup, shakes extra grain into its crevices, and finally heaps it up to overflowing as he throws it into the fold of the (Christian) shopper's garment. But this is an image of God rewarding Christian conduct, not an image of the Christian himself, which is what we are seeking here. Also in 6:39–42 there is an extended series of metaphors of the blind man who judges his brother, but this refers not to the Christian empowered for new Christian action but to the Christian who ignores his own weakness and acts according to the judgmental standards of the world, and so not as a Christian at all. No help for our search.

The good tree bringing forth good fruit (6:43–45) is an image of the Christian whose conduct is judged worthy. This is a crystal-clear literary way of saying *agere sequitur esse:* if someone's conduct manifests the other-worldly goodness of the Sermon's ethics, there must be some special kind of goodness in the man himself. But the image is not so specifically Christian as that in 6:35c–36.

Finally, in 6:47–49, the Christian doing the Lord's words is likened to one building his house on rock. But this image refers more to the judgment made on such a Christian, rather than on the existential status from which his Christian conduct flows.

In conclusion, then, the Sermon itself contains five figures (the paradoxical Beatitudes, sons of the Most High, the shopkeeper, the good tree, the good builder) which point to the singularity of the Sermon's ethics. Of these, two point directly to the ethical person. But while the good tree points to the *agere sequitur esse* principle, it seems more interested in giving a benign standard of judgment than in describing the ethical person's powers. The figure of the son of the

Most High, however, arises out of an explicit contrast between the (mediocre) good actions of sinners and the extraordinary self-giving conduct of the Christian who hears.
In that context it affirms that such Christian ethics has its
reward of becoming sons of the Most High (6:35c). However
that sonship then in 6:35d–36 becomes the present principle
by which one's actions in this world conform to the compassionate way of the Father with all mankind. Clearly of all
these images, it is "sons of the Most High" whose content
seems most likely to bear preconsciously Luke's understanding of the ontological relationships which ground the Christian's ethical conduct. Our next step of the investigation,
then, should be to inquire if Luke has himself composed the
middle section of the Sermon in such a way as to highlight
the image.

(b) The Love Commandment Has Been Structured in Many Ways[22]

Rhetorically, it has long been noted that 6:27–38 is
built on the imperative mood, while 6:39–43 returns
to the indicative mood for its figurative argumentation and exhortation to do its commands. This
seems to indicate that 6:27–38 should be taken as a
unity, but by itself does not help us locate the role of
6:35f in the love commandment.

Thematically we note that themes of doing (unmerited) good (6:27c, 33a, 35b) and loving one's enemies
(6:27b, 32a, 35a) begin, intertwine, and end in 6:27–
35. But themes of giving and lending freely (6:30a,
34a, 35c, 38a) and rewards (6:32b, 33b, 34b, 35d,
37ab, 38e) begin in 6:27–35 and "spill over" into
6:37f. And so thematically there are grounds for
taking 6:27–35 as a unit and also for taking 6:27–38
as the basic unit.

Strophically: J. Ernst[23] divides this section into
three strophes: a double rhythmed (6:27–31), a triple
rhythmed (6:32–35b), and a final double rhythmed
(6:35c–38c). Upon closer examination, however, the
expansions he admits into the last strophe really

destroy the pattern he has created. Ernst's problem is that he wants v. 36 to go with v. 37f to form a unit on judging, and that theological perception has distorted his literary arrangement.

Staying somewhat closer to the *rhetorical* (not poetic!) patterns, I believe that I can discover *three movements*:

a. a four-beat pattern (6:27b–28, 29f), with a summary rule (6:31) *not* in rhythmic form;

b. a three-beat pattern (6:32–34, containing three rhetorically nearly identical sentences);

c. a three-beat pattern (6:35abc, containing three imperatives, and 35def, an explanatory expansion in three clauses) with a summary statement (6:36), *not* in rhythmic form.

In this scheme, then, 6:36 is added to conclude the third "strophe" just as v. 31 had been added to conclude the first. Moreover, 6:36 serves as a summary statement not only for 6:35, but also for all three preceding "strophes" (6:27–35), giving the largest sense underlying the Christian ethic of the love command. Since it resumes the figure of sonship in 6:35d, such a summary indicates that such sonship accounts for the intent and the source of such radical ethic. Further, the imitation of the Father's compassion leads into the theme of not judging in 6:27f. The image of sonship is, then, structurally central not only as the climax of 6:27–35, but also as the hinge introducing 6:37f, as Schürmann saw so clearly.

If this structural analysis is correct, it confirms our preceding suspicion that "sons of the Most High" is the image by which Luke wishes to convey the underlying relationships which ground his Christian ethic. If that is the case, then we must now turn to the Jewish and Hellenistic usages of the term which would have formed Luke's background and finally to his usage of the term to see if we can tease out what he might have meant by the term here in his Sermon.

(Space allows us to present only the topical headings and the summarizing conclusions of the next two sections.)

(c) The Religious Background of the Term "Son of God" (= "Sons of the Most High")

(a) The Jewish Background

(b) The Greco-Roman Background

(c) The Christian Tradition

Paul's Notion of Son(s) of God

The (Pre-)Synoptic Tradition

CONCLUSION

Our survey indicates that before Luke began to write, "son of God" had already gone through three or four stages of Christological development, ranging from establishment in power at the resurrection to pre-existent relationship with God, from ignorance and weakness in Jesus' earthly career to the heights of wonderworking and intimate personal knowledge of his "Abba." Some of these uses fairly demand a metaphysical basis for intelligibility, even if they do not use philosophical language. Finally, we found the titles already developed in all strands of the pre-Lukan tradition: Pauline, Markan, Q, and the early catechetical material behind Acts.[24] Since Luke as an ancient author gives every indication both in practice and profession (Luke 1:3) of living in and absorbing the traditions of his community, we can assume that a considerable range of development underlies his use of "sons of God."

(d) Luke's Own Use of Son(s) of God

We will read Luke-Acts from top to bottom by methods of literary analysis, looking first for Luke's explicit meaning, and then for possible larger meanings carried by his symbols. After that we will comment on the ontological implications of his usage. The most important verses and passages (which space does not allow us to comment on further) are: *Luke 1:26–38; 1:39–80; 2:41–52; 3:1—4:13; 3:21–22; 4:1–13; 4:14–44; 4:31–44; 6:35d–36; 6:41; 6:45; 9:28–36; 10:1–24; 11:2b–4; 11:13; 12:12; 20:36; 22:70–71.*

(e) Conclusion of Our Survey of the Title

(1) For Jesus as Son of God

(a) There is in Luke-Acts a residual theology of sonship by the power of the Spirit in the resurrection (Acts 2:36; 13:33; Luke 9:21–36);

(b) Luke more fully represents the Synoptic Christology in which Jesus is Son of God in his ministry (3:21–22)—indeed, he intensifies this Christology by making Jesus Son of God from his conception (1:32–35). In general, such sonship is of the royal sonship kind, but stretched out of clearly definable categories (cf. 22:67–71) by its reinterpretation in terms of the Servant of Yahweh (3:22; 4:18–22, etc.);

(c) This is not a de-eschatologizing of the notion of Son of God, since Lukan theology rather considers the historical time of Jesus and the Church to be eschatological reality now moved into time;

[*In Luke 11:20 Jesus' work in the Spirit is the presence of the Kingdom; in Acts 2:3–4, 17 the Spirit in the Church is a continuation of this eschatological time (cf. following paragraph). I believe that, of all the evangelists, Luke's eschatology is closest to the already/not yet eschatology of Paul. It is impossible to see how this can be so unless some ontological incursion of God into history through Jesus and the Spirit has transformed time by divine presence from inside time.*

Jesus' mission was to baptize his disciples in the Holy Spirit and fire (Luke 3:16). Such a baptism is promised in Luke 24:49 and Acts 2:4–5 and occurs in Acts 2:3–4, designated a phenomenon of the last days (Acts 2:17). The disciples go out to do the very works which Jesus had done in the Spirit (curing a cripple, Luke 5:25; Acts 3:1–10; 9:32–35; 14:8–10); raising the dead, Luke 7:11–17; 8:49–56; Acts 9:36–42; 20:7– 10). This wonderworking power in which Peter and Paul parallel the works of the Lord manifests that the Spirit which had already signalized the presence of the Kingdom in Jesus' ministry (Luke 11:20) is now making the Kingdom present in the life of the Church (Luke 9:27). I hope to demonstrate this presence of the Kingdom in the Church at greater length in a subsequent article.]

(d) The sonship is effected and empowered by the Spirit of God, whether in Jesus' conception (1:32–35), or his baptism (3:21–22 with 14:1, 14), or his ministry of preaching (4:18) or of exorcising (11:20);

(e) The special emphasis of Luke is on Jesus' conception as Son of God. It is prominent in the prologue's foreshadowing of Jesus' career and destiny, and from that pre-eminent position it influences subsequent uses of the title (3:22–23, 38; 4:3, 9, 22) or of other titles (1:43, 76, etc.). Conception sonship adds depths of relationship which intensify Q's notion of sonship (Luke 10:2, the intimate, exclusive, reciprocal knowledge of Father and Son; Luke 11:2, the address of God as "Abba"; cf. 22:42; 23:34). Indeed, it seems to me that sonship by conception, by the very nature of the symbol of sonship, implies a deeper metaphysical relationship to a Father of the same species than do some forms of pre-existence Christology (e.g., a pre-existent Wisdom Christology).

(2) For the Disciples

(a) The disciples are called to receive Jesus' Spirit, in their own baptism (3:16; 24:49; Acts 2:3–4), as extensions of Jesus' own mission (10:9, 16), as their advocate in persecution (12:12) and simply as the gift which is their real possession (11:3);

(b) Since that Spirit made Jesus a Son (Acts 13:33; Luke 3:22) in a special way (1:32–35), so it establishes the disciples already in a special relationship of sons to their Father, so they can call God Father (11:2b; 8:21; 10:22);

(c) And so Christians as special sons of God will not only be so in a new way (angelic sons of God) at the resurrection (22:70–71), but now enjoy this new relationship in their present (eschatological) existence. Therefore they can act in the radically new imitation of the Father which is the basis of Jesus' ethic of forgiveness (11:4; 15:1–32, etc.) and compassion (6:35d–36).

(f) The Existential Function of "Sons of the Most High" in the Lukan Sermon's Ethics

Our survey of exegesis of the Sermon's ethics called attention to its radical nature. Jesus' demands so far exceed the requirements of a "rational" human ethics that exegetes can hardly categorize them as ethics in the accepted sense of that term. And so we are driven to seek an underlying (formal) cause for such a radical new ethic (see above 180–182). Since Luke is not a philosopher but a literary author, we have to seek his understanding of the ontological relationships which explain such a new ethic in his literary figures and symbols.

Luke appears to have centered the title "Sons of the Most High" in his structure of the Sermon so as to make it the explanation of its radical demands. Christians are called to, and live out, a superhuman ethic of selfless love of the neighbor because they "will be sons of the Most High" (see above 188–191). *How* being sons of God affects our conduct is what must finally be concluded.

It may be that Christians are to do these works of love out of hope of that eschatological reward of becoming sons of God. This interpretation takes *kai esesthe* (6:35c) as epexegetical of the great reward of 6:35b.[25] This interpretation coheres with the Jewish expectation of the people's being revealed and acknowledged as sons of God in the eschatological age. However this interpretation labors under two difficulties: (1) Such a hope for a final goal seems to put the efficient cause of such radical living in the human will. One strives with all one's human means for a goal which will later be conferred as a reward for such a virtue. This is foreign not only to the general New Testament sense of gratuitous justification, but also to Luke's (cf. Fitzmyer 235–37). (2) Such an eschatological reward is hardly attested in

Luke's theology of Son of God. For Luke, Jesus is already in human history the (eschatological) Son of God. The power of the final Kingdom is already operative in him (11:20; 17:21). This same presence of sonship now is true of Christians themselves.

And so a second interpretation seems more likely: Besides the great reward, Christians will (now) be (eschatological) "sons of the Most High," who can be requested now to measure their present acts of selfless generosity (Luke 6:27–35) and forbearance (6:37–38) by the standards of their Father (6:36) whose divine Spirit they already share. As Schürmann pointed out, this sonship forms the link to the summons to be compassionate now in 6:36.[26] This coheres with Luke's theology of sons of God: Christians who receive Jesus' unique personal revelation of the Father are able in this present life to call on the Father by Jesus' own intimate name "Abba" (11:2b) and are able in such prayer to obtain from the Father the gift of the Spirit (11:13) to be their advocate in the trials of present historical persecution (12:12), and to empower their work of healing and preaching (10:1–16; cf. the miracles of Acts which parallel Jesus' works in the Spirit). Christians, then, doing the will of their Father, are brothers and sisters of Jesus (8:21). Thus sonship through the power of the Spirit as a present reality which enables us to do the Sermon's radical ethics.

Whether Luke saw that this made us "partakers of the divine nature" (2 Peter 1:4) is not clear. Certainly there is nothing as explicit as the vital union of vine and branches in John, nor as clear as the baptism into Christ as members of his body, as in Paul. Rather Luke appears to have seen personal relationship of the Christian to the Father to be mediated by the agency of the Spirit. As the Spirit made Jesus Son of God in his conception, baptism, and resurrection, so the Spirit makes Christians sons of God and so able to do Jesus' works of preaching and healing (Luke 10 and Acts), and to do that forgiving which is the work of the Father himself (Luke 5:21, etc.).

Still, the very symbol "Son" inevitably carries with it the notion of an offspring of a father of the same species. It is highly doubtful that the term could be reduced to such a dead metaphor as to lose totally its original meaning of conception from the same nature. Luke's need to push Jesus' own sonship back to his conception may be a clue to the fact that sonship for Luke carries this resonance of specific relationship from birth also for Christians. They then do the works of their compassionate Father because their Christian *action* flows from their eschatological *existence* as sons and daughters through the Spirit in Christ.

Notes

1. In earlier years, works on the Matthaean Sermon outnumbered those on the Lukan Sermon by about 20 to 1. This ratio has improved with the years, but even after the rise of redaction criticism, it is still more than 3 to 1. Cf. W. S. Kissinger, *The Sermon on the Mount: A History of Interpretation and Bibliography* (ATLA Bibliog. Series 3; Metuchen, N.J.: Scarecrow, 1975) and the bibliographical material in *Biblica,* the *Revue Biblique* and *NTA*.

2. The material in this section, esp. in a. and b., has been drastically reduced from the form in which it appeared in my "The Lukan Version of the Lord's Sermon," *BTB* 11 (1981) 48–53.

3. J. Dupont, *Les Béatitudes* I (2nd ed.; Paris: Gabalda, 1958) seems to assign a "priority" to the Matthaean version. H. Schürmann takes the opposite view. (In this chapter, names of authors without titles refer to their commentary·on Luke; when the commentary has a title other than "Commentary . . ." it will be given.)

4. This agrees with the approach of J. Tyson, "Source Criticism of the Gospel of Luke," *Perspectives on Luke-Acts* (ed. C.H. Talbert; Edinburgh: T. & T. Clark, 1978) 39. For a brief description of such an approach, cf. W.G. Thompson, "Reflections on the Composition of Mt 8:1—9:34," *CBQ* 33 (1971) 365–66 and the literature cited there.

5. This division has been popular since G. Heinrici, *Die Bergpredigt* I (Leipzig: Dürr, 1899) 43.

6. E.g., Schanz, Hahn, B. Weiss, Klostermann, Rose, Easton, Creed, Schlatter, Hauck, Rengstorf, Leaney, Tinsley, Stuhlmueller, Harrington, etc.

7. Cf. Lagrange 83; Rigaux, *Témoignage de l'Evangile du Luc* (Bruges/Paris: Desclée de Brouwer, 1970) 169; C.G. Montefiore, *The Synoptic Gospels (S.G.)* II (2nd ed.; London: Macmillan, 1927) 416–17; W.C. Van Unnik, "Die Motivierung der Feindesliebe In Lukas VI, 32–35," *NovT* 8 (1966) 284–300; Easton 82.

8. E.g., Danker, *Jesus and the New Age* (St. Louis: Clayton, 1972) 84; B.M. Chevignard, "Bienhereux vous qui êtes pauvres," *LumetVie* 7 (1958) 53–60; Jeremias, *The Sermon on the Mount* (ET N. Perrin; Philadelphia: Fortress, 1963) 30–35; Ellis.

9. E.g., J. Ernst 213; H. W. Bartsch, *Wachet aber zu jeder Zeit* (Hamburg—Bergstedt: H. Reich, 1973) 70; "Feldrede und Bergpredigt. Redaktionsarbeit in Luk. 6," *TZ* 16 (1960) 16–17.

10. H. Kahlefeld, *Der Jünger. Eine Auslegung der Rede Lk 6, 20–49* (Frankfurt: Knecht, 1962) 77–80.

11. Cf. Montefiore, *S.G.* II 419; Loisy 207; D. Lührmann, "Liebet eure Feinde (Lk 6,27–36/Mt 5,39–48)," *ZTK* 69 (1972) 412–38, esp. 426.

12. Cf. Lagrange 183–84, 191–98 and esp. G.L. Hahn 438.

13. Cf. K. Truhlar, "The Earthly Cast of the Beatitudes," *Concilium* 39 (1968) 35–43; E.W. Hirst, "The Implications of the Golden Rule," *ExpTim* 26 (1914f.) 555–58.

14. Cf. J. Ernst, "Das Evangelium nach Lukas—kein soziales Evangelium," *TGl* 67 (1977) 415–21.

15. B.W. Bacon, "The Order of the Lukan Interpolations. II The Smaller Interpolation, Lk 6:20—8:3," *JBL* 36 (1917) 122. Montefiore, *S.G.* II, 417 describes this ethic by saying the Sermon's ethic is not grounded in personal interest, but in looking at what our conduct will cause in the other: "Love knows no limits but those which love itself imposes."

16. Cf. E.A. Sonnenschein, "The Golden Rule and Its Application to Present Conditions," *HibJ* 13 (1914f) 863 argues (but not exegetically) yes.

17. Cf. P. Hoffman, "Selig die Armen," *BibLeb* 10 (1969) 111–22, esp. 114–15; H. Frankemölle, "Die Makarismen (Mt 5, 1–12; Lk 6, 20–23). Motive und Umfang der redaktionellen Komposition," *BZ* 15 (1971) 52–75; H.W. Bartsch, "Der soziale Aspekt der urchristlichen Paränese von ihrem Ansatzpunkt her," *CommViat* 5 (1962) 255–60, esp. 255–56; H. Diem, "Predigt über Lukas 6, 20–21," *EvT* 14 (1954) 241–46; P. Bläser, "Las Bienaventuranzas (Mt. 5, 3–10; Lc. 6, 20–26)," *RB* 18 (1956) 20–24, 91–97, esp. 20–22.

18. In spite of his herculean work of clearing the underbrush, I do not find that Ricoeur has as yet arrived at a hermeneutical theory which can explain this translation from the symbolic to the more systematic structures of the author's world-view.

19. Cf. R.E. Brown, "The Beatitudes according to St. Luke," *BibTod* 18 (1965) 1176–80.

20. Cf. J. Fischer, "Ethics and Wisdom," *CBQ* 40 (1978) 293–310 and the bibliography cited there, as well as his contributions in this book, esp. "Biblical Paradox" above 103–107.

21. Cf. W.C. van Unnik, "Die Motivierung" for an account of the difference between the Greek ethical standards and the Christian ones embodied in these verses.

22. In "The Lukan Version" I sketched in some detail the general lack of agreement on the structure of Luke 6:27–45. The

extensive and subtly articulated arguments I have been assembling in support of my proposed structure cannot be reproduced or even convincingly summarized here. Therefore the reader should try to take the present suggestion in its best light and, even if he or she must reject what I here advance without argument, remember that our immediately preceding section (a) has already vindicated in some measure the centrality of the figure "sons of the Most High" in this section of the Sermon.

23. Taking his inspiration from C.F. Burney, *The Poetry of the Lord* (Oxford: Clarendon, 1925) 113–14.

24. Cf. Acts 2:36; 3:14–15; 5:31; 13:33, which we have not investigated because in such a short sketch it would take too much space to separate tradition from Lukan redactional interests.

25. Cf. *BGD* s.v. *kai,* I, 3, p. 393.

26. In this case, *kai* can be epexegetical of 6:35b as a present reward, or it can give a present consequence in addition to the eschatological reward—their present power to be summoned to the divine ethics of their Father and empowered to live it out here and now manifests them as (the eschatological) sons of God. This coheres with Paul's notion of our manifestation as sons in the resurrection.

Chapter Two

LIVING UP TO MATTHEW'S SERMON ON THE MOUNT: AN APPROACH

(Frederick E. Schuele)

The Sermon on the Mount has long been the subject of serious questioning. Are Christians expected to take it literally? Did Jesus mean it as a pattern for everyday living? Is it possible to live this way? Christians have clearly found it difficult not only to live up to the demands of the Sermon, but also, in some instances, even to admit that they were all called to do so. Our attempt here will be to see what light some recent studies on Matthew can shed on this. While space will allow us to do little more than sketch conclusions, we will, of course, be striving for the greatest possible methodological clarity. This is particularly needed in relation to the various sources of Matthew as we find it, and in regard to the relationship to the in some ways quite similar and in some ways quite different Sermon on the Plain in Luke. Does one or the other Sermon have priority of place or import?

A second methodological concern regards the starting point of our inquiry. Should it be our faith-questions and life-situations, or should it be Matthew 5—7 in its own context and on its own terms? Modern hermeneutics has made it clear that an adequate answer must find some balance between these alternatives. But, while we can never climb completely out of our own presuppositions or hermeneutical circle, any valid interpretation of a text, and of Matthew's Sermon in particular, must be an interpretation of *the text.*[1] That alone is the normative guide for validating or rejecting one's views about what living according to Jesus' teachings means, and not vice versa. For the central questions of this chapter—what Matthew's Sermon demands of a follower of Jesus, and what it says about the possibility of living up to those demands—one can list at least six important consequences or implications of making the text itself the focal point of our research:

1. The Sermon itself (and not someone's views about it) should be the ruling point under discussion.

2. Interpretations of the text and commentary on it should be judged by the text (as nearly as we can make out its meaning) and not vice versa.

3. Some concrete questions about what living as a Christian should mean may not be answerable by a study of the Sermon in Matthew alone. Assertions and commands which are found in the Sermon must be examined closely and with careful attention to their Matthaean context.

4. History, past and present, is full of sad examples of individuals and communities who have falsely judged the Bible to be on their side. The Sermon itself seems to give a direct example of this in 7:21–23, and an indirect example when one compares 5:14–16 with 6:1–18. Humility, distrust of the conviction that one's own claims are always right, and a constant striving to read the Bible objectively and apply it honestly are needed.

5. What a text such as the Matthaean Sermon *means* is not always exactly the same as what it *says* or what its *author meant* or a later redactor adapted it to say in a new context. Increasingly, doubts are expressed that "traditional" historical-critical methods alone can do justice to biblical texts. Beyond these methods, one must, as suggested by Gadamer, Ricoeur and many others, give renewed literary attention to the texts *as texts* and be alert to the so-called "superfluity

of meaning" over and above the meaning consciously intended by a text's human authors.

6. We will be dealing with the finished unity (final redaction) of the Matthaean Sermon in the larger context of all of Matthew in order to bring some results of recent investigations on Matthew to bear on the question of whether and how the Sermon can be taken as a guide to a Christian approach to life today.

The question whether the Sermon is a practical guide for Christian life has been under discussion since biblical criticism rose to prominence in the last century, especially among German Protestant scholars. A survey of how German biblical scholars treated the "theological question of the Sermon" can provide helpful background here, especially in alerting us to the limitations that theological viewpoints can impose on the results of biblical research.[2] Grundmann uses the Law-Gospel theme, first by showing the inadequacy of some earlier attempts to understand the Sermon predominantly in terms of Law, and then by stressing its reality as Gospel, specifically by seeing it as an eschatological-Christological proclamation of the will of God. That is, because it is proclaimed *now*, with the Christological authority of Jesus, it has the power now to break through the demonic cycle of sin, revenge and isolation by creating a new fellowship based on forgiveness, reconciliation and peace.

But has not Grundmann gone beyond the text in doing this? Here one must carefully distinguish. In pointing out that the Sermon, on its own terms and as a text in its own context, makes far more sense as Gospel than as Law, he has not gone beyond the text. However, he does seem to have gone beyond the text in using Law and Gospel as comprehensive categories belonging to biblical theology in general and as the ruling categories of theology in general. Nevertheless, even though he goes beyond the text and emphasizes only one aspect of the Sermon, one can say that he does so legitimately, especially as a representative of the evangelical tradition which understands most of its theology as having a "Pauline" cast. Here, Grundmann, and, like him, E. Schweizer,[3] seem to be *doing theology*, or doing Christian

ethics. And as long as this is done with reasonable methodological precision and sufficient hermeneutical awareness,
one need have no fundamental argument with it.

The authors of this book, however, are working out of a
tradition which sees theology and ethics as separate "sacred
sciences." This has made it possible, especially in recent
years, to delineate much more clearly the boundaries between exegesis, ethics and theology. One can deal more
openly and productively with the various presuppositions of
one's confessional position or theological school. And one is
also more conscious of the various areas of competence
from exegesis through biblical theology to ethics. But this
situation has also made it extremely difficult to do Christian biblical ethics as defined in this study. For within our
tradition, we tend to think of the task of the exegete as
providing the material which the theologian is to systematize and the ethician is to apply. There is very little direct
conversation or cooperation between exegete and ethi-
cian/theologian. This makes it possible for exegesis to be
done not only in a way that is free from the particular or
narrowing presuppositions of a religious tradition, but also,
at times, in a way that is irrelevant to it. For theology/ethics,
the situation is similar: the "independence" of theology and
ethics as separate sciences is assured, but it has also become
very difficult for these sciences to appropriate the findings
and insights of exegesis and biblical theology.

It is with this situation and its challenges in mind that
we now move to consider the Sermon as we find it in Matthew and ask how Matthew regards the question of whether
and how the Sermon is meant to be taken as a guide for
practical behavior by Christians. Our main guides will be
the continental scholars W. Grundmann, R. Schnackenburg
and E. Schweizer, and the American scholars J. Meier and
N. McEleney.[4] They, and many others with them, while
disagreeing on the actual structure of the Sermon, do agree
that it has a unity as a text and thus can and should be so
analyzed. In doing so, form criticism and other appropriate
methods of analysis must be duly applied to the great variety of literary forms that appear in the Sermon.

In addition, one must examine the different levels or
settings in or behind the Sermon. The Pontifical Biblical
Commission's document "On the Historical Truth of the

Gospels" (1964) recognized at least three different settings
for a passage or unit: (1) in Jesus' ministry, (2) in the oral
tradition of the apostles and early Church, (3) in the final,
written Gospel. Most scholars, in dealing with such passages as the Beatitudes (5:3–12)[5] or the section on Jesus and
the Law (5:17–20), would now work with a much more complex division of these settings such as: (1) Jesus' oral teaching, (2) the oral teaching and preaching of the apostles and
others in the early Church, (3) the writing down of some
blocks of material, (4) the influence of the writing of the
first document (Mark) on the literary form "Gospel," (5) the
written material "Q" which circulated separately from
Mark, (6) the special material M which Matthew and his
community had access to, (7) the final theological shaping
and editing by the redactor we call Matthew. Not surpris-
ingly, scholars differ on how these various levels relate to
the final redaction, but it is clear that all of these different
levels and their concerns are given *through* Matthew's final
redaction. This viewpoint and "message" is the controlling
one, and often the only one we can be reasonably sure about.
It is this that we will concentrate on as we attempt to
reconstruct the situation in Matthew's Church and the answers he offers, in order to discern what his answers to our
questions might be.[6]

As a starting point, we can list five qualities or themes
in the Sermon on which our five authors generally agree,
and which also have their place in the Gospel as a whole,
which is , of course, the guiding point of our interpretation.

(1) The *eschatological tone* of Matthew. "Now," and "in
the last days," now that Christ has come, things are now
demanded and are possible which would have been impossible before. Matthew is moving in the direction of a more
"realized" eschatology like John's, but has not yet arrived at
that point.[7]

(2) It is the "event" of Christ, portrayed within the
framework of a high Christology, which makes possible
now the things demanded by Christ and thus provides the
Christological key to the radical demands of the Sermon.[8]

(3) Christ is the *Teacher* who definitively fulfills (even overfulfills) the Law which he interprets *prophetically*. Jesus demands *more* than the Pharisees and other teachers, he demands *more* than "the Law and the prophets" (this phrase in 5:17 and 7:12 serves as a *conclusio*), and brings a wisdom that teaches what God really intended by his Law.[9]

(4) These eschatological, Christological and prophetic themes provide the basis for Matthew's message that *a new level of existence is given* by God in Jesus so that *as the Father's children we can love as God loves his children*. This is the *gift* which makes it *possible* for us to *be perfect as the Father is perfect* (5:48).[10] In other words:

(a) loving all people, good and bad, brother and enemy, is the heart of Jesus' commands about our moral conduct with other human beings;

(b) this is made necessary by the fact that our Father is himself this way and his expectation, mediated through Jesus' authoritative exposition of his Father's will for us, is that we also be like our Father (perfect);

(c) this is possible for us because we are in fact the Father's children; and

(d) this is all revealed to us and made possible for us by the revelation that comes through Jesus, incarnate Wisdom (Matthew is unique among the Synoptics in identifying Jesus with Wisdom) and by the example of such love that he shows and enables us to show like him.[11]

Grundmann sums this up by stating that the Lord's Prayer is the theological center, the heart, the "outline" of the Sermon. Or, as Tertullian put it, the Lord's Prayer is the *"breviarium totius evangelii."*[12] Another way of putting it is to observe that Matthew has in his unique way revealed the "ontological" sonship of Jesus in Chapters 1–4, while the Sermon expresses the fatherhood of God as a gift and sonship as a promise to its hearers, a gift and promse that oblige them to the brotherhood of love toward all.[13] *The gift of this new level of existence is the guiding viewpoint or image* of the whole Sermon and Gospel.

(5) The *nexus between Christ and his Church* (to use Meier's phrase) is a further characteristic of Matthew. One can speak of this as the mode of Christ's continuing and empowering presence among his followers whom he calls and expects to behave in a unique way as God's children. A key concept here is the relationship of Christians to the Law. Matthew reflects a deliberately anti-Pharisee concept of the Law. This in turn reflects the situation in Judaism at the time (80–90 A.D.) when only the Pharisees had survived the Jewish war and the temple destruction. They had become, without significant competition, the major force within Judaism, and they had already begun the systematic expulsion of Christians from the synagogues. However, Matthew is by no means anti-Law. It seems, in fact, that he is consciously combatting an antinomian tendency in the Church which might trace back to a misunderstanding of Paul's position on the Law. Matthew proclaims Christ as reinforcing and deepening the need to obey the Law; Christians are called to a stricter observance of the spirit of the Law than are their Jewish contemporaries.[14] The role of the Church in regard to the morality taught by Christ who is *the* Teacher (No. 3 of the five "qualities or themes in the Sermon" we have just mentioned) and *the* basis (Nos. 2 and 4) of Christian morality is to hand on, explain, and enforce the teachings of Jesus.[15] This eschatological theme is integral to Matthew (in contrast to Luke whose ecclesiology, or preaching of Christian life in the Spirit, is proclaimed not in his Gospel but predominantly in Acts).

We can summarize our findings to this point by listing Matthew's answers to our questions about whether and how Christians are bound to live out the demands of the Sermon:

(1) Christians *are bound* to live up to the practical commands of the Sermon. They cannot dodge these demands; they must do the Father's will, as Jesus interprets and expounds it, even more radically than the Pharisees.

(2) Christians are bound in principle by *all* the demands of the Sermon, taken to their practical conclusions. They cannot pick and choose, living up to the easy commands and pleading impossibility as an excuse for not living up to the difficult ones.

(3) This, difficult as it is, is possible because the Christian is living in a new age. Jesus came, died, and rose, and is eternally present and empowering the Christian in a community of children of God. We are raised to a kind of divine level by being made God's children, who are taught to pray and strive that the *will of our Father* be done. We are empowered by the eschatological fullness of God's power revealed in his Son.

(4) This call to obedience to the will of the Father as the Son authoritatively expounds it is not meant as a temptation to try to justify ourselves by our own power, but is a call to radical following of Jesus as part of a community that is created by God and depends on his power. Humble dependence on God's power and seeking his will, rather than human pride or doing "pious acts" to be seen and admired, is needed.

(5) The Church was "established" by Christ with the duty and power of preserving, teaching and carrying out Jesus' teachings until the end of this world. The community in which "I am with you always" (28:20) is where we are jointly taught and empowered by the living Christ to live as the Father's children, the "salt of the earth" (5:13).

This enables us to formulate now some practical guidelines for Christian morality based on Matthew's Sermon. They do not of themselves constitute a comprehensive base for moral theology, but they do constitute some fundamental elements which cannot be overlooked in the attempt to formulate a Christian biblical ethics.

1. The Sermon is not a whole new Law code to be "literally" interpreted. Jesus in Matthew opposed the Pharisees' practice of "building a fence around the

Law." Jesus cut to the heart of the moral conduct governed by the Torah. Although he was against a narrow, self-righteous legalism, he did seem to mean that his commands should be kept and lived out in practical action.

2. The Sermon is characterized by a strong anti-legalistic, anti-judgmental and anti-hypocritical tone, a humble admission of sinfulness and need for forgiveness and reconciliation, which is to result in disciples who are themselves compassionate and responsive to the call to be (not "perfectionistic" but) "perfect"—like their Father.

3. Weakness and failure should not lead to giving up but to renewed prayer to the compassionate Father for forgiveness and renewed striving to be like him. This grows from a God-centered rather than from a human- or law-centered faith and morality.

4. Following Jesus as a disciple will lead to doing God's will. Listening to him and maintaining contact with his powerful presence among us gives us the way to discern and live up to what God expects of us in morality.

5. Hyperbole is probably used in some of the Sermon's commands, and Jesus himself does not always follow them literally elsewhere in Matthew.[16] There is need for a mature reading of the "spirit" and intent of the commands to understand the limits of Matthew's images and judge individual cases. One must be aware of the limits of literary forms and allow plenty of room for the practical wisdom of moral theology.

6. One must be aware that different times make for different answers or emphases. For example, the Pharisees were probably "heroes" in many teachings in Jesus' lifetime, but are the "villains" in much of Matthew. Particularly valuable for us here is the lesson that *our link with the teaching of Jesus is through a community* that holds his teachings sa-

cred yet applies and adapts them to situations not previously covered. An example in the Sermon is specifying *porneia* as an exception to the no-divorce teaching of Jesus.[17] This example of Matthew's community (in dialogue with Matthew, an inspired "authority" figure) in dealing with a new pastoral problem in a continuity-yet-development framework is instructive.

7. Different calls are given to different individuals who share common discipleship. This is not, however, reducible to two "levels" of morality, for *all* are called to serve God.[18]

8. The answers and approach of Matthew are not identical with those of Mark or John or Paul. A searching for the moral teaching of other New Testament books also must be done at the biblical theological level,[19] so that moral theology can have this fundamental data in its task of appropriating the experience of the Christ-guided Church and the lessons from wider human experience. Matthew provides an authoritative and gripping moral challenge in a Christological context—but it is only one of the voices which need to be heard.

Notes

1. See our previous treatments of method and hermeneutics, esp. 23–32 and 45–54.

2. For a summary of German scholarship (which we draw upon here), cf. W. Grundmann, *Das Evangelium nach Matthaeus* (THKNT 1; Berlin: Evangelische Verlagsanstalt, 1972) 182–90.

3. E. Schweizer, *The Good News According to Matthew* (trans. D. Green; Atlanta: John Knox, 1975) 204–9.

4. Grundmann, *Das Evangelium* 182–90; R. Schnackenburg in *Christian Existence in the New Testament* (2 vols.; trans. F. Wieck; Notre Dame: University of Notre Dame, 1968): "The Sermon on the Mount and Modern Man" 2. 128–57; "Christian Perfection According to Matthew" 2. 158–89; E. Schweizer, *Good News* 204–9; J. Meier, *Law and History in Matthew's Gospel* (An Bib 71; Rome: Pontifical Biblical Institute, 1976); *The Vision of Matthew: Christ, Church and Morality in the First Gospel* (Theological In-

lew York: Paulist, 1979); N. McEleney, "The Principles of
on on the Mount," *CBQ* 41 (1979) 552–70.

Many good studies have attempted to discern the original
form, ...e intermediate stages, and the final form given the Beatitudes by Luke and Matthew. Two brief studies might be mentioned: K. Koch, *The Growth of the Biblical Tradition* (trans. S.
Cupitt; New York: Scribner, 1969); N. McEleney, "The Beatitudes
of the Sermon on the Mount/Plain," *CBQ* 43 (1981) 1–13. J. Dupont's *Les Béatitudes* (3 vols.; Paris: Gabalda, 1958–73) shows how
complex the subject is. Cf. also the bibliographic review of modern
research on the Sermon: W.S. Kissinger, *The Sermon on the
Mount: A History of Interpretation and Bibliography* (American
Theological Library Association Bibliog. Series 3; Metuchen;
Scarecrow, 1975).

6. Cf. the listing of recent studies of the situation in Matthew's community in Meier, *The Vision of Matthew* 6–29. These
include works by G. Bornkamm, D. Hare, D. Harrington, G.
Strecker, and W. Thompson.

7. Meier, *Vision* 29–39.

8. Cf. Meier, *Vision* 75–82, 248–62 [Meier acknowledges particular indebtedness to J.D. Kingsbury, *Matthew: Structure, Christology, Kingdom* (Philadelphia: Fortress, 1975); *Matthew*
(Proclamation Commentaries; Philadelphia: Fortress, 1977) 30–57];
McEleney, "The Principles" 556–58; Grundmann, *Das Evangelium*
190.

9. Cf. Meier, *Law and History* 71, 86–89; *Vision* 116–17, 141–
42, 199–203, 224–25, 227–28.

10. Cf. Schnackenburg, "Christian Perfection" 176–78; "The
Sermon on the Mount" 153; Schweizer, *The Good News* 201–02.

11. Schweizer, *The Good News* 446–47. He cites Matthew 11:19,
11:25–30 and 26:34–39 as key texts.

12. Schweizer, *The Good News* 204–06.

13. Grundmann, *Das Evangelium* 241–42.

14. Cf. Meier, *Vision* 13, 19–21, 28, 238 n. 11; Schweizer, *The
Good News* 15, 200; Grundmann, *Das Evangelium* 47–48.

15. Cf. Meier, *Vision* 210–16, 237–39; Schweizer, *The Good
News* 201–03.

16. Cf. Schnackenburg, "The Sermon on the Mount" 149–50;
Schweizer, *The Good News* 204.

17. Cf. Meier, *Vision* 249–57.

18. Cf. Schnackenburg, "Christian Perfection" 179–89.

19. R. Schnackenburg's *The Moral Teaching of the New Testament* (New York: Herder, 1965) is still a valuable overview of the
various New Testament books and the probable traditions behind
them, but it should be used with an awareness of more recent work
done on the individual sources and books it studies.

Chapter Three

THE NEW TESTAMENT LOVE COMMAND AND THE CALL TO NON-VIOLENCE[1]

(Robert J. Daly, S.J.)

This chapter is a brief biblical-theological reflection on a theme which was central to the two preceding chapters: the demands of Jesus regarding love of enemies and non-violence. The investigations of Topel on the Lukan Sermon and Schuele on the Matthaean Sermon show the radicality of these demands. They show that Jesus quite obviously calls and expects (and Luke and Matthew understand Jesus as calling and expecting) his followers to live that way. Among other things, this chapter will indicate how necessary sociological analysis is to understand what texts such as these meant or could have meant as they were being formulated in the New Testament. It will also give another example of how one must often "move beyond the text"— but not against it—in order to discover its full range of meaning.

Christians are accustomed to speak of the "first" or "greatest" or "central" Christian commandment as the "love command" or the "law of love." Based as it is on a dominical saying, such language is quite authoritative. But it is also paradoxical. For genuine love can never be "commanded" in the strict sense of the word. A different approach which, conceptually, at least, might help us out of this impasse would be to focus the obligatory aspects of Christian life less on the "Law" of love and more on the

211

missionary command to preach the good news. The central New Testament command would thus be centered more on the missionary command to "make disciples of all nations ... teaching them to observe all that I have commanded you" (Mt 28:19–20), to be "witnesses to Jesus to the ends of the earth" (Acts 1:8), to be "ambassadors for Christ" with his message of reconciliation (2 Cor 5:19–20), i.e., *to preach the good news of Jesus Christ.*[2] (This is, of course, theological reflection which goes beyond the direct meaning of the texts we have just quoted.) In any case, the missionary command heightens the Christian obligation to non-violence. For against those who would like to impose religion one can ask how it is possible, if one has really listened to the Gospels, to think of being a witness to the true Jesus by means of force or violence.

Another way of approaching the same point is to point out that emphasis on love as *commanded* might push us too strongly in the direction of a purely heteronomic ethic in which one acts virtuously simply because one is so commanded. That is, the motive for an ethical act comes *entirely* from outside, in this case, from God. When pushed to extremes, this view ends in what can be called a theonomic moral positivism, a position not only at odds with popular modern views of human autonomy and human dignity, but also quite inconsistent with a mature understanding of what it means to be created in God's image and likeness (Gen 1:26) and to have God's own Spirit dwelling within us.

These and similar motives (although I cannot pause here to speculate in what particular combination) were undoubtedly behind some modern attempts, e.g., those of Bultmann and Braun, to locate the essence of the love command in the subject who is to love. But these too are unsatisfactory: they tend toward the extremes of a purely autonomic ethic which is quite difficult to reconcile with Christian faith. But, most decisively, such interpretations don't seem to be reconcilable with those texts which are a Christian's primary source for the love command.[3] These texts are Matthew 5:38–48, Luke 6:27–36, and Romans 12:14, 19–21. These are the texts which tell us to love our enemies, to pray for those who persecute us, not to resist one who is evil, and to return good for evil.

After confirming the reliability of the text itself, the

scholarly analysis of text

exegete turns to source criticism to see what can be determined about the prior history and the process of formation and tradition behind these texts as we now have them. The earliest text is from Paul in Romans 12:14, 17, 19: "Bless those who persecute you; bless and do not curse. . . . To no one render evil for evil, but provide good things. . . . Do not avenge yourselves, beloved, but give place to the wrath." Written in the late 50's, Paul's Letter to the Romans clearly contains the same teaching as Matthew and Luke whose Gospels took their final form some twenty years later. The verbal variation, however, suggests that Romans gives us an independent example of a tradition derived from Jesus and formulated in a manner distinctive of Paul.

But what seems to be most significant is that the Matthaean and Lukan texts form part of the hypothetical Q document.[4] Happily, the beginning of the wider context needed to resolve the ambiguities and tensions which a study of Q alone suggests (cf. note 4) is to be found within the New Testament, within the Gospels themselves; for it is from Matthew 5:35–38 and Luke 6:27–36 that we know Jesus' teaching on non-violence. It is these Gospels, not a hypothetical Q, that the Christian Church reveres as God's Word. This is not to dismiss Q as unimportant, for it provides us with an invaluable means toward reconstructing some of the sayings of Jesus. If a significant number of these sayings could be reconstructed beyond all doubt, their authority and normativity would be recognized by most as unparalleled. However, such a reconstruction is not within our grasp. Thus it is that the Gospel witness to and interpretation of the words and works of Jesus, as received by the Christian community of faith, must serve as our basic starting point. Q, and what we can reconstruct of its "theology," helps us to interpret the Gospels, but the Gospels themselves in their contexts remain the authoritative and inceptively normative sources for Christian life.

Now what we can piece together of the Lukan and Matthaean communities which produced these Gospels *"there"* gives us a picture in which community expectations of an imminent parousia remained fairly strong, but it also gives us a picture of communities beginning to settle down for the long haul. Further, the way Matthew and Luke incorporate the Q material and material from other sources suggests that they are conflating earlier "theologies" into their own redactional framework (cf. Edwards 150). Thus, the practical exhortation of Gospels produced in this context cannot be dismissed by us as mere interim-ethic, no more than it was so dismissed by the early Christians. Our inquiry thus comes down to two interrelated (and not necessarily completely different) questions: What did Matthew 5:38–48 and Luke 6:27–36 mean in their respective Gospels (i.e., final redactional) contexts? What do they mean for us today? (see above 26–32).

Following very closely Schottroff's exposition, we can remark first that the existential interpretations of Bultmann and Braun fail to do justice to the Gospel texts. One must rather look to an interpretation which is not so much interested in what goes on internally in the heart of the one who loves, but rather looks to the effect that loving one's enemy and renouncing violence will have in the heart of the enemy. This view takes love of the enemy as a concrete social event. As Schürmann explains: "Here is required that ultimate, creative goodness which makes all malice disappear ... such love takes evil to its heart and crushes it to death."[5] But most importantly, this does not seem to be a universally applicable ethical rule but rather is the attitude expected of Christians when they encounter resistance. It can be practiced only by the weak toward the strong, and only those who are involved in resistance can teach or demand it. When it is recommended from outside it is perverted into a demand to give up resistance (Schottroff 13).

This understanding of love for the enemy can be easily verified as a valid interpretation of Matthew 5:38–48 and Luke 6:27–36, for the passage is indeed addressing the problem of the enmity between Christians and their persecutors, and it is quite clear that the early Christians were socially at a disadvantage in this conflict. But if love of enemy is understood in this way—i.e., not as passively accepting but actively seeking to turn evil into good, to change, to convert the enemy—how can we explain it in relation to the clear prohibition of resistance in Matthew 5:39–41 and Luke 6:29? In other words, why is resistance forbidden, and at the same time an active love of the enemy enjoined?

Some solve this by seeing the prohibition of resistance as an attack on the zealot position, rejecting the idea of violent rebellion against the Romans. But for this interpretation to make sense, we would have to be able to see the text as being formed at a time when the enemies (persecutors) of the Jews were the same as the enemies (persecutors) of the Christians. From what we know of the formation of the Gospel traditions, this does not seem possible. But this interpretation still makes an important point which will be a key element in any adequate solution: the combination of the prohibition of resistance and the injunction to love the enemy has political implications. In order to determine what these might be, one should be able to distinguish what is here being preached to the Christian community from the various ways in which "love of enemy" could be conceived in non-Christian antiquity.

Some of these parallels in non-Christian antiquity are:

a. The attitude and reactions of the underdog, the person who does not resist evil or avenge himself/herself because he or she is powerless to do so. This seems to fit the actual social situations of those being addressed in Matthew 5:38–48 par, 1 Peter 2:18–25 and by the early Christian (ca. A.D. 177) apologist Athenagoras. None of these Christian texts pay any attention to the social relation of dependence which did not give the Christian any other realistic option than to submit to injustice peaceably and non-violently. Does this mean that we, too, should ignore social differences and interpret Matthew 5:38–48 par as inculcating a universal ethic intended for everyone under all circumstances?

b. The renunciation of revenge by the powerful is a constant theme in classical ethics. But this theme is always talking about the benefits of clemency, patience and leniency by one who is in power. Matthew 5:38–48 par presupposes a fundamentally different situation which cannot be prescinded from if we wish to avoid misunderstanding and misusing this text.

c. Antiquity also knows of the non-violent protest of the powerless, associated especially with the figure of

Socrates, and made popular in a variety of legendary embellishments. But the common theme here is that the philosopher accepts even the physical abuse of his tormenters in order to proclaim the rottenness of society. This is quite different from what is going on in Matthew 5:38–48 and Luke 6:27–36 (cf. Schottroff 15–23).

What one can draw from all this is the importance of knowing the concrete social situation of the authors and audience of a text in order to discern accurately what is the meaning and intended message of that text. For since biblical texts are not just of divine provenance (doctrine of inspiration) but are also human productions, we cannot ignore the concrete social situation of their original human authors and audience.

Close analysis of the Matthaean and Lukan call to nonviolence, renunciation of revenge and love of the enemy enables us to reconstruct the general nature of the common tradition behind Matthew 5:38–48 and Luke 6:27–36, but not the original order of these injunctions. It seems clear that the tradition behind both evangelists defined "your enemies" as "those who persecute you." It seems equally clear that the parallel material in the rest of the New Testament (e.g. Rom 12:14; 1 Cor 4:12–13; 1 Pet 2:12, 23; 3:9, 16; 4:4, 14) teaches the same thing, and understands "doing good to," "praying for" and "blessing" one's enemies in a thoroughly active and even "aggressive" sense. That is, "the command to love the enemy is an appeal to take up a missionary attitude toward one's persecutors, to convert them from their enmity and bring them into the fold of the Christian community. This is the meaning of Romans 12:21: 'Do not be overcome by evil, but overcome evil with good' " (Schottroff 23).[6] Despite verbal variations, this attitude of active, converting love that a Christian is expected to show toward enemies of the community seems to be very much the same at all levels of the New Testament tradition. Its authority and normativity, in terms of biblical foundations for basic Christian attitudes, could not be much more firmly established.

Taking social distinctions into account, we can see that this "desire of the powerless for the salvation of their enemies is the precise opposite of the desire of the ruling classes to integrate their enemies or rebellious subjects into their dominion after they have defeated them" (Schottroff 24). Thus, whether or not the identification of enemies with persecutors goes back to the historical Jesus, the essential meaning of the dominical teaching is that we should love our enemies, i.e., work to make them our brothers and sisters in the Lord, even when they are truly our enemies. And thus again, "Insistence on the love of enemy has a public and implicitly political dimension because it explicitly refers to the identity of the social group" (Schottroff 25).

With this meaning of love for one's enemy (= the active desire of the powerless for the salvation of their persecutors) fairly well established as the basic New Testament meaning, the combination of love for the enemy with non-violence or non-resistance in the face of injustice—for these appear together in all levels of the tradition—appears to be an insoluble enigma. For if love of one's enemy is a genuinely *active* love, as explained above, this is inconsistent with a passive, non-violent acceptance of an enemy's unjust demands. It seems that we must, as Schottroff suggests (25–27), go beyond what can be established by exegesis alone and see non-resistance in these texts as applying specifically and concretely in the area of politics, and most specifically to the area of insurrectional or revolutionary politics. Christians are not revolutionaries. But non-cooperation with evil (e.g., Martin Luther King, Jr.) is consistent with the prohibition against resisting one who is evil (Matthew 5:39), for this prohibition is not a fundamental rejection of every type of resistance. In other words, as Tertullian puts it, Christians are, and precisely as Christians, factors of resistance in society.[7] They resist injustice and oppression. They are impelled to this by their active and aggressively missionary love by which they strive by non-violent yet quite active means to bring all, including their enemies, into the one flock of Christ. They are impelled to this, as Topel and Schuele have shown in the preceding chapters, by their being as "sons of the Most High" and children of their heavenly Father.

It is in this way, or at least in a way very similar to this, that it seems we must try to make sense of the way the various strata of the New Testament have presented the

[handwritten margin note: moving beyond the text (but not against it)]

"love command" side by side with the call to non-violence. It also seems to be the predominant way in which the early Christian writers also understood the relationship between non-violence and love. It is an active, missionary, "aggressive" love that makes sense of the whole picture. The "command" part of the love command can be thus quite logically and comfortably associated with the command to "make disciples of all nations" (Matthew 28:19). Love is the motivating heart of this commandment. Non-violence, its inseparable corollary, specifies the mode and style of its fulfillment.

Notes

1. This chapter was originally published as the final part of "The New Testament and Early Church," *Non-Violence—Central to Christian Spirituality: Perspectives from Scripture to the Present* (ed. Joseph T. Culliton; Toronto: Edwin Mellen, 1982) 33–62. Thanks are gratefully rendered for the permission to reproduce it here in slightly revised form. As I indicated there, I rely extensively on L. Schottroff, "Non-Violence and the Love of One's Enemies," *Essays on the Love Commandment* (trans. R.H. and I. Fuller; Philadelphia: Fortress, 1978) 9–39. For numerous criticisms and suggestions reflected throughout this chapter I am indebted to my colleague at Boston College, Dr. Pheme Perkins, whose own fine study of this theme, *Love Commandments in the New Testament* (New York/Ramsey: Paulist, 1982), has recently appeared.
2. Cf. H.-W. Bartsch, "The Foundation and Meaning of Christian Pacifism," *New Theology No. 6* (ed. M.E. Marty and D.G. Peerman; London/New York: Macmillan, 1969), 185–98.
3. Cf. L. Schottroff 9–12.
4. The "two-source theory," favored by the great majority of exegetes, states that the Gospels of Matthew and Luke, besides material that is unique to each of them, drew upon two other common sources or documents: Mark and the Q document, a collection of Jesus' sayings. This collection of sayings accounts for some 230 to 250 verses in Matthew and Luke which are so similar (and often identical) in content and style that exegetes commonly assume that a common document lies behind them. The existence of the extra-canonical *Gospel of Thomas,* a collection of 114 sayings of Jesus which may well have been based on a collection similar to Q, tends to support this theory. Exegetes have been familiar with this hypothesis for over a century, but only recently, after the flowering of redaction criticism in the last three decades,

has there been a concerted effort to study the theology of Q and to reconstruct the religious situation of the communities which formed this collection of Jesus' sayings (cf. R.A. Edwards, *A Theology of Q: Eschatology, Prophecy, and Wisdom* [Philadelphia: Fortress, 1976]). A prominent feature of this situation, as reflected in Q, is the pervasiveness of eschatology. For example, Howard Kee's division of Q into themes or subjects finds one narrative, three parenetic and thirty-seven eschatological themes (cf. H.C. Kee, *Jesus in History* [New York: Harcourt, Brace and World, 1970] 62–103, as cited by Edwards 25; cf. also 32–43). Also quite prominent in Q, and especially in Matthew 5:38–48 and Luke 6:27–36, are motifs and forms of exhortation from the wisdom tradition (Edwards 58–79). A reconstruction of the religious situation of the community which gathered the sayings of Jesus into the Q collection would describe a group whose whole vision of reality was both colored by their imminent expectation of Jesus' return, but also tempered by the worldly-wise traditions and forms of expression of the wisdom tradition. But here we must be careful; for this reconstruction is itself a hypothesis built upon another hypothesis (the two-source or documentary theory). Thus, this evidence alone cannot support the often-made conclusion that the non-violent ethic of the Sermon on the Mount was an interim-ethic with little relevance for the modern world. But neither can one exclude eschatology from a careful consideration of the New Testament. To resolve this tension, a wider context than just the New Testament texts is needed.

5. H. Schürmann, *Das Lukasevangelium I* (HTKNT 3; Freiburg: Herder, 1969) 344, 349, as cited by Schottroff 12.

6. In actual fact, the relationships of the early Christian minorities to their sometimes persecuting enemies were profoundly complicated, and the spotty evidence we have allows only conjectural conclusions as to the extent to which the persecutions may have been engendered by missionary activity on the part of the Christians.

7. Tertullian, *Apology* 37; ANF 3.45; cf. Schottroff 27.

Chapter Four

PAUL'S DYING/RISING ETHICS IN 1 CORINTHIANS

(Terence J. Keegan, O.P.)

To the Corinthians who thought they knew what Christian life was all about Paul wrote: "I decided to know nothing among you except Jesus Christ and him crucified" (1 Cor 2:2). This chapter will examine Paul's approach to the problem of Christian living especially as it emerges from a study of 1 Corinthians, a letter which, among the Pauline writings, has the highest incidence of moral directives.

1. INTRODUCTION

For Paul, Christian life is at one and the same time life in the Spirit and life in the body. Paul can write to the Galatians: "Because you are sons, God has sent the Spirit of his Son into our hearts, crying, 'Abba! Father!' So through God you are no longer a slave but a son" (Gal 4:6–7). He can also write to the Corinthians: "We have this treasure in earthen vessels, to show that the transcendent power belongs to God and not to us" (2 Cor 4:7).

Paul maintains, on the one hand, that we are already delivered from the bondage of sin and death by the free gift of God apart from any efforts on our part (Rom 5:12–17), and maintains, on the other hand, that we must work out our salvation with fear and trembling (Phil 2:12). Paul insists that Christians are no longer subject to any code of behavior (Gal 5:1), but he insists on the Christian's ethical obligation to live the new life that has been freely given him (Gal 5:25). Paul also issues an abundance of specific moral directives, including what I believe to be the directive which governs all others, "Glorify God in your body" (1 Cor 6:20).

There is a tension in the Pauline teachings about Christian living, a tension that is deliberate. We live in a world that groans for redemption (Rom 8:22). We are subject to temptation, suffering and death. We even sin. Yet the saving action of God in Jesus has already accomplished our salvation. We are already recipients of the Holy Spirit. Paul can proclaim: "It is no longer I who live, but Christ who lives in me" (Gal 2:20).

The tension of Christian existence is a tension that natural inclination seeks to avoid and that logical minds seek to resolve. Paul, however, strove mightily to retain this tension. His efforts involved warding off opponents at various extremes and having almost to retract his arguments on one front to confront his opponents on another. At times Paul sounds quite illogical and perhaps he is.

2. THE LANGUAGE OF CHRISTIAN ETHICS

Christian moral behavior cannot be discussed using ordinary human language. Christian moral behavior is distinctive precisely because it is Christian, i.e., what one does follows upon what is (*agere sequitur esse*). How we talk about what a Christian does will therefore depend on how we talk about what a Christian is. What is involved here is the Christian's new mode of existence in the God-man. The problem of talking about Christian ethics is rooted, therefore, in the problem of talking about God.

Though some would limit the possibilities of human expression to what is called empirical language and thus deny the possibility of God-talk, most theologians recognize the possibility of speaking about God in non-empirical language. Scholastics used analogy. Scripture uses parable, paradox and various other forms of non-discursive language. Contemporaries use such forms as disclosure-language and limit-language. We shall see that the kind of language Paul uses in speaking about moral behavior is precisely this kind of non-discursive language which makes God-talk possible.

The discussion above has, however, leaped from talking about moral behavior to talking about God. Have we ignored the importance of the man Jesus? Is not talk about Christian ethics concerned primarily with talking about Jesus who precisely as one of us symbolizes and effects in us the new life we live as Christians?

Being able to talk about Jesus is indeed crucial for biblical ethics but is it possible to talk about Jesus in ways that differ from God-talk? Many today are convinced of the possibility and even the necessity of using the tools of historical criticism to recover the actual words and deeds of the historical Jesus. Some even use the results of such studies as the basis for Christian ethics. I would suggest, however, that although, whether, and what we can know about the historical Jesus are interesting questions they do not really (or necessarily) affect the moral lives of Christians. Christians lived their faith for centuries before modern critical studies enabled us to distinguish between the words of the historical Jesus and the theology of the apostolic community.

There is, indeed, a genuine danger involved in seeking access to the life of Jesus, the danger that was manifested in nineteenth century liberalism and is reappearing today in a variety of forms, the danger of losing sight of the universal significance of the death and resurrection of Jesus. W. Marxsen and other post-Bultmannians maintain that Christian faith was equally possible during Jesus' life or after Easter.[1] Process Christologists regard the resurrection as so non-essential to Christian faith that some choose not even to discuss it.[2]

Paul, however, maintains that everything a Christian is and does derives its being, its power and its significance from the death and resurrection of Jesus. I will suggest later in this chapter that, for Paul, the death and resurrection of Jesus, precisely as an event involving God, constitutes a paradox that remains unresolved. What I am suggesting here is that the Jesus-talk most necessary for biblical ethics is essentially God-talk.

The parable, the most familiar form of non-discursive language in the New Testament, has been aptly defined as:

> a metaphor or simile drawn from nature or common life, arresting the hearer by its vividness or strangeness, and leaving the mind in sufficient doubt about its precise application to tease it into active thought.[3]

Most of the types of non-discursive language found in the New Testament function in precisely the same way as the parable, by teasing the mind. Paradoxes especially, pairs of statements both of which are affirmed as true but which on the level of ordinary logic are irreconcilable, function by teasing the mind to go beyond the possibilities of logic, of ordinary human expression, and arrive at a higher level of appreciation. What will be discussed later in this chapter is how Paul confronted the situation at Corinth with a paradox, the paradox of the death and resurrection of Jesus. The supreme ethical content of 1 Corinthians is a paradox teasing the Corinthians to look beyond their inadequate conceptions of Christian existence.

3. EXCURSUS ON SCHUMACHER

E.F. Schumacher, a German-born, British economist, was a recent, somewhat unorthodox writer whose insights can be helpful. In his later life he came to realize that the "science" of economics (a part of ethics) as presently practiced ought to be scrapped and a fresh start made.[4] His study of presuppositions and principles of economics (meta-economics) led him to the study of philosophy and eventually religion. In his latter years he became a Roman Catholic. In his last book, published in the year of his death, he proceeds in good Aristotelian fashion from ontology to epistemology to ethics.[5]

Schumacher's basic epistemological principle is that real thinking involves dealing with opposites. The real problems of life are what he calls "divergent problems." It is true that we sometimes confront problems that do not involve opposites. These problems are "convergent problems." The statement of the problem demands or converges upon the solution. No matter how difficult or complex the problem may be there is a solution and someone with sufficient intelligence and resources will probably arrive at the solution. Problems in mathematics and most textbook problems in other disciplines are of this nature. The real problems of life, however, are not.[6]

The real problems of life tend to diverge. The statement of the problem does not demand a unique solution. The more we seek a straight line logical solution the more people of sound character and intelligence will arrive at opposing positions. Divergent problems can only be dealt with by breaking out of a straight line logical approach and ascending to a higher level of being.

Most parents face the problem of how to raise an adolescent child. The child needs freedom in order to mature and develop as an autonomous person. The child also needs discipline in order not to self-destroy through an immature exercise of freedom. How does the parent reconcile these irreconcilable opposites, freedom and discipline? One way is to compromise, to limit the freedom by a measure of discipline and to limit the discipline by a measure of freedom. This approach, however, is to remain on the plane of the problem, to treat the problem as a convergent problem, to attempt to solve the problem. Most parents know how to handle this problem instinctively. The opposites can only be reconciled by rising to a higher level, reconciling freedom and discipline in love.

Though Schumacher does not elaborate on paradox here, paradox functions in exactly the same way, teasing the mind through opposites to a higher level of reality. Schumacher does point out, however, that to solve a problem is to kill it. While there is nothing wrong with killing a convergent problem, any attempt to solve a divergent problem will merely inhibit our ability to profit from it.[7]

Divergent problems offend the logical mind which wishes to remove tension by coming down on one side or the other. However, the opposites that are basic to human existence, e.g., freedom and order, growth and decay, bring a tension that sharpens our sensitivity and increases our self-awareness. The dynamism provided by these tensions propels the human being to a higher form of human existence. Without these tensions the human being is nothing but a clever animal.[8]

Ethical problems are, by their nature, divergent problems. There is no solution to true ethical problems in the sense of a convergent solution. "It is not good enough to decide that virtue is good and vice is bad (which they are) ... the important thing is whether a person *rises* to his higher potentialities or *falls* away from them."[9] At the conclusion of his work Schumacher sets out in three stages what he considers to be the ideal ethical advance of a human person.

1. To learn from society and "tradition" and to find one's temporary happiness in receiving direction from outside.

2. To interiorize the knowledge one has gained, sift it, sort it out ... becoming self-directed.

3. "Dying to oneself," to all one's likes and dislikes, to all one's egocentric preoccupations . . . one has gained freedom or, one might say, one is then God-directed.[10]

I have gone through this excursus on Schumacher because we find here an approach to ethics similar to Paul's.

4. LEGALISM AND ANTINOMIANISM

Throughout the Christian centuries Paul's ethical teaching has been subjected to a wide spectrum of interpretations. Two extreme positions which regularly recur are legalism and antinomianism. A recent advocate of the legalist position, whose views are shared with a sizable number of scholars and churchmen, is C.H. Dodd. His article "Ennomos Christou" analyzes the phrase "under the law of Christ" which appears in 1 Corinthians 9:21.[11] In this article Dodd maintained that maxims which formed a part of the tradition of the sayings of Jesus were treated as if they were elements of a new Torah. To fulfill the Law of Christ "connotes the intention to carry out . . . the precepts which Jesus Christ was believed to have given to his disciples, and which they handed down in the Church."[12] He further suggests that while the commands of Jesus remain the nucleus, the Law of Christ is not restricted to the sayings of Jesus.[13]

I feel that Dodd not only has severely exaggerated the importance and role of the commands of Christ, but, more seriously, has come dangerously close to reducing New Testament ethics to Old Testament legalism. I will simply make two observations at this point and allow the later discussion to shed further light on Paul's original thought.

First in his analysis of 1 Corinthians 7:10 Dodd refers to 1 Corinthians 7:25 where Paul says he has no command (*epitagē*) of the Lord. Dodd claims the precept cited in 7:10 is also an *epitagē* of the Lord though here Paul uses "a more colorless term."[14] I would ask: If Paul wanted to cite an *epitagē* why did he choose a more colorless term? Is it not because he wanted to avoid giving an *epitagē*?

The term *epitagē* appears four times in the acknowledged Paulines (three times in the Pastorals). In 1 Corinthians 7:6 Paul does not give an *epitagē*; in 1 Corinthians 7:25 there is no *epitagē* from the Lord; in 2 Corinthians 8:8 Paul does not give an *epitagē*. Only in Romans 16:26 is the sense positive and here the subject is God and the command is that Jesus be preached everywhere to bring about the obedience of faith. What we can see here is that Paul consciously avoids doing that which Dodd claimed he had done.

Second, and more seriously, what we see in this article by Dodd is the tendency, commented upon by Schumacher, to eliminate tension by reducing divergent problems to convergent problems. A Law of Christ which can be specified as a code of precepts is one that our logical minds can handle; not so a Law of Christ that teases us to strain beyond ourselves to a level of being that no human person has yet attained. It is the latter that Paul has in mind when he says "not being without law toward God but under the law of Christ" (1 Cor 9:21).

The rejection of legalism, however, opens up the opposite danger, antinomianism. At least from the time of Marcion, if not even in Paul's own day, there have been people who interpreted Paul with a logic Paul never intended. Since Christian life is not a code of behavior through which we can earn the reward of eternal life, since we have been justified by the free gift of God apart from any efforts on our part, it follows, they would say, that ethical obligations are really of no consequence for Christian living.

Paul, however, vigorously (perhaps illogically) rejects all forms of antinomianism. Christian life is not passively, quietly, accepting the redemption Christ gave us as if we need contribute nothing (Phil 2:12). It is not amorality, i.e., a situation in which, because of the redemption already accomplished, it makes no difference what we do (Rom 6:11). It is not an existence of blissful spiritual communion with the risen Lord in which what happens in the body (e.g., abnormal or abusive use of sex, drugs, etc.) is of no consequence (1 Cor 6:20). Paul rejects all of the above by setting Christian life within the framework of the death and resurrection of Jesus.

5. PAULINE TENSIONS

Paul's rejection of both legalism and antinomianism involves expressing his ethical teaching non-discursively. The modes of expression he uses produce tensions with which our logical minds are often uncomfortable.

a. INDICATIVE/IMPERATIVE

A tension-producing opposition found in Paul and much of the New Testament is the indicative/imperative opposition. The New Testament has an abundance of moral imperatives but usually (almost always in Paul) they are associated with indicatives. "You are not your own; you were bought with a price. So glorify God in your body" (1 Cor 6:19–20). Here and elsewhere Paul appears to be saying: "The goal is accomplished; therefore work to accomplish the goal."

In one way the indicative/imperative opposition can be understood in terms of our actions flowing from our being (*agere sequitur esse*). A parent might say to an adolescent child: "If you want to be treated like an adult, then act like an adult." So also Paul might say to his churches: "If you are really filled with the Holy Spirit, then act like one filled with the Holy Spirit" (cf. Gal 5:25).

In other ways, however, the matter is more complex. First, for Paul the indicative is an accomplished fact, accomplished by God in Jesus. In passages like Galatians 2:20 Christian living is presented almost as an inevitable consequence of being a Christian. Because of one's new mode of being in Christ one necessarily behaves like a Christian. Elsewhere, however, Paul presents his imperatives in a way that clearly does not consider Christian living to be a necessary consequence of Christian being (e.g., Gal 5:13; Phil 4:9; 2 Cor 7:1). Never, however, does Paul retreat from his conviction that the indicative is an accomplished fact. Never does he suggest that our fulfillment of his imperatives can accomplish what God has already accomplished for us in Jesus. Here lies the tension. Because a stone is heavier than air it falls to the ground when dropped. One never has to command a dropped stone to fall to the ground. Paul does have to exhort redeemed Christians to behave like redeemed Christians because sometimes we do not.

A second complication involved in this Pauline tension is the presence in Paul of a double indicative framing his imperatives, the double indicative itself constituting an opposition. "If while we were enemies we were reconciled to God by the death of his Son, much more, now that we are reconciled, shall we be saved by his life" (Rom 5:10). The imperatives in Paul are connected not only with the indicative that we are already justified by our faith in the risen Lord, that already it is no longer I who live but Christ who lives in me, but also in the future and equally certain indicative of the soon to come salvation of the entire created order. "Salvation is nearer to us now than when we first believed; the night is far gone, the day is at hand. Let us then cast off the works of darkness and put on the armor of light" (Rom 13:11–12; cf. Gal 6:10; 1 Cor 4:5).

The tension between these two indicatives is quite apparent in 2 Corinthians 5 where Paul says, on the one hand, "Here indeed we groan, and long to put on our heavenly dwelling" (2 Cor 5:2; cf. Rom 8:18–23), and, on the other hand, "If anyone is in Christ, he is a new creation; the old has passed away; behold, the new has come. All this is from God who through Christ reconciled us to himself" (2 Cor 5:17–18). At the present time only Jesus is victorious over the enemies of God. Our lives in the world remain susceptible to the powers still to be overcome (1 Cor 15:24–26; 2 Cor 5:17; Gal 6:15).

Paul's imperatives derive their meaning primarily from the yet to come future indicative. Our lives in the body are meaningful precisely because our body is destined for glory (1 Cor 6:13–14; cf. 2 Cor 5:10; Rom 14:12). Yet, at the same time, Paul's ethical demands can be made only because, in some sense, we are already what we will be (Gal 5:25).

The whole of Paul's ethical teaching is rooted in this tension between the reconciliation already accomplished and the salvation soon to come. The delay of the parousia altered the perspective of some later New Testament writers and much of later Christianity but it did not alter Paul's perspective. Paul did, it seems, change his mind about how soon the parousia would be. At first he thought he would live to see it (1 Thes 4:15; 1 Cor 15:50–52), but then began to realize he might not (Phil 1:20; 2 Cor 5:1–11). Nevertheless he continued to ground his ethical teaching in the imminent parousia whenever that might be (Rom 13:11–12).

b. FREEDOM

Another tension in Paul's ethical teaching results from the peculiar Pauline notion of freedom. His idea of freedom is strange and even disconcerting for people living in modern democracies. The common American understanding of freedom is strongly affected by the deistic conceptions of Thomas Jefferson and others of our founding fathers. Paul, however, was no deist. For Paul God was intimately involved with his creation on every level, especially on the level of human behavior.

The concept of freedom is prominent in Greek philosophy, especially in connection with the Stoic notion of self-sufficiency, but it is not to be found in the Old Testament. Human autonomy is an ideal connected with the Greek man-centered universe but it is foreign to the Semitic God-centered universe. The Old Testament does speak of God leading his people out of the house of bondage but never of leading them into a state of freedom.

Paul introduced the idea of freedom into the Christian understanding of human existence. For Paul life before Christ was life in slavery, slavery to sin (Rom 6:17), held captive by the Law (Rom 7:6), in bondage to beings that are not gods (Gal 4:8). "For freedom Christ has set us free" (Gal 5:1). Yet in one sense true freedom awaits the final victory of God over all enemies. "The Jerusalem above is free" (Gal 4:26). "Creation itself will be set free from its bondage to decay and obtain the glorious liberty of the children of God" (Rom 8:21). In another sense, however, we are already free. "The Law of the Spirit of life in Christ Jesus has set me free from the law of sin and death" (Rom 8:2). "Where the Spirit of the Lord is, there is freedom" (2 Cor 3:17).

The greatest difficulty in understanding the Pauline concept of freedom comes when one asks what this present freedom involves. For Paul there is no such thing as human autonomy. All human existence involves slavery. What is to be determined is to what we are enslaved. "You who were once slaves of sin ... having been set free from sin, have become slaves of righteousness" (Rom 6:17–18). Paul speaks of himself as a "slave of Jesus Christ" (Rom 1:1). He warns the Galatians not to distort the Christian notion of freedom into Greek freedom. "Do not use your freedom as an opportunity for the flesh, but through love be slaves of one another" (Gal 5:13).

The Pauline concept of freedom involves the paradox that we have already been set free from whatever may once have held us in bondage but still must await the true freedom of the new creation. Furthermore, though we are not yet free, we are already free but only if we accept our status as slaves of Jesus and slaves of one another.

Paul's notion of freedom would clearly set him at odds with the second stage of Schumacher's ethical advance. Self-direction is not an ideal for Christian existence, nor is it even a suitable stage for arriving at what Paul and Schumacher agree is the ideal, God-direction.

c. GRACE

How is it possible to be both free and a slave at the same time? Paul reconciles these opposites not by compromising either freedom or slavery but by ascending to a higher plane and introducing the non-discursive concept of grace (*charis*). "You are not under law but under grace" (Rom 6:14). "By the grace of God I am what I am" (1 Cor 15:10).

Grace, like freedom, is a concept not found in the Old Testament. Grace has often been related to the Old Testament notion of *ḥesed,*[15] a term used to express God's loving kindness or mercy toward his people. The Septuagint, however, never translates *ḥesed* as *charis,* Paul's term for grace, but instead uses the Greek term for mercy, *eleos.*

Charis was a term less precise than *eleos* but rich in sensuous and even sexual overtones. The Septuagint does use this term but uses it to translate the Hebrew term *hen* where it has the sense of favor or attractiveness—e.g., "if she finds no favor in his eyes because he has found some indecency in her" (Deut 24:1), "she will place on your head an attractive garland" (Prov 4:9). *Charis,* however, is never a theological word in the Septuagint.[16]

In Judaism God's mercy (*hesed*) was related to his justice. God, in his mercy, would supply what a person lacked in works. Paul had a radically different understanding of the Christian's relation to God, one in which God's attitude toward a person was radically indifferent with respect to works. Paul's understanding, then, could not be spelled out in the neat categories of justice and mercy. He wanted to express the possibility of freedom and slavery at the same time. He wanted to express the radically new attitude of God resulting from the saving action of God in Jesus. He avoided the term *eleos*[17] and chose instead *charis* which can be translated as "charm," a word which curiously is now being used in theoretical physics as science pushes beyond the realm of logical expression.[18]

Paul never attempted to systematize grace. Questions like whether grace is imputed or infused would be entirely foreign to Paul. The folly of subjecting grace to logic is aptly expressed in the alleged Jansenist petition: "From sufficient grace deliver our souls, O Lord."

For Paul grace was that aspect of God's dealings with us by which we are justified apart from any works of our own (Rom 3:24; 4:4, 16; 5:15–17, 20–21; 6:14, 23; 11:6; Gal 2:21; 5:4; 2 Cor 8:9). Grace, however, is not only that which constitutes us in our new state of freedom; it is also that by which we are established in our new state of slavery, each in our own peculiar vocation whatever that might be (Rom 1:5; 5:2; 12:3, 6; 15:15; Gal 1:15; 2:9; 1 Cor 1:4; 3:10; 15:10; 2 Cor 1:12; 12:9; Phil 1:7).

6. GALATIA AND CORINTH

All of the letters Paul wrote (including, I believe, Romans) were written not to present a systematic analysis of the Gospel or of Christian theology but rather to address specific problems that had arisen in various communities. The problems that provoked Galatians and 1 Corinthians had at least one element in common. In both communities the tension of Christian existence had been relaxed although in almost diametrically opposed ways.

The Galatians had relaxed the tension of Christian existence by focusing on the imperative at the expense of the indicative. Paul had given them no law, so they eagerly accepted the Law brought to them by the Judaizers. Paul's letter to them, therefore, insists on the indicative, on their unmerited justification (Gal 2:16), on their freedom as sons of God and recipients of the Spirit (Gal 4:6–7; 5:1). The Galatians were retreating from freedom, so Paul urged them to live the freedom Christ had won for them.

At Corinth the problem was quite different. The Corinthians had also relaxed the tension of Christian existence but by focusing on the indicative at the expense of the imperative. Their relaxation of the tension of Christian existence was actually twofold, for they not only focused on the indicative of their already being reconciled to God but they collapsed the twofold indicative of past justification and future salvation into a present indicative of being already filled with the Spirit.

The Corinthians conceived of themselves as having arrived at the freedom which Paul so vigorously promoted in his Letter to the Galatians. Having lost sight of the future expectation of the fullness of the Spirit they regarded their present life in the Spirit as complete. The Spirit had become almost their personal possession, and through the Spirit they had arrived at autonomy.

Autonomy or Greek freedom is not, however, what Paul had in mind when he wrote to the Galatians. Self-direction, Schumacher's second stage in the ethical advance, plays no role in Paul's understanding of Christian existence. Self-direction, in fact, was the cause of various problems that had arisen within the Corinthian community, chief among them being the problem of factions (1 Cor 1:11; 3:3; 11:18–19). In response to their presumed autonomy Paul accused them of pride, of being "puffed up in favor of one against another" (1 Cor 4:6). Paul's concern with pride is shown by his sixfold use of the verb *phusioō* in this letter (4:6, 18, 19;

5:2; 8:1; 13:4), a verb used only once in the rest of the New Testament (Col 2:18). Paul speaks of the Corinthians as being already filled (1 Cor 4:8) possibly using a play on words in describing the *Korinthioi* with the verb *korennumai,* his sole use of this verb. He sarcastically criticizes their presumed maturity (1 Cor 3:1–2) and suggests that their unedifying behavior is a clear sign that they do not yet know as they ought to know (1 Cor 8:2).

Though there are many concrete ethical problems to be dealt with at Corinth, Paul does not solve them by laying down rules of behavior. Paul recognizes that their denial of the imperative of Christian existence is rooted in their failure to appreciate the tension in the double indicative of Christian existence. Paul's concern is not so much with the individual problems that had arisen as it is with the Corinthians' having lost the dynamism of Christian existence. They are all talk but without power (1 Cor 4:19–20). The dynamism could only return if they would accept the paradox that power lies in weakness. "The word of the cross . . . is the power of God" (1 Cor 1:18). Paul came to them in weakness precisely so that the power of God might operate in them (1 Cor 2:3–5). Indeed the whole of Christian existence is cast in the perspective of this pair of opposites, "It is sown in weakness, it is raised in power" (1 Cor 15:43).

Throughout the letter Paul lays down no simple indicative about justification by faith with which, for example, he responded to the problem at Galatia. Rather he utilizes various paradoxical affirmations to lead the Corinthians to an appreciation of the tension of Christian existence. In a similar way Paul solves none of their ethical problems with clear imperatives but rather teases them in various ways to appreciate the demands of Christian existence as they flow especially from the future indicative of our resurrected life with the Lord.

Paul does indeed offer advice in each of the problem areas brought to his attention. He does this, however, in such a way as not to subject the Corinthians to outside-direction (the situation that the Galatians desired). Concerning the unmarried he gives his opinion "as one who by the Lord's mercy is trustworthy" (1 Cor 7:25). This outside-direction, however, is clearly not affirmed as a hard and fast rule but simply as a helpful aid for a divided community, "for your own benefit ... to promote good order and to secure your undivided devotion to the Lord" (1 Cor 7:35).

Paul would probably regard all the concrete admonitions he gives in 1 Corinthians in this same light. He has different degrees of commitment to the various admonitions he gives. He gives them all in response to immediate needs. He consciously avoids laying down commands (*epitagē*) either from himself or from the Lord. Even the admonitions about which he is most certain he deliberately sets in the context of future glory, e.g., the passage on prostitution ends with the advice: "Glorify God in your body" (1 Cor 6:20).

The ethical advance for Paul involves arriving at God-direction. Self-direction is a side track that could terminate the journey. The whole tenor of 1 Corinthians manifests Paul's urgent desire that the Corinthians should advance. The example of the Israelites in Chapter 10 illustrates the fate of those who set out on a journey without reaching the goal. Paul feels that he has experienced God-direction. "We have the mind of Christ" (1 Cor 2:16); "I think I have the Spirit of God" (1 Cor 7:4). His desire is that the Corinthians should advance as well, taking him as their example. "Be imitators of me" (1 Cor 4:16); "Be imitators of me as I am of Christ" (1 Cor 11:1).

7. TEASING PARADOXES

When opposites are brought together two things can happen: the plane of opposition can be transcended or the opposition can solidify. The latter is what Paul observed at Corinth. "When you come together it is not for the better but for the worse" (1 Cor 11:17). The diverse members of the community at Corinth, when they came together for the Lord's supper, rather than ascending to a higher plane by transcending their diversity, chose to remain as they were, untouched by the sacrament of unity.

When divergences are not transcended (e.g., when a

divergent problem is treated as if it were a convergent problem), diversity yields disarray and destruction. When the divergence is correctly dealt with, edification results. In the prayer meetings diversity was allowed and encouraged with only one stipulation: "Let all things be done for edification" (1 Cor 14:26; cf. 14:4, 12).

Throughout the letter Paul confronts the problems of the Corinthians not by solving their problems but by teasing them to a deeper appreciation of what Christian existence is all about. He frequently devises paradoxes that are intended not to divide but to unify and elevate.

The Corinthians had chosen to belong to factions (*haireseis*) (1 Cor 11:19), realizing with their human wisdom that one cannot stand on both sides: You can't be both a Democrat and a Republican, both a hawk and a dove. Paul, however, says you can:

> For all things are yours,
> whether Paul or Apollos
> or Cephas or the world
> or life or death
> or the present or the future,
> all are yours (1 Cor 3:21–22).

How is this possible? It is possible because "you are Christ's; and Christ is God's" (1 Cor 3:22). It is no longer necessary to remain on the plane of division. One can now transcend that plane and unify the opposites.

Paul presents himself as an example of one who has unified opposites in his own person. He is both free and a slave; in short he is "all things to all men" (1 Cor 9:22). Why does he display this diversity? How does he do it? Is it real or simulated? Paul gives a twofold answer: "I do it all for the sake of the Gospel, that I may share in its blessings" (1 Cor 9:23). A more literal and less interpretative translation would read: "I do it all because of the Gospel, that I may become a sharer of it." Leaving *dia* ambiguous allows it to convey the full paradoxical sense of both cause and effect. Paul's behavior is no mere simulation for the sake of spreading the Gospel; the Gospel is itself both cause and effect of Paul's behavior. Further, by unifying in himself various opposites through being both effect and cause of the

Gospel, Paul enters ever more profoundly into that very Gospel.

Even in those passages where he is most concrete and specific Paul is teasing the Corinthians to a deeper awareness, a higher level of existence. Twice he initiates a discussion with the paradoxical assertion: "All things are lawful but not all things are helpful" (1 Cor 6:12; 10:23). To which shall we give priority, that which is permissible or that which is expedient? Paul never answers this question. Paul never dissolves the paradox. In both passages he gives a good deal of concrete advice on the problems discussed but he concludes each by raising the discussion to a higher plane: "Glorify your body" (1 Cor 6:20); "Do all to the glory of God" (1 Cor 10:31).

Paul never tries to tell the Corinthians how to live their lives. He does, however, tell them to be imitators of him as he is of Christ (1 Cor 11:1; cf. 4:16). How is Paul an imitator of Christ? What does he do in imitation? Paul preaches the Gospel, not by his own will, but by vocation (1 Cor 9:16–17). Paul's words about himself echo Jesus' in Mark: "Remove this cup from me; yet not what I will but what thou wilt" (Mark 14:36). Paul says of himself: "I bear on my body the marks of Jesus" (Gal 6:17). He encourages the Corinthians in their Eucharist to "proclaim the Lord's death until he comes" (1 Cor 11:26).

Each has an appointed role in the time between the death of Jesus and the final resurrection. Paul was called to be an apostle (1 Cor 1:1). "To each is given the manifestation of the Spirit for the common good" (1 Cor 12:7). Precisely because we are called to share, at some future time, in the glory of God we should even now glorify God in our bodies (1 Cor 6:20), a glorification of God that involves proclaiming the Lord's death (1 Cor 11:26).

Paul assists the Corinthians in overcoming their immediate problems—first, by providing specific advice that both renders the Christian more free to pursue the glory of God and also heightens the paradox-producing tensions that impel the Christian toward this goal; second, by framing his entire presentation of the paradoxes of Christian existence in the fundamental paradoxes: Christ's death and resurrection, our dying and rising; paradoxes that give meaning and impetus to all other paradoxes.

8. DEATH/RESURRECTION PARADOX

According to Schumacher the most basic pairs of opposites are freedom/order and growth/decay. These opposites bring about the tensions that sharpen our sensitivity and increase our self-awareness. Both of these pairs are utilized by Paul in his exposition in 1 Corinthians, especially the second which appears as the specifically Christian paradox of dying/rising. This paradox provides both the unity and the open-ended dynamism of this letter.

For Paul, Christ died and is risen; we, on the other hand, have died with Christ but await our final resurrection (Rom 6:5). The fundamental tension of Christian existence arises from attempting to unify our death with Jesus and our equally certain future resurrection with him. Some of the Corinthians had relaxed this tension by denying the futurity of our resurrection (1 Cor 15:12) and consequently losing as well the tension between the indicative and imperative of Christian existence. The paradoxical tension between our dying and rising with Jesus, however, can only be appreciated if we first appreciate the paradoxical tension between Jesus' own dying and rising.

Later New Testament writers, for various reasons and in various ways, began to relax this tension between Jesus' death and resurrection. John unites death and resurrection into one event in such a way that the cross represents not mankind's darkest hour but rather the entrance into glory (Jn 13:27–33). The author of Luke/Acts sees the death and resurrection of Jesus as distinct events but relaxes the tension between them by presenting the resurrection as God's reversal of an ignominious death (Acts 2:23–24). Paul, however, never relaxes the tension between Jesus' death and resurrection.

For Paul, Jesus' death and resurrection are parallel events whose full meaning requires that they be affirmed together (Rom 4:25; 8:34; 1 Cor 15:3–4; 2 Cor 5:15; 1 Thes 4:14). At the same time, however, they are opposites whose opposition Paul never attempts to relax or resolve. Jesus died the ignominious death of one condemned by hostile powers (Gal 3:13). His death was and remains a scandal to

Jews and folly to Gentiles (1 Cor 1:23). It is foolishness, it contradicts wisdom, it is a manifestation of weakness (1 Cor 1:14, 18, 25). Jesus also has risen into glory where he reigns even now though the hostile powers are not yet defeated (1 Cor 15:20–26).

Precisely as standing in paradoxical tension with this death, Jesus' resurrection is the guarantee of our soon to be accomplished resurrection. Jesus is the "first fruits" (1 Cor 15:23), "the first-born among many brethren" (Rom 8:29). The death of Christ, however, had not been undone. Our lives as Christians involve being weak and foolish in the eyes of the world (1 Cor 3:18; 4:10). Paul can say, therefore, "I decided to know nothing among you except Jesus Christ and him crucified" (1 Cor 2:2).

Paul's purpose in writing to the Corinthians was to tease them out of their Greek self-direction and lead them into God-direction. The contrast between the *psychikos* (natural) and the *pneumatikos* (spiritual) illustrates Paul's concern. This contrast appears only twice in the letter, at the beginning (1 Cor 2:14–15) and at the end (1 Cor 15:44–46). The Corinthians think they are already *pneumatikoi* but Paul is able to show them by their behavior that they are still *psychikoi.* At the end of the letter he explains that it is at the final resurrection that we become *pneumatikoi.* The Corinthians had lost sight of this future dimension. The ethical thrust of the letter, however, is that we can and should, even now, live as *pneumatikoi,* i.e., be God-directed, but this is possible only by now living under the sign of the cross.

The climactic chapter of this letter, Chapter 15, presents, in all of its dimensions, the fundamental Pauline paradox, dying/rising: "What you sow does not come to life unless it dies" (1 Cor 15:36). The resurrection of the dead, the final and perfect coming to life, is treated in this chapter not out of speculative interest but because it provides the dynamism for Christian existence. The goal of our existence is glory (*doxa*)—our glory and God's glory. It is in the resurrection that our glory is God's glory. Until then we are in between, we are on the way, we are being God-directed. Where does this movement toward glory get its power? Paul's answer is clear: the cross of Christ. The whole of 1 Corinthians is framed by the cross and resurrection of Jesus. The resurrection of Jesus is the guarantee of our resurrection; the cross of Jesus provides the power which moves us to that goal.

Paul speaks of cross and crucifixion only at the beginning of this letter, just as he speaks of resurrection only at the end (1 Cor 6:14 is the sole exception). The two, however, are presented as that pair of opposites which, when their unity is grasped, provide both the impetus and goal for Christian living.

The first two chapters are clear in asserting that it is the power of the cross that provided the dynamism for all that Paul seeks to accomplish (1 Cor 1:17–18, 23; 2:2). Chapter 15 shows the essential relationship between Christ's resurrection and ours. What is that relationship? Paul does not state it in categorical terms; he simply presents it with his chiastic use of the term *egeirō*.

A.	15:4	he was raised on the third day
B.	15:12	Christ is preached as raised
C.	15:13f	then if Christ has not been raised
D.	15:15	he raised Christ
E.	15:15	whom he did not raise
F.	15:15	if the dead are not raised
F^1.	15:16	if the dead are not raised
E^1.	15:16	then Christ has not been raised
D^1.	15:20	in fact Christ has been raised
C^1.	15:29, 32	if the dead are not raised
B^1.	15:35	how are the dead raised
A^1.	15:42ff	what is raised is imperishable
		raised in glory
		raised in power
		raised a spiritual body

The unity of these two opposites, death and resurrection, is brought out by Paul's concern for glory, ours and God's, as the goal of Christian existence. His first reference to glory comes in the passage with the last reference to the crucifixion:

We impart a secret and hidden wisdom of God which God decreed before the ages for our glorification. None of the rulers of this age understood this; for if they had, they would not have crucified the Lord of glory (1 Cor 2:8–9).

Glory appears at various points in the body of the letter as a transcendent principle which for Paul governs our behavior. The final reference to glory appears in the climactic passage of Chapter 15 in which our resurrection (A^1) is related to the resurrection of Jesus (A). "It is sown in dishonor, it is raised in glory" (1 Cor 15:43). Glory is not yet ours but it is, nevertheless, the certain future indicative of Paul's Gospel. For this reason Paul can urge the Corinthians, even now while living under the cross of Jesus, to do all for the glory of God (1 Cor 10:31; cf. 6:20).

We live as Christians, we enter into the paradox of Christ, by realizing in our lives both the dying and rising of Jesus. 1 Corinthians, far from dissolving the paradox of death/resurrection, leaves the paradox wide open. It is a unified letter setting the mystery of Christian existence in the mystery of Christ and providing the open-ended dynamism necessary for Christian living.

9. CONCLUSION

Christian living, for Paul, does not consist in abiding by a determined set of ethical norms. Neither does it consist in an autonomous form of existence in which ethical obligation plays no part. Rather it consists in living the life Jesus has already won for us although we do not yet possess this life. It consists in transcending the plane of ordinary human existence and being God-directed. It is rather like the heroics occasionally performed by quite ordinary people on the scene of a tragedy, e.g., the man who jumped into the river near the Fourteenth St. Bridge in Washington, D.C., in the winter of 1982, to rescue a victim of an airplane crash, or even more strikingly, that unknown hero who kept passing the helicopter rescue sling to others and who, when the helicopter came back for him, had already slipped anonymously beneath the ice. Such people usually insist that they do not consider themselves extraordinary. They only did what they feel anyone would have done facing a similar crisis.

As Christians we are not yet glorified but we are already taken into the crisis situation of the death and resurrection of Jesus. Though we remain quite ordinary people we are inspired to respond to the needs of the moment by glorifying God in whatever situation we encounter. The difference between the momentary hero and the Christian is that, for the Christian, the crisis is never over; there is no return to ordinary living (cf. Galatians). For Paul, the tension of Christian existence is never to be relaxed. Throughout his letters he teases his readers with paradoxes that force them to appreciate the urgency of the present situation and respond by rising above themselves into God-direction.

Christian living, however, does not demand the kind of heroic sanctity that might lead to canonization. Only a few were called to be apostles as Paul was. Only a few are called to work with the poorest of the poor as Mother Teresa is. Everyone, however, is called "to lead the life which the Lord has assigned to him, and in which God has called him" (1 Cor 7:17).

Mother Teresa is a person whose life exemplifies the Christian living urged by Paul. She has been accorded considerable praise and admiration all over the world. Unfortunately she is usually admired for the wrong reasons. She is praised for the good works she does, but few seem to realize how and why she does these works. Her own words are worth quoting:

> A few weeks back one of our brothers came to me distressed and said: "My vocation is to work for the lepers." He loves the lepers. "And I want to spend all my life, my every day in this my vocation." And then I said to him, "You're making a mistake, brother. Your vocation is to belong to Jesus. He has chosen you for himself, and the work is only a means of your love for him in action. Therefore it doesn't matter what work you are doing but the main thing is that you belong to him, that you are his, and that he gives you the means to do this for him."

And so, all of us, it doesn't matter what we do or where we are as long as we remember that we belong to him, that we are his, that he can do with us what he wants, that we are in love with him. And the means he gives us, whether we are working for the rich or we are working for the poor, whether we are working with high class people or low class people, it makes no difference. But how much love we are putting in the work we do is what matters. And maybe you and I are the only people in that work where Jesus can come to the people that we are touching.[19]

Paul's own words point to what is fundamentally the same understanding of Christian living:

Paul, a slave of Jesus Christ, called to be an apostle ... to bring about the obedience of faith ... among all the nations, including yourselves who are called to belong to Jesus Christ (Rom 1:1–6).

Do not use your freedom as an opportunity for the flesh, but through love be slaves of one another (Gal 5:13).

Do you not know that your body is a temple of the Holy Spirit within you, which you have from God? You are not your own; you were bought with a price. So glorify God in your body (1 Cor 6:19–20).

Notes

1. W. Marxsen, *The Beginnings of Christology* (Philadelphia: Fortress, 1969) 69.

2. D. Griffin, *A Process Christology* (Philadelphia: Westminster, 1973) 12.

3. C.H. Dodd, *The Parables of the Kingdom* (New York: Charles Scribner's, 1961) 5.

4. E.F. Schumacher, *Small Is Beautiful* (New York: Harper and Row, 1973) 75.

5. E.F. Schumacher, *A Guide for the Perplexed* (New York: Harper and Row, 1977).

6. Schumacher, *Guide* 123.

7. Schumacher, *Guide* 126.

8. Schumacher, *Guide* 127–28.

9. Schumacher, *Guide* 131.

10. Schumacher, *Guide* 135. What Schumacher says about the three stages is roughly equivalent to Franz Böckle's assertion that the dualism of autonomy and heteronomy can only be overcome in a theonomic human autonomy (*Fundamentalmoral*; Munich: Kösel, 1977) 19, 158.

11. C.H. Dodd, "Ennomos Christou," *More New Testament Studies* (Grand Rapids: Eerdmans, 1968) 134–48.

12. Dodd, "Ennomos Christou" 147.

13. Dodd, "Ennomos Christou" 148.

14. Dodd, "Ennomos Christou" 142.

15. H. Conzelmann and W. Zimmerli, "*Charis*," *TDNT* 9 (1974) 381–87.

16. Conzelmann and Zimmerli, "*Charis*" 389.

17. Paul does use *eleos* and *eleeo* (*eleao*) thirteen times, twice with reference to human mercy and the remainder in passages concerning God's dealings with the people of the Old Testament (ten times in Rom 9—11 and once in Rom 15:9, a passage introducing Old Testament quotations).

18. For a non-technical discussion of the use of non-discursive language by contemporary physicists see Alan McGlashen, *Gravity and Levity* (Boston: Houghton Mifflin, 1976).

19. From a talk given by Mother Teresa of Calcutta at the National Presbyterian Church, Washington, D.C., Spring 1975.

Chapter Five

1 COR 7:8–24—MARRIAGE AND DIVORCE

(James A. Fischer, C.M.)

1. THE EXEGESIS

1 Corinthians 7 is directed toward various people: the married, the widowed, virgins, slaves, freemen, children. Although the chapter is ordinarily thought of as referring to marriage problems, the broad sweep of the persons noted may cast some initial doubt on the validity of this impression.

1 Corinthians 7:8–24 contains no noteworthy textual variants. The pericope begins with the rubric: "It would be well ..."[1] *Kalos* has no precise ethical sense either in biblical Greek or in Pauline usage. Paul's use of *kalos* (sixteen times in the ordinary Paulines + twenty-four if the Pastorals are considered as pertinent in some way) ranges from a word to describe the beauty of the Christian life to something that is right, valuable or praiseworthy. *TDNT* seems correct in concluding that "no precise sense can be distinguished in Paul."[2]

1 Corinthians 7:10 is translated by the *NAB* as, "I give this command ..." *Paraggellō* is not the precise word for command (*keleuō*) but is often used for it both in profane and biblical Greek. The Pauline usage is neither precise nor frequent (1 Cor 7:10; 1 Thess 4:11; 2 Thess 3:4, 6, 10, 12). In some cases it is natural enough to understand it as a com-

mand—e.g., 2 Thess 3:10, "We used to lay down the rule that anyone who would not work should not eat." However, it is not clear even in this case how Paul commanded this or how he expected it to be enforced. In 2 Thessalonians 3:12 he seems to repeat the *logion* but now it is prefaced: "We enjoin (*paraggellomen*) and urge them strongly (*parakaloumen*) . . ." Paul's usage seems to fall somewhere between gnomic exhortation and administrative decision.

Finally, 1 Corinthians 7:10 admonishes the married that they "must not separate" (*mē chōrizisthēnai*). This is paralleled by *mē aphienai* in 1 Corinthians 7:11, 12, 13. Neither word is a technical expression for "divorce" or "separate" although both are used in the sense of "divorce" in other New Testament passages. Although the conclusion cannot be apodictic, Paul seems to be using both words interchangeably for the condition of divorce under whatever technicalities of law existed or whatever state resulted.[3]

The analysis of the literary form of the passage here follows the model I have proposed in a previous paper.[4] Basically, I have argued that the body of a Pauline letter can best be understood on the models of Jewish wisdom writing. The thought begins not with abstractions but with concrete realities, as the words chosen indicate. The word patterns indicate that the thought progresses by using catchwords which stand out clearly as antithetical. The end of the pericope is often a paradox rather than an absolute conclusion from an argument.

The initial step in this method of diagnosing the form is to mark off what we call paragraphs. Based on an *inclusio* in the uses of the word "remain" in 7:8 and 7:24 and a distinctive vocabulary in these verses, it would seem that the pericope extends from 7:8 to 7:24 with 7:8–16 being a specific application which is followed by a more generic teaching in 7:17–24.

The chain of most frequently used words in this passage centers on "remain," "dwell" (in the sense of continuing to cohabit), "go about" (in the sense of walking in the Way), and the exhortations to stay in the state of circumcision or slavery; cf. vv. 8, 11, 12, 13, 17, 18, 20, 21, 24. A controlling verb governing these concepts is "call"; cf. vv. 15, 17, 18, 20, 21, 22. A "slave-free" antithesis dominates the concluding verses; cf. vv. 21, 22, 23. Overall, this distribution of key words suggests that the topic of men and women in marriage as introduced in 7:8–16 is tied into the following verses 17–24 on the basis of the "call" and "enslaved-free" words and that the second section is more tightly organized around "call" and climaxes in an antithesis between "free" and "slave," and that whatever is said about marriage in the first section is governed by the second section. In my article on Pauline literary forms,[4] I have argued that the Pauline literature is largely sapiential in form. In this pericope three passages have something of a gnomic form:

9b "It is better to marry than to be on fire."

15b "God has called you to live in peace."

19 "Circumcision counts for nothing
and its lack makes no difference either.
What matters is keeping God's commandments."

The first is generally accepted as a proverbial saying or at least formed on such a model. The second is not strictly a proverb, but it has the pithiness of proverbial form and embodies the unexpectedness which is found in proverb. Here it is tied into the context by the catchword "call." The third, which has a better balance in Greek than in the *NAB* translation, is carefully constructed and embodies an unusual antithesis for Paul. Works are usually contrasted with faith in Paul; here he contrasts two works with what appears to be a general summary of all works. One might suspect that "commandments" doesn't mean what it seems to mean but that in the context it expresses a living way of achieving freedom.

The *Sitz im Leben* adds little data. My reading of the vocabulary and of Strabo does not convince me that there was excessive sexual license in Corinth nor that there was a contrasting esoteric wisdom.[5] The range of sexual problems seems to be fairly normal; the wisdom of the Corinthians was managerial competency. The problem of Paul was to face the *de facto* conditions and read into them a Christian meaning.[6]

The logical analysis can now be attempted on the basis of the preceding data. An outline of the passage would fall out in some such manner:

1 COR 7:8–24—AN INSIGHT INTO CHRISTIAN FREEDOM AND MARRIAGE

(The title is dictated by the analysis that the passage does not include all these verses and that it climaxes with an insight into the meaning of Christian freedom within the conditions imposed by life.)

A. CHRISTIAN FREEDOM WITHIN THE LIVED CIRCUMSTANCES OF THREE GROUPS—7:8–16

1. THE UNMARRIED AND WIDOWS—7:8–9

Paul's advice is that they stay "as I am." From the immediate context this would seem to identify him with the unmarried (m) or by extension with the widows (f). However, the inclusion suggests that the meaning may be that they remain as Paul "before God." There is freedom in such a remaining since marriage is an option if continence proves impossible. A proverb or proverb-like saying concludes the exhortation: "It is better to marry than to burn," an experiential observation.

2. THE MARRIED—7:10–11

The *logion* of the Lord is introduced to assert that a wife must not separate from her husband. The reason for such action is not further stated. Later discussion under function will indicate that the basic dynamic behind all the *logia* about marriage is the insight that men and women can be like God or Christ in uniting themselves to one another. The dominical saying is used here within a context which speaks of freedom to indicate that a decision to remain married can indeed be a free choice even if it is a dominical precept. On the other hand, if a break-up of the marriage has occurred, there is still the freedom to observe the Lord's injunction by remaining single or becoming reconciled. How the separation has been affected, whether by civil divorce or by simple leaving, is not clear from the words *chōrizō* or *aphiēmi,* but more probably a formal divorce is meant.

3. THE MARRIED WITH MARRIAGE TENSION—7:12–16

The insight from the dominical saying is not applied to those whose marriages are filled with tensions. The cause of the tensions is not mentioned, but presumably it has something to do with the new status of becoming a Christian.

a. THE VIABLE MARRIAGE—7:12–14

In this case the unbeliever is willing and yet the believer is contemplating divorce. If 1 Corinthians 7:25–35 is connected to this case, then the Christian's involvement in the new religion has introduced tensions; if 1 Corinthians 7:36–40 is cited, then it is community pressure which is causing the trouble.[7] The pericope in general urges the Christian partner in marriage to preserve the union. Paul sees a consecrating power flowing out of the Christian partner. Then 1 Corinthians 7:14b adds enigmatically: "If it were otherwise, your children would be unclean; but as it is, they are holy." "Consecrated," "unclean," "holy" have religious connotations, possibly even cultic ones. The concept of "uncleanness" also enters the Matthaean divorce sayings (Mt 5:32; 19:9) as an enigmatic factor. Whatever the precise meaning expressed in diverse words (*akathartos* and *porneia*) may be, these texts seem to reflect an early Christian understanding that some things could tarnish the "two in one flesh" potential in the marriages of Christians and some did not. If so, Paul is protesting that Christian practice does not sustain the view that marriage to a pagan is somehow unclean. Just what the practice is that he had in mind is unknown, but he does speak of it as a *de facto* situation. Perhaps the Corinthians had not yet evolved the practice of excluding the non-baptized from the eucharistic celebrations.

If the above fits together on a literary pattern analysis, then the principal approach is flexibility in marriage. The believer need not be running off on Christian duties and leaving the non-believer behind; he (or she) can be made part of the Christian community. If a prejudice exists in the Corinthian community that mixed-marriage Christians are second-rate citizens and should divorce, one should resist this kind of pressure and look at the facts of unprejudiced reception of non-baptized children into its midst.

b. THE NON-VIABLE MARRIAGE—7:15–16

The final case concerns a marriage in which the unbeliever desires to separate. The cause of the marriage problem is not stated, but the invocation of the God of peace in verse 15b suggests that such a serious rift has taken place that a minimally peaceful co-existence is no longer possible. If the unbeliever takes the initiative the Christian can accept the separation. Verse 15, however, introduces the term "not bound." This is the tie-in to the following 1 Corinthians 7:17–24. Considering what the following section has to say about slavery—viz., that it is an indifferent condition in itself—the thought here seems to be that the Christian should not be bothered by worries over "bound" or "not bound" in marriage; the true freedom comes from within as one seeks to live within the peace of God which can exist in any *de facto* situation.

B. THE BASIS OF TRUE FREEDOM—7:17–24

The sub-section is tied together by the inclusion that each should continue in the condition of life that existed when he or she was called (cf. 7:17 and 24). One hardly expects Paul to propose status quo outcomes. So here the insight is basically dynamic: freedom does not come from changing external conditions but from admitting that one has been freed internally. "You have been bought at a price" (1 Cor 7:22). So also changing the external mark of circumcision (*peritomē* vs. *akrobustia,* an embarrassingly concrete way of putting it, 7:19), or changing one's legal status from slave to freedman (7:21) can leave the person unchanged. The question is: How does one change one's attitude toward the imposed conditions of life when one becomes a Christian? One can again enslave oneself to human opinion (7:23 and the following context 7:25–40). The essential freedom comes from acceptance that God has called one to serve as a freedman of Christ, or to remain "before God" in such circumstances. The present tense of *menō* indicates the continuing challenge to find freedom in existing circumstances.

The conclusion to this logical analysis is that marriage is treated as a *de facto* condition, not as a juridic entity about which regulations are being made. Given that the Corinthians are married, they have freedom and therefore an imperative to make the most out of such freedom. If the marriage cannot survive, they are not freed from obligation; they must make the most of the existing conditions to achieve as much of God's peace as is possible.

2. THE FUNCTION

By "function" I mean the way in which the text operated in the society in which it was fashioned. Some may consider this under *Sitz im Leben;* I simply want to pay special attention to it whatever it is called. Since the Pauline text cites a dominical *logion* and the Lord's sayings cite a Genesis text on marriage and a Deuteronomic saying on divorce, I shall simply try to evolve briefly a trajectory of how such texts may have functioned.

The Genesis 2:24 *logion* on two in one flesh is a sapiential reflection within the Yahwist's creation narrative. The literary evidence indicates that it is probably contemporaneous with the narrative. So the question is: How did the *logion* in Genesis 2:24, which strongly affirms the spiritual significance of monogamous marriage, function in the Davidic-Solomonic society? One must presume that it exists at all because it addressed some need in that society.[8] The history seems to affirm that the Genesis *logion* did not function at all in royal circles. One should presume, therefore, that the saying is in the genre of popular proverb and represents the wisdom and desires of the common people. The *logion* never appears again in the Old Testament, but seems to be implied in such proverbial sayings as Proverbs 5:15–23 *inter alia.* Only Sirach 25:25, which advocates getting rid of an impossible wife, is an exception.

The divorce sayings of Deuteronomy 24:1–4 (and 22:13–19, 28–29) seem to be in the genre of Deuteronomic legal form, dating vaguely to a time after Genesis 2:24. The point of such legislation is basically a regulation of property rights, not personal rights. As for divorce itself, the sayings simply take for granted that it exists without giving religious significance of any sort to it. How these "laws" were administered is uncertain; whether indeed they were "laws" or pragmatic admonitions to divorce-bound husbands is uncertain.[9]

The dominical sayings are of various kinds: Matthew 19:9 usually called a pronouncement story; Mark 10:11 a dominical saying after a pronouncement story; Luke 16:18 an independent saying and Matthew 5:32 a *logion* within a wisdom context. If any of them is in the genre of legal statement, it is odd that no penalty is attached. Whatever the *Sitz im Leben* adduced, there is no evidence of a court system to enforce such sayings. To the contrary, the literary form is always closer to proverb than legal statement and so the major presumption should be that such sayings functioned as advice to individuals and community during the period of the formation of the Gospels.

All of these texts affirm in various degrees an insight into the meaning of marriage as reflecting something about God. Matthew 5:32 falls under the introductory rubric of perfecting the Law (5:17) and the concluding rubric to be perfect as the heavenly Father is perfect (5:48). Matthew 19:4–5 and Mark 10:6–8 specifically cite Genesis 2:24 as the basis of their teaching. Luke 16:17 refers to the impossibility of a single iota of the Law passing away. The teaching of the Essenes, the Qumran Covenanters and the rabbinic schools basically supports monogamous marriage. We know relatively little about the legalities of divorce procedures in early Judaism.[10] From the earlier legislation, if such it was, courts seem to have become involved only because of financial complications. John 8:1–11, an interpolated but ancient story, presents the case of a woman taken in adultery who now had to be condemned and stoned. The action apparently was going to be taken by a crowd, not by court and police proceedings.

The Pauline citation of the dominical *logion* cannot be traced with assurance to any of the Gospel texts of Q.[11] The

Matthaean and Markan versions show evidence of interpretation of the basic insight to meet developing situations within the Christian communities. This is much more possible within a wisdom genre than within a legal form. Paul's use of the generic saying indicates that it operated at least as community *mores* which would be accepted without question. However, while he reinforced the basic saying with his own authority, he felt free to elaborate on the underlying insight into the meaning of marriage as reflecting an image of God to make room for personal freedom in the face of too much community pressure. I can only conclude that Paul is writing as a wise man and that his whole aggregate of sayings functions as an insight into deeper meanings of the Genesis 2:24 starting point. The trajectory continues into Ephesians 5:22–23 where the Genesis 2:24 *logion* is the basis for a vision of the possibilities of the sanctifying power within the body of Christ. Ephesians 5:22–33 is certainly not a picture of how the Ephesian churches actually existed, nor is it legislation about how they ought to exist.

The trajectory should be carried through the Christian tradition until today. For this enterprise I do not have the expertise, and a brief reading of the data as presented by Roman Catholics reveals only a fragile consensus.[12] In the prelegal state of the Church the dominical and Pauline *logia* seem to have functioned as "teachings." Christians entered marriage through the legalities of Roman law. The purpose of the *didachē* was to read Christian insight into this civil state. This continued down through the early patristic period. Legal and liturgical applications of the teaching began to emerge in the post-Constantine Church. Councils made decrees; sanctions were imposed by clergy through such measures as public penance, refusal of Communion, etc. The Gospel *dicta* with their exceptive clauses were finally accepted in the Western Church virtually without the exceptive clauses. The Eastern Churches eventually applied the exceptive clauses as functional. On the other hand, the Western Church extended the Pauline attitude into such procedures as "Pauline Privilege," "Petrine Privilege," etc. The authority to do so obviously does not depend on the marriage and divorce texts, but on the more general mandate to the Church to bind and loose.

Today both factors appear to be still at work. I accept that inspiration, canonicity, tradition and magisterium form as a continuum in which the Holy Spirit is at work in each age. But the Spirit does not reveal everything. Today we find the gnomic approach very suitable for pastoral counseling; the escape valve from external regulation is found in the moralist's saying that one must obey one's conscience and in the canonist's recognition of the internal forum. Yet gnomic sayings never functioned simply as personal morality. They also functioned as formative of community values. If they have been formulated into laws, one may regret this or wish that they were modified; but the gnomic sayings must operate somehow in a societal framework. So we have tension in the Church. One cannot eliminate it either by suppressing the legislation or by telling Christians what their consciences must be. Above all, one cannot eliminate an imperative.

The final imperative of the wise man is to know. In the present circumstances of our lives the biblical *logia* operate in the area of marriage and divorce to make us find deeper meanings in such realities. Individuals are not free do as they please; they must judge themselves in the light of the total Gospel and often walk in darkness through difficult times to discover the truth which lies hidden. Society is not free to impose any regulations it wishes to make human affairs more efficient; law is revelation and its primary function is teaching. How these two are to be combined is a matter which we do not fully know.[13] Indeed, the whole matter is full of paradoxes. That is why wisdom is an imperative—an imperative to understand the inscrutable God and to be like him.

Notes

1. The English text used is the *NAB;* the Greek text is the *UBSGNT.*

2. *TDNT* 3 (1965) 550.

3. Joseph Fitzmyer, "The Matthaean Divorce Texts and Some New Palestinian Evidence," *TS* 37 (1976) 211–13; R.L. Roberts, "The Meaning of *chōrizō* and *douloō* in 1 Cor 7:10.17," *Restoration Quarterly* 3 (1965) 179–84; J.E. Elliott, "Paul's Teaching on Marriage in 1 Cor," *NTS* 19 (1972–3) 219–25.

4. James A. Fischer, "Pauline Literary Forms and Thought Patterns," *CBQ* 39 (1977) 209–23; cf. Addison G. Wright, "The Structure of the Book of Wisdom," *Bib* 48 (1967) (165–84 for the seminal ideas.

5. *The Geography of Strabo* (tr. H.L. Jones; Cambridge: Harvard University, 1961) 4. 189–95; *TDNT* 7 (1971) 467.

6. James A. Fischer, "Paul on Virginity," *The Bible Today* 7 (1974) 1633–38.

7. Fischer, "Virginity" discusses the central theme of "busyness" as affecting all classes in Corinthian society.

8. R.N. Whybray, *The Succession Narrative* (Naperville: Allenson, 1968) is the usual source for the function of the Yahwist in Davidic-Solomonic times.

9. Moshe Weinfeld, *Deuteronomy and the Deuteronomic School* (Oxford: Clarendon, 1972) examines the influence of wisdom on Deuteronomy; cf. also Harry W. Gilmer, *The If-You Form in Israelite Law* (SBL Dissertation Series, 1975) 99 and 110–11 for summary statements.

10. Leonard Swidler, *Women in Judaism* (Metuchen, N.J.: Scarecrow, 1976) 154.

11. Fitzmyer, "Matthaen Divorce Texts" prefers to tie 1 Cor 7:10 most closely to Luke 16:18 as a declaratory legal statement, but notes the lack of a penalty. David L. Dungan, *The Sayings of Jesus in the Churches of Paul* (Philadelphia: Fortress, 1971) 83–138 has an ample discussion on the relationship of the sayings. D.L. Balch, "Backgrounds of 1 Cor 7: Sayings of the Lord in Q," *NTS* 18 (1971–2) 351–58 reviews recent attempts to trace these sayings to an ascetic tradition in Q.

12. Charles Curran, "Divorce," *AER* 168 (1974) 8–83 for a brief summary by an ethicist; Anthony J. Bevilacqua, "The History of the Indissolubility of Marriage," *Proceedings of the Catholic Theological Society of America* 22 (1967) 253–308 for a voluminous documenting of early texts; Henri Crouzel, *L'Eglise Primitive Face au Divorce* (Paris: Beauchesne, 1971) which advocates a minimalist view of divorce and Victor J. Popishil, *Divorce and Remarriage* (New York: Herder and Herder, 1967) which proposes a maximalist view; Richard McCormick, "Notes on Moral Theology, April–September, 1974," *TS* 36 (1975) 100–17; Leopold Sabourin, "Notes and Views: The Divorce Clauses," *Biblical Theology Bulletin* 2 (1972) 80–86

13. The problem of the relationship of the science of ethics to biblical teaching is treated by James A. Fischer, "Ethics and Wisdom," *CBQ* 40 (1978) 293–310.

Chapter Six

DISSENT WITHIN A RELIGIOUS COMMUNITY: ROMANS 9—11[1]

(James A. Fischer, C.M.)

Dissent has always been an ethical problem for both the dissenters and those against whom they dissent. When either party is Christian, the Bible is apt to be cited as justification for one stand or another. This has been particularly true of dissent within the Christian Church, local or universal, diocesan or religious community. That the Bible has some relevance to the questions discussed may be granted. However, the way in which the Bible is relevant is as difficult to define in this particular problem as in the more general question of the relevance of the Bible to "Christian" ethics.

An attempt will be made here to examine one example of religious dissent within a religious community and to locate this within a larger context of an approach to the total ethical problem. The example concerns Paul as a dissenter within his own Jewish community. Paul never separated himself from the community into which he was born. As the Acts of the Apostles testifies, he continued until the end of that story to preach first to synagogue Jews. At the time the Epistle to the Romans was written (ca. A.D. 55) there was no completely clear separation between the groups of Christians and Jews. Yet Paul's prophetic message set him at odds with the Jewish groups. It was an uncomfortable relationship for him.

(Cf. the methodology outlined above 175–177.)

1. ROMANS 9—11: INTEGRAL

The relevance of Romans 9—11 has usually tested the mettle of commentators. To some it has seemed a fragment from a lost letter; to others it has appealed as an abstract treatise on "the Jewish Question." The approach taken here is that Romans 9—11 is an integral part of the epistle as an application of some of the basic insights of the first eight chapters to a personal problem of Paul. As usual, Paul is aware that his own problems are the problems of many of this audience also, but the approach is through the personal dimension.

The methodology used here has developed out of a more general consideration of the relevance of the Bible to ethical topics. It begins with the observation that most human decisions are reached on the basis more of images than of reasoning. Whether the problem is a national one or a personal one, the nub of the problem is probably one of self-imaging, however that may be wrapped up in abstract rationalizing. On this level the Bible becomes relevant if authentic images bearing on the decision can be located both in the text and in the decision-maker. Behind these literary images are the psychological self-images of the authors, and behind these psychological self-images are those enduring pictures in which we have to express our inner nature. In contemporary ethical studies this final level of images is often referred to as "character," "root of being," "vision," "value," etc.

2. ANTITHESIS AND PARADOX

These images challenge one another both in the biblical text and in the decision-maker. Antithesis and paradox are frequent literary ways in which the author seeks for understanding. The same conflict goes on in the decision-maker; without a conflict there would be no problem. The dynamism in the conflict eventually concentrates on a necessity for an act of faith. Far from being cut and dried, Christian ethics is a continual challenge to gain a deeper understanding of what is involved in the stance which the Christian takes. The only place that the Christian can find peace eventually is in surrendering self to a person who is ultimately responsible for the problem. This is the point on which the Bible, Old Testament as well as New, continually operates. It is "revelation"; i.e., it discloses the presence of God. Whatever the abstract reasoning may be which leads to preferring one decision over another, the Christian must finally make an individual decision in faith. Otherwise, it is not a Christian decision. In effect, the Bible is better at challenging the decisions one makes than at presenting a solution to problems. It is within this general framework that Paul's problem of dissent is to be considered. He carried out a ministry which provoked his brother Jews because he was convinced that he had been given a mandate from God. He discovered that they were unwilling to listen and rejected him.

3. OUTLINE OF ROMANS 9—11

A brief and somewhat conventional outline of the passage will serve as a reminder of what is in these chapters and locate the material to be used later. The whole matter might be entitled: "The Problem of God's Freedom and Power in Choosing a People."

1. BLESSINGS ARE A FREE ACT OF GOD'S LIMITLESS POWER

   a. All nations are blessed through Israel even though Israel is not now blessed since that is God's free choice (Rom 9:1–13).

   b. What God's free choice is now is that his name be announced to all the world (Rom 9:14–19).

   c. He achieves his purpose despite human opposition or weakness; he shows his glory by choosing us whom he prepares for glory (Rom 9:19–29).

   d. We cooperate by faith in Jesus, a rock of scandal; we do not rely on our own works (Rom 9:30–33).

2. DISBELIEF AS AN ACT OF THE HUMAN BEING

   a. Sincere belief was rare among the Jews, but not unknown (Rom 10:1–13).

   b. The unbelief of the Jews has led to the believing of the Gentiles (Rom 10:14–21).

3. CAN GOD SAVE THE JEWS?

   a. Questions and answers (Rom 11:1–12).

   b. An admonition to Gentiles: don't boast (Rom 11:13–24).

   c. Explanation of the mystery of salvation (Rom 11:25–32).

   d. Final doxology (Rom 11:33–36).

4. LITERARY ANALYSIS OF THE IMAGES

Romans 9—11 abounds in images, most of which come in pairs. Isaac-Jacob, Moses-Pharaoh, the talking pot and the potter, Christ and the Law, the broken branches of the olive tree and the engrafted branches, friends-enemies, the people-the remnant, etc. The central contrasting image seems to be "no people"—"my people" (Rom 9:25). These are not abstract terms, but names for definite entities taken from the prophetic preaching. In the prophetic vocabulary "my people" was Israel as it perceived itself; the odd expression "no people" was clearly the non-Jew who had no entity before God. The paradox was that the prophets so often converted the identities involved.

Paul employs a great number of sub-images in the passage to picture the same reality. Thus Romans 9:22–23 contrasts "vessels of wrath" and "vessels of mercy"; Romans 9:30–32 has the "Israel of works" and "nations of faith"; Romans 9:25 sets side by side "not loved" and "beloved"; Romans 9:8 has "children of flesh" and "children of promise"; Romans 10:17–18 and 11:8 image the community as "non-hearing" and "hearing"; Romans 10:4 speaks of "the Law" and "Christ" as the end of the Law. In summary, as Paul looks at the community to which he belongs, he sees them as consciously boastful of ethnic background, achievement, and law-abiding although they know that all has not gone well, and yet on the other side he knows that they have experienced mercy, that they have a stability of faith in a promise and that they experience the presence of Christ as the "end" of the Law. All of this is expressed in a series of images which were not spun off by Paul as literary approximations but which had a concrete entity before he used them.

Nor is Paul uninvolved in the images. Each of the three chapters begins with a statement of his personal and emotional involvement:

> 9:1 "I speak the truth in Christ: I do not lie. My conscience bears me witness in the Holy Spirit that there is great grief and constant pain in my heart."

> 10:1 "Brothers, my heart's desire, my prayer to God for the Israelites, is that they may be saved."

> 11:1 "I ask then, has God rejected his people? Of course not! I myself am an Israelite, descended from Abraham, of the tribe of Benjamin."

Romans 9—11 is not an abstract treatise on the "Jewish Question," but a problem for Paul.

5. OPPONENTS

The same conclusion must be reached by asking: Who is the imagined opponent in the diatribe sections of the passage? Diatribe (a technique of popular preachers in asking questions and giving succinct, often ironic answers) appears first in Romans 9:14 and 30 with the standard introduction: "What then shall we say?" and a following set of answers. These questions concern God's governance of the world: Is God unjust? Why does he find fault? Do the Gentiles succeed by failing and the Israelites by working? Romans 10:14, 15, 18, 19 use diatribe in a series of questions which ask "how" or begin "But I ask . . ." They all concern the question of how it was that Israel received the message of God but did not act on it. 11:1, 2, 4, 11 are questions introduced by "I ask"; Romans 11:7 is introduced by "What" and 11:15 by "Who." The center of the questioning concerns whether God has forsaken his people. It is impossible to identify from historical evidence who might have posed these questions, and it is somewhat irrelevant to the diatribe technique to do so. The personal references at the beginning of the chapters give an indication that Paul, like other preachers who employ diatribe, was posing problems which first arose within himself, and which he then projected with. good sense would be questions that his readers had or should have had.

To exemplify, Romans 11:14–21 raises the question whether the good news has been preached to the Israelites since they have not responded. It was a perplexing problem to Paul since he had just reflected on his own self-image as a preacher to the nations: "I say this now to you Gentiles: Inasmuch as I am the apostle of the Gentiles, I glory in my ministry" (Rom 11:13). That mission had been successful. On the other hand, he had frequently referred to himself as an Israelite and a preacher to them (cf. Rom 9:1–5; 10:1–2, 13; 11:1–2). They had not listened. It is precisely in this conflict of images within Paul, the successful preacher to the nations and the spurned preacher to Israelites, that the conflict arose.

6. THE CHALLENGE

The literary images point to the conflict within Paul. The mystery of choice and rejection arises from the way in which the situation is pictured. Yet there is a paradox. The Israelites are not rejected (Rom 11:1–3). It is not ethnic descent or performance on the basis of the Law which makes a true Israelite. Within "my people" is a remnant and a Gentile group of hearers. Even the non-hearers have a future (Rom 11:25–29). The paradox is expressed in a literary way by the contrasting words which form the center of the discourse. Thus in Romans 9 the words with multiple uses center around the contrast between mercy (Rom 9:9, 15, 16, 18, 23) and wrath (Rom 9:15, 17, 19, 28). At the end of this chapter a new concentration begins and continues into Romans 11. This is based on faith (Rom 9:30, 33; 10:6, 8, 10, 11, 14, 16, 17) and justness (Rom 9:30; 10:3, 4, 5, 6, 10). The antithesis to this is Law and works (cf. Rom 10:4 for law; the rest comes from the context). Concentrating on Romans 11, this centering of words on faith and justness indicates that the challenge of the opposing images must somehow result in a deeper insight into what faith and justness really mean. This can then be fed back into the images, and a hermeneutic loop results which eventually culminates in the doxology that ends the whole passage.

7. PAUL AND THE JEWS

To put this in terms of decision-making, Paul was confronted with the problem of how he could continue to perform a God-given mission to his own people when it seemed to be totally fruitless. He could see himself as a prophet admonishing them against overconfidence (cf. Rom 11:13–24) and that was just a matter of common sense. But when he pictured himself as preaching to his own people, he cringed. Had God's word failed? They had certainly heard the word of God from Moses on and they were zealous for it

(Rom 10:1–7). But somehow they had never made the connection that Jesus was "the end of the Law" (Rom 10:4). The Gentiles, who didn't even pretend to understand this, seemed to have arrived at understanding. Isaiah had experienced the same thing: "All day long I stretched out my hands to an unbelieving and contentious people" (Rom 10:21 quoting Isa 65:2). Indeed, this message of rejection had been part of Isaiah's inaugural mission (cf. Isa 6:9–10). Paul could not avoid the prophetic image. The mission was to preach; it was not to preach successfully. That had its mysterious place within God's design as Chapter 11 goes on to say. But the preacher does not fully understand the mystery. He could only join himself to God as an apostle, but not as a counselor (Rom 11:34).

8. CONTINUING REVELATION

A good deal of attention has been given to technical details in order to show that a contemporary application is not an exercise in subjective eisegesis. The test portrays Paul caught in a conflict of images as prophetic preacher. The literary expression is basically a series of antithetical images from the past. These chapters contain more quotations from the Old Testament than any other Pauline passage; poetic sayings from Deuteronomy, Psalms, Isaiah and Jeremiah abound. Paul's identification with those previous Israelites is strong. The final stance which Paul adopted depended on how he pictured Israel and Israel's prophets in previous ages. It was the images which were trans-temporal in his time.

Our application depends on the same transference of images. How the present author and reader react to the material presented here depends far more on self-imaging and self-understanding than on logical argument. Any dissenter worthy of the name must have a self-image of being a spokesperson for God or a higher morality, and probably creates that impression. Yet such a position tests the honesty of any human being. Actual experience of protesting reveals unsuspected and cunning self-interests. The desire to win an argument, to vindicate a position, to manipulate policy, to demonstrate superior knowledge inevitably intrudes. In the final analysis, there is no way of proving infallibly that one is right in the *ad hoc* situation. Yet the protester must adopt an unambiguous stance, knowing all this. The test of the prophetic image is important: the prophet speaks for God and knows that he will not be heard. Such was the tradition of old: Jesus quoted the proverb, "No man is a prophet in his own country." The test of honesty (but not rightness) is whether one is willing to be ignored.

Yet this is not all that is involved. Since the protesting is within one's own community, the reactions are not neutral but predictably unpleasant. Can one ignore the message because of personal loss? What shall be one's stance toward those who do not hear? It is easy enough to dismiss them as a "no-people." But is this true? One's own community is still one's own community. As Paul realized, God had not rejected his own people. Conversely, God had not canonized them. One may say that these are good people. They may not be. They are simply chosen and chosen for mysterious reasons.

In the end, one can only make a decision out of faith. The images from the past illuminate one's own self-images, good and bad. Such images are human psychological drives which can both exalt and debase. Behind them somewhere lies an ultimate reality of who the protestor really is before God. In facing that reality one defines both one's potential and one's limitations. One is forced to ask if one is really honest. If the answer is yes, then the only part of the mission which is visible is that I am convinced that my decision somehow connects me with God, whether it is objectively right or not. I know no more than an honest conviction and a willingness to allow God to act. "For who has known the mind of the Lord? Or who has been his counselor?" (Rom 11:34). Even less can one manipulate the outcome and expect a reward. "Who has given him anything so as to deserve return? For from him and through him and for him all things are. To him be glory forever. Amen" (Rom 11:35).

Note

1. The source material for this chapter is: James A. Fischer, "Pauline Literary Forms and Thought Patterns," *CBQ* 39 (1977)

209–23; "Ethics and Wisdom," *CBQ* 40 (1978) 293–310; John A.T. Robinson, *Wrestling with Romans* (London: SCM, 1979); B.C. Birch and L.L. Rasmussen, *Bible and Ethics in the Christian Life* (Minneapolis: Augsburg, 1976); James Gustafson, "The Place of Scripture in Christian Ethics: A Methodological Study," *Interpretation* 24 (1970) 430–55; Robert W. Funk, *Language, Hermeneutics and Word of God* (New York: Harper, 1966); Ernest Käsemann, *Perspectives on Paul* (Philadelphia: Fortress, 1971); H. Edward Everding and Dana Wilbanks, *Decision Making and the Bible* (Valley Forge, Pa.: Judson, 1975).

Chapter Seven

POLITICS AND BIBLICAL ETHICS: ROMANS 13:1-7

(James A. Fischer, C.M.)

1. THE PROBLEM

"All authority that exists is established by God" (Rom 13:1b). The problem is too clear both exegetically and historically to need much amplification. As a conclusion applied to contemporary problems, it appears to be an example of ethical overkill.

The temptation for the establishment—any establishment—to use it for political purposes has been irresistible down through the ages. In the official pronouncements of the Roman Catholic Church, Romans 13 first appears as a probative text in the declaration of Boniface VIII in A.D. 1320. After citing Romans 13:2 Boniface concluded: "Furthermore, we declare, say, define and proclaim to every human creature that they are by necessity for salvation entirely subject to the Roman Pontiff."[1] However, in the condemnation of Gallicanism in 1690 Alexander VIII used Romans 13:1 to illustrate the opposite: "Therefore, by the command of God, kings and princes cannot be subject to ecclesiastical power in temporal affairs. . . ."[2] By the time of Pius IX in 1873 Romans 13:3 was being used to show how the Church had always supported civil obedience. "And from him, surely by divine mandate, the Church has never turned aside, which always and everywhere strives to nurture obedience in the souls of her faithful; and they should inviolably keep (this obedience) to the supreme princes and their laws insofar as they are secular."[3]

Martin Hengel has a similar difficulty in dealing with the Lutheran tradition of concentric circles of power in Church and state.[4] John Yoder considers that this tradition met its final disaster in the experience of Hitler.[5] Karl Barth represents perhaps the darkest view in considering that all government is as corrupt as man himself and that the only thing for a Christian to do is to retire within himself and simply let civil government stand under the judgment of God.[6]

On the other hand, if one avoids historical usage and political theory, the text offers its own problems on the level of individual conscience. It is almost impossible to make a summary of standard approaches to the text. Perhaps in a general way one can distinguish between "ideal" solutions and "realistic" explanations. The "ideal" solutions tend to remove the problem to some supernal or extra-temporal sphere. John Yoder adopts Cullmann's and Barth's view that the "authorities" are to be identified with the "powers, dominations and thrones" which Paul mentions elsewhere as cosmic forces.[7] J.A.T. Robinson and J.C. O'Neill connect Romans 13:1–7 with the older Jewish tradition of God as the absolute Lord of history who exercises his ministry of control through earthly powers of Church and state.[8] The "realistic" approach may be exemplified by Carl Herman Schelkle who considers the state as a servant of God only when it represents the true order established by God.[9] A bridge between the two views is sometimes attempted by connecting Romans 13:1–7 with the following context on love of neighbor and by seeing a Christian imperative to love officials of the state even when they are evil.[10] Of course, the text provides woeful difficulties for liberation theology and perhaps for anyone who believes in the separation of Church and state.

(Cf. the methodology outlined above 175–177.)

2. CONTENT AND OUTLINE
OF ROMANS 12—15

The Epistle to the Romans has been outlined in many ways; Chapters 12 to 15 have been especially subject to dissection.[11] However, the keynote in Romans 1:16–17 will still function as a unifying theme in Romans 12 to 15 if that theme is in some way defined as freedom from wrath through the power of the Gospel.

Romans 11 concludes its treatise on the Christian stance toward the Jewish heritage by leaving all in the hands of God (Rom 11:33–36). The remaining chapters then consider the stance of the freed Christian toward other societal problems. They begin with what is close to a general rubric:

And now, brothers, I beg you through the mercy of God to offer your bodies as a living sacrifice holy and acceptable to God, your spiritual worship. Do not conform yourselves to this age but be transformed by the renewal of your mind, so that you may judge what is God's will, what is good, pleasing and perfect (Rom 12:1–2).[12]

Shortly before the end of the following parenesis occurs a phrase which almost duplicates this and seems to serve as an *inclusio*:

Use the faith you have as your rule of life in the sight of God: Happy the man whose conscience does not condemn what he has chosen to do (Rom 14:22).

Such general rubrics occur elsewhere in Paul. 1 Corinthians 1:1—4:21 is organized around the paradox of wisdom and folly in 1 Corinthians 1:25; the whole of 1 Corinthians 9:10 to 14:40 is apparently a spin-off from the one-in-many theme of 1 Corinthians 8:5–6. These are not principles from which specific ethical conclusions can be reached, but insights into confusing situations which arise in the lives of Christians. Romans 12:1–2 states that the Christians must stand apart from the world's ways and use their renewed mind to judge what is God's will. No specific mandates are given. What follows is a discussion of the Christian's attitude toward the gifts (Rom 12:3–8), toward love (Rom 12:9–21), toward authorities (Rom 13:1–7), toward commandments (Rom 13:8–10), toward the pressing time (Rom 13:11–14), toward various religious practices (Rom 14:1–22) and toward God (Rom 15:1–13).

3. WORD STUDY AND DISTRIBUTION IN ROMANS 13:1–7[13]

Romans 13:1–7 is obviously a pericope by itself due to its content. But it is tied into the context by a catch-word technique. Vengeance and wrath appear in Romans 12:19–20 immediately before and abound in Romans 13:1–7. Romans 13:7 ends on a note of "dues" and this is where Romans 13:8 begins.

This tying together of words and compounds, often in antithetical meanings, dominates Romans 13:1–7. The topic is introduced as "authority" in Romans 13:1 (bis), 2 and 3. What is said about authority emerges in the very group centering on "arrange" (*tassō*) in 1, arrange oneself "against" (*antitassō*) in 2. We lose the word play by translating "obey" and "rebel" (*NAB*) and we lose the peculiar Pauline meaning of "obey" which he applies to Christ vis-à-vis God or the Church, to wives and to Christians in relation to one another.[14] In the final usage here Paul observes: "You must obey (i.e., take your proper stance) not only to escape punishment, but also for conscience' sake."

Spinning off from this basic vocabulary are other words which are polarized and which affect the context. "Good" (*agathos*) and "bad" (*kakos*) conduct are opposed in 4 but in some way affect the whole passage. Authority is presumed to be good in 1 where it is "under God"; it is also good as found in the deacon in 4 and in the liturgical minister in 6. On the other hand judgment in 1, wrath in 4 and 5, fear in 3, 4 and 7 (bis), avenger in 4 and necessity in 5 are all associated with something bad. This ties in well with the whole wrath-redemption (power) antithesis which inhabits the

Epistle to the Romans. The word distribution alone would suggest that what is being said here refers to the results of the stance which one takes toward authority. It may involve the power of the Gospel to transform authorities into good, or it may provoke a wrath which is invincibly evil.

4. *SITZ IM LEBEN*

The quasi-mechanical technique above merely highlights the topic and the antitheses which surround it. The interpretative methodology used is that of sapiential literature; i.e., (1) the statement begins from an observation of the facts of life, (2) behind them some sort of mystery or paradox is discerned, and (3) the antitheses do reveal unsuspected facets of God and man in their various actions. The first approach to the interpretation is to describe the *Sitz im Leben* as accurately as possible.

The Roman converts appear to have been good Roman subjects. Such was the later tradition of the Roman Church as evidenced in patristic writings and in the acts of the Christian martyrs. Indeed, the first Latin acts of the martyrs evidences that the martyrs protested that they were law-abiding taxpayers and tied this to the teaching of Paul.[15] So it may be assumed that the readers prerformed the same civic actions before and after conversion. The need was for an explanation of what difference conversion had made.

5. IMAGES

Although the passage sounds to us like a discussion of principles couched in abstract terms, it really proceeds by using concrete images. "Authority" or "authorities" is not simply an abstraction; it existed in visible symbols of military and governmental power such as the standard of a Roman legion or the *bona fortuna,* the picture of a patron goddess on the coins of free cities (which may be what the mysterious "authority on the head" of Christian women means in 1 Corinthians 11:10), or in the religious symbols of cults which talk about "powers and principalities" (cf. Eph 2:2; 3:10; 6:12; Col 1:16; 2:15). Such authority can be put down by Christ (1 Cor 15:24) or disarmed (Col 2:15). The authority is pictured on the one hand as holding a sword, i.e., an image of a Roman soldier who is inflexiby brutal, or on the other hand as dressed in cultic robes as one who serves or mediates with the divine. The passage abounds in gnomic sayings which are usually phrased in concrete imagery; the final picture is of a citizen clinking down taxes or tolls at a government office bowing deferentially to officials. In this welter of images the Christian must picture the self.

6. PARAPHRASE INTERPRETATION

To get at my understanding of the text, I submit the following rough translation and explanation. However clumsy, the translation attempts to bring out the word-play.

1. "Let every soul be properly arranged toward the authorities which are over (us), for there is no authority except from God; those which exist have been arranged by God."[16]

   The statement begins in a non-religious way by accepting that there are authorities over us and that one must take a proper stance toward this inevitability. The following context defines the authorities as police forces, tax collectors, toll agents, presumably Roman (13:7). Then follows the insight that there is no authority except from God. That God is behind everything that occurs is a constant theme in the Old Testament, but that says nothing about the moral goodness or badness of the agents. Amos asks: "If evil befalls the city, has not the Lord caused it?" (Amos 3:6b). Romans is filled with the theme of the wrath of God; that wrath is exercised by humans who are bad for themselves and others. All that the introductory gnomic saying does is to introduce us to the mystery of a God who is behind all authority and who demands that we take a proper stance toward it.

2. "So he who takes a stance against the authority stands against the arrangement of God, and those who stand against it will receive judgment for themselves."

The statement simply escalates the problem; if the existing order is opposed, the opposition is against God. That may not be bad; Job opposed God and was praised. However, it is dangerous. On a human level, it is simply street knowledge that governments do not remain passive in the face of rebellion. However, Paul uses the word judgment in a more religious way. It is not entirely a pejorative word; Romans 11:33 had concluded: "How deep are the riches and the wisdom and the knowledge of God! How inscrutable his judgments. . . ." The most striking thing about God's judgments are their inscrutability. The obedient subject as well as the revolutionary must make a decision about God's will. On this the Christian will be judged. He does not know what the judgment will be, but only that it will come from God.

3. "Rulers are no fear to a good work but to the bad. Do you wish not to be afraid of the authority? Do good and you will have a blessing from it."

This is a gnomic saying which has nothing religious about it. Life does not work out that way all the time, but such sapiential sayings simply capture a customary part of human experience. They also leave us wondering if that is all there is.

4. "[It] is a deacon of God for you unto good. If you do evil, fear; not in vain does it bear a sword. For it is a deacon of God, an avenger for wrath to him who practices evil."

Deacon may have a secular meaning, but Christian usage and the context here persuade that it is given a religious sense. Obviously Roman authorities have not been appointed Church ministers by the saying. It is the Christian who can give them this significance: "It is a deacon of God for you." Conversely, the authority bears a sword. However, civil punishment is not seen simply as a way of making people obey laws. It is the agent of "wrath." How this wrath works is a mystery since it often seems senseless to us.

5. "Wherefore, there is a necessity to take a proper stance, not only on account of the wrath, but also on account of conscience."

An additional faith consideration comes into play here—namely, conscience. To Paul conscience is first of all consciousness of our relationship to God and only then a moral guide. So 1 Corinthians 8:10 has: "If someone sees you with your knowledge (*gnosis*) reclining at table in the temple of an idol, may not his conscience (*syneidēsis*) in its weak state be influenced to the point that he eats the idol-offering?" There is a necessity for all citizens to take some stance toward authority; whether it will be the proper stance depends on how one interprets the wrath which government obviously exercises and on how one interprets the way in which God is involved in this.

6. "On account of this, you pay taxes. The officials of God (*leitourgoi*) for this purpose are doing their work carefully."

Grammatically, this is a difficult sentence. *Leitourgos* is a word from a Christian vocabulary even though we know little about sacred officials in the New Testament. At any rate, they are "of God." The context demands that it is the tax collectors who are being referred to. The connotation of *leitourgos* and the modifier "of God" demand that such officials be seen in a different light. It is a common observation that tax collectors are among the most assiduous civil servants. Paying taxes is regarded as serious business. One may pay taxes because the civil servants are so assiduous, or one may see them as servants of God.

7. "Give to all their dues:
tax to whom tax (is due),
fear to whom fear (is due),
honor to whom honor (is due)."

The saying has all the brevity and balance of the proverb form. In itself it is a purely secular piece of advice. Only in the following context does it pick up its real Christian meaning. "Owe nothing to anyone except to love one another" (Rom 13:18). In the secular order once dues have been paid, nothing more can be asked. Not so for the Christian. Anything which one recognizes as "due" must be seen as an act of love.

7. POLITICAL THEORY

Reading political theory into Romans 13:1–7 on a principle-conclusion basis seems to be a penchant of Western thought. If the first premise is that Paul stated principles, then inevitably we must live with the conclusions. Since these conclusions are not now to our liking (as with slavery or wives being submissive to husbands), we seek some escape. Interpretations which call Pauline parenesis "time-conditioned conclusions of a middle-class society" or those which seek eschatological or idealistic contexts seem suspect of such self-justifying intent. The obverse is the self-serving application of the texts to bolster up the existing order. Francis Xavier Murphy remarked after a study of pagan and patristic thought on political theory: "What seems difficult to explain is the fact that in both the experience of the pagan whose religious thinking was not buttressed by a direct divine revelation, and in the Judaeo-Christian experience where this over-reaching element is present, there does not seem to be a substantial difference in the matter of achieving terrestrial justice."[17] The actual practice of Christians persuades that some other explanation must be found for Romans 13:1–7 than a philosophy of politics.

8. CONCLUSION

This chapter has attempted to develop an understanding of the text by using a sapiential approach and an ethical methodology of images. In effect, Paul has caught the Christian in the act of standing between an armed soldier and a minister of God. Who really are these people? The soldier is not simply the state; he is the avenger of God. Who is the liturgical minister? He is the agent of the caring God. The soldier represents a wrath which is mysteriously beyond judicial justice. Christian goodness also operates in this mysterious area. The Christian is free to obey, but if he obeys it must be from some deeper understanding than simple acquiescence to the power of government. He has mysterious power to transform the government officials into ministers of God. Doing so will not ensure that they act more justly than previously. The gnomic sayings express a confidence in the usual order of society, but the proverb maker is too sophisticated to believe that this will always be so. The pericope addressed the individual Christian in the struggle to perceive what is behind the usual order. He must discover for himself out of the renewal of his own mind what is God's will.

Notes

1. Roy J. Defarrari, *The Sources of Catholic Dogma* (St. Louis: Herder, 1957), 187. The Latin text may be found in DS 469.
2. Defarrari, *Sources* 341; cf. DS 1322.
3. Defarrari, *Sources* 458; cf. DS 1841.

4. Martin Hengel, *Christ and Power* (Philadelphia: Fortress, 1977) 33–50.

5. John Howard Yoder, *The Politics of Jesus* (Grand Rapids: Eerdmans, 1972). Yoder devotes a chapter to explaining Romans 13 (193–214). Yoder's methodology and coherence are not particularly clear in this chapter.

6. Karl Barth, *The Epistle to the Romans* (London: Oxford U., 1933). Barth devotes a chapter entitled "The Great Negative Possibility" to Romans 13:1–7 (481–92). His presentation is more in the genre of polemic than of scientific exegesis and yet he does raise substantial problems. His question is not whether we should obey this or that government, but whether we do not seize control of our fate, call it the will of God, and then refuse to stand under judgment.

7. Yoder, *Politics* 200.

8. J.A.T. Robinson, *Wrestling with Romans* (London: SCM, 1979) 136–39. Robinson rejects the Cullmann-Barth explanation of *exousia* with reluctance. J.C. O'Neill, *Paul's Letter to the Romans* (Harmondsworth: Penguin, 1975), considers Romans 13:1–7 a series of eight Stoic injunctions which were only accidentally attached to the text because of the previous Jewish tradition and the verbal agreement between Romans 13:7 (Stoic) and Romans 13:8 (Pauline) in the word "owe."

9. Carl Herman Schelkle, *The Epistle to the Romans* (New York: Herder and Herder, 1964) 209.

10. Emil Brunner, *The Letter to the Romans* (Philadelphia: Westminster, 1959) 107–11.

11. Karl Paul Donfried, "False Presuppositions in the Study of Romans," with a response by Robert J. Karris, *CBQ* 35 (1974) 356–85, and Wilhelm Wuellner, "Paul's Rhetoric of Argumentation in Romans: An Alternative to the Donfried-Karris Debate over Romans," *CBQ* 38 (1976) 330–51 are recent examples of discussion concerning the unity and *Sitz im Leben* of Romans 12—15.

12. The *NAB* text is used for the English quotations.

13. James A. Fischer, "Pauline Literary Forms and Thought Patterns," *CBQ* 39 (1977) 209–23.

14. Nigel Turner, *Grammatical Insights into the New Testament* (Edinburgh: Clark, 1965), 165 has a full discussion of *hypotassō*.

15. The earliest Latin acts of the martyrs are those of the Scillitan martyrs, dated July 17, 180 A.D. The leader of the Christian group answers the charges thus: "Speratus said: 'I do not recognize the empire of this world. Rather, I serve that God whom no man has seen, nor can see, with these eyes. I have not stolen; and on any purchase I pay the tax, for I acknowledge my lord who is the emperor of kings and of all nations.'" Later, Donata, one of

the martyrs, says: "Pay honor to Caesar as Caesar; but it is God we fear." *Honor* and *timor* are the Latin words used in the Vulgate of Romans 13:7. When Speratus is asked: "What have you in your case?" he replies: "Books and letters of a just man named Paul." The reference seems obvious. Cf. Herbert Musurillo, *The Acts of the Christian Martyrs* (Oxford: Clarendon, 1972), 87–89.

16. All explanations which attempt to define *exousia* as referring to heavenly powers seem suspect to me. Paul uses this meaning only in combinations of powers, principalities, sovereignties, etc., or in contexts in which it is clear that he is speaking of extraterrestrial forces. Rom 13:2, 3, 6, 7 clearly indicate that Paul is speaking of known people. Although the word is in itself abstract, there is nothing abstract about the context.

17. Francis Xavier Murphy, *Politics and the Early Christian* (New York: Desclée, 1967) 168.

Chapter Eight

HUMAN SEXUALITY AND CHRISTIAN BIBLICAL REVELATION

On several occasions the task force discussed the 1977 CTSA study Human Sexuality *or issues related to it.*[1] *But it was only in the final stages of redaction in the spring of 1983, when the articulation of our methodological insights was most developed and the structure of this book had already evolved, that the editor sat down to assemble in this form the collective wisdom of its authors and editors on this topic. It was subsequently slightly edited on the basis of suggestions from the co-editors. What has resulted is a fairly critical comparison and contrast of the method used by the CTSA study with that worked out by this task force. We recognize that it is largely six years' worth of hindsight that has made our criticism possible, and we acknowledge our grateful indebtedness to the authors of the CTSA study which has indeed been for us, in accordance with their hopes, "a stimulus for the kind of theological discussion that will contribute to a better understanding and more effective articulation of the Christian values we share in common."*[2]

The CTSA study *Human Sexuality (HS)* has the following structure: I. The Bible and Human Sexuality (7–32); II. Christian Tradition and Human Sexuality (33–52); III. The Empirical Sciences and Human Sexuality (53–77); IV. Toward a Theology of Human Sexuality (78–98); V. Pastoral Guidelines for Human Sexuality (99–239). This structure facilitates comparison with our work, particularly with the way we summarize our insights in the section "The Science and the Art of Christian Biblical Ethics" (above 114–138) and with our outline of the process of "doing Christian biblical ethics" in Figure 1 (above 117). Chapters I and IV of the CTSA study are the ones which offer the most fruitful points of comparison. The Preface leads into these chapters with the following respective comments:

> "As followers of Jesus Christ, we begin our study by looking to the Scriptures as a primary witness to the revelation of God and insight into the divine plan for the human race, specifically as it pertains to human sexuality. The first chapter, therefore, reviews the pertinent biblical material of the Old and New Testaments. With the help of contemporary critical biblical scholarship, special effort has been made to separate what is revealed and lasting in the Bible from what is culturally conditioned and subject to change" (*HS* xii).

> "The fourth chapter attempts to integrate the biblical, historical and anthropological data into a theological synthesis. Theological and cultural experiences of the past and present provide a source from which to discern the basic human values and principles that have been constant in Catholic teaching. These values furnish the foundation from which we have attempted to elaborate principles for interpreting and evaluating sexual behavior. We have strived to accomplish this task by taking cognizance of the plurality of theological opinions and approaches that have characterized Catholic tradition in the past and that constitute the state of Catholic theology today" (*HS* xiii).

Chapter I begins with the obvious caution that "the Bible should not be seen as giving absolute prescriptions with regard to sex," and that "one should not look to the Bible for a systematic presentation on sex" (*HS* 7). It then briefly summarizes the teaching of the Old Testament under the following headings: the views of Genesis, the theme of cultic purity, remarks of patriarchal society, and the theme of fidelity and personhood (*HS* 8–17). The New Testa-

ment is introduced with remarks about the occasional, non-systematized nature of the sayings of
Jesus and the writings of the New Testament
Church on sexuality, and the historical conditioned-
ness of the theology of the New Testament on this
subject. It then summarizes the New Testament
teaching under the headings of "Jesus" and "St.
Paul." In view of the various limitations under
which the study committee was working, it provides
a passable, if not wholly satisfactory, summary of
the way critical biblical scholars of the mid-1970's
tended to answer the questions of moral theologians
as to what the teaching of the Bible was on sexual
matters. (An analogous judgment could be made
about Chapter II of *HS*.)

Chapter IV, "Toward a Theology of Human Sexuality," presents the pivotal insights and methodology
of the book (*HS* 78–98). It identifies *four* "levels of
moral evaluation as one moves from abstract principle to concrete decision. The first level is that of
universal principle." This is seen as "the nature of
the person and his acts," or "the basic principle of
creative growth toward integration" (*HS* 96). A *second level* further unfolds this basic principle by
identifying "the more particular values associated
with human sexuality: self-liberation, other-enrichment, honesty, fidelity, service to life, social responsibility, joy" (*HS* 96–97). The *third level* "consists of
more concrete norms, rules, precepts, or guidelines"
(*HS* 97). The *fourth and final level* is that of the
individual concrete decision (*HS* 98).

This clear delineation of a process of "moral evaluation
as one moves from abstract principle to concrete decision"
(*HS* 96) obviously suggests comparison with our outline of
the ideal process of doing Christian biblical ethics from the
level of "Christian Biblical Revelation" to that of "The Art
of Christian Biblical Ethics" which we outlined above in
Figure 1 of the section: "The Science and the Art of Christian Biblical Ethics" (114–138). On the basis of this comparison (and benefiting, we must humbly acknowledge, from a

great deal of hindsight), it is our judgment that the approach of *HS* is flawed and inadequate. This is not because the process or methodology of *HS* does not exactly fit into or measure up to ours, for we do not presume our outline of the process to be definitive. But two fundamental aspects of any adequately conceived process of doing Christian ethics seem, in our view, to be totally missing or badly neglected in *HS*. These are: *first,* that the Bible, or "Christian Biblical Revelation" as we have been defining it in this study, must be integral to the very process of doing ethics. Otherwise ethics is not, in the full sense, truly Christian. Second, the central reality, the basic or universal principle (Alpha and Omega, if you will) of any ethics that is truly Christian, no matter how it might be conceived or systematized, is our life in and with Jesus Christ, the Jesus who has died and is risen.

> Thus, if one is searching for an ultimate universal principle, it is not enough to speak of "the nature of the person and his acts" (Vatican II, "The Church in the Modern World" 51) or "the basic principle of creative growth toward integration" (*HS* 96). One must go back beyond these to what von Balthasar has called the "concrete universal,"[3] namely to Jesus Christ, and to our incorporation into Christ. In other words, the ultimate operational principle of Christian life and morality is the paschal mystery. This is more precise than merely the law of love, for it specifies the actual mode of realization of the law of love.

The first of these faults is not surprising. The moral theological and ethical traditions from which the authors of *HS* came generally did not even think of attempting, let alone actually attempt, to make the Bible or Christian biblical revelation integral to the process of doing ethics. It is not surprising that a study which relied heavily on a fairly small selection of scholars for its views of the Bible and the Christian tradition did not look beyond the presuppositions of those scholars.[4]

The second fault is more critical and embarrassing, even if it is an embarrassment that reflects more on a weakness of the whole tradition of Catholic moral theology than just on the authors of *HS*. How could Christian theologians fail to put the mystery of Christ at the center of something—human sexuality—that is so central to human and Christian existence? *HS* itself suggests the answer:

> "Traditionally the question of evaluating the morality of sexual behavior has been approached by asking the simple, direct question: 'Is this act moral or immoral?' Such an approach is flawed in two highly significant ways. First, it does a disservice to the complexity of the human moral enterprise . . . in the second place, it implies a greatly oversimplified understanding of sexuality" (*HS* 91).

HS recognizes that the simple, direct question "Is this act moral or immoral?" is inadequate. But it apparently did not realize that its own approach to the Bible suffered from a similar inadequacy. For in effect, although the authors of *HS* were aware that one cannot look to the Bible for a systematized set of concrete rules for Christian sexual behavior, they were, nevertheless, implicitly still asking the kind of question which Christian ethicists traditionally asked when they began work on a given problem: "What does the Bible say about such-and-such—in this case, human sexuality?" Such an approach is flawed or inadequate in at least two vitally significant ways. First, it fails to recognize adequately the complex literary and imaginative modes of expression which go to make up so much of the Bible. Second, it fails to take into account the dynamic, imaginative ways in which the Bible, through "Christian Biblical Revelation," is taken up into "Christian Life" and becomes an integral part of the process of doing Christian biblical ethics.

In other words, the way the authors of *HS* formulated their basic questions resulted, for all practical purposes, in the Bible and biblical revelation becoming largely irrelevant to their work. The way they methodologically conceived their task made this inevitable. We have no argument with "creative growth toward integration" as a "basic principle" (*HS* 92). And indeed it is both helpful and necessary to keep in mind the values of "self-liberation, other-enrichment, honesty, fidelity, service to life, social responsibility, joy" (*HS* 96). But unless these are seen in the full context of the paschal mystery coming to be in our lives, then we have clearly lost sight of something essential.[5] Any method or theory which is not attempting to come to terms with this reality is condemned to inadequacy from the outset. One can criticize the adequacy and correctness of the biblical scholarship in *HS,* and one can criticize points of detail and application, and one can question whether *HS* represents fairly enough the broad spectrum of contemporary Catholic thought. All of these points have become commonplace in the reaction to *HS.* But our major criticism is that the core principle of Christian conduct, the law of love in its specifically Christian realizations in the Law of the cross and the paschal mystery, does not have its proper place as centrally integral to the whole process.

One might illustrate this by asking: "What kind of *discrimen,* what kind of Christian self-image seems to be implicit in the approach of *HS*?" One could describe this as that of a sexual human being striving for maturity and self-fulfillment while standing in tension between two poles. The first pole is the (largely autonomic) "basic principle of creative growth toward integration" being realized through "the more particular values associated with human sexuality: self-liberation, other-enrichment, honesty, fidelity, service to life, social responsibility, joy" (*HS* 96–97). The second pole is the (largely heteronomic) pole of the call to live one's sexual life in fidelity to the principles and rules of sexual morality as taught by the Roman Catholic Church.

This is, in itself, a situation fraught with tension and paradox. It is, in the terminology which Keegan takes from Schumacher (above 223–226) and which Fischer successfully applies (above 166), a "divergent" problem. It is our impression that *HS* tries to solve (ie., "kill") the problem by eliminating the tension and paradox and reducing it to a "convergent" problem. Conservative criticism claims that it did this by resolving the tension in favor of the first

pole we just described. But be that as it may, it
seems that neither *HS* nor those who criticized or
agreed with it in terms of resolving the tensions
between these two poles took the further necessary
step of "breaking out of [this] straight line logical
approach and ascending to a higher level of being"
(above 224). This higher level of being is, of course,
life in Jesus Christ "and him crucified"; it is life in
this "body of death" which is also the "temple of
God"; it is life in this body in which is being made
up "all that is lacking in the sufferings of Christ"; it
is life which is sown "perishable," "in dishonor,"
and "in weakness," but is raised "imperishable," "in
glory," and "in power."

Thus, this bodily life in Christ is the center, the
beginning and the end of the hermeneutic circle
which constitutes Christian existence. Our challenge, it seems, is to develop a moral theology, a
Christian ethics of sexuality which does not try to
reduce profoundly divergent problems—for no part
of human existence is more filled with tension, paradox and mystery—to convergent ones, but which
remains open to that higher level of being which we
already have and are in Christ dying and rising.

Notes

1. In addition, there was a plenary session discussion of it
during the 1978 CBA Annual Meeting on August 23, 1978.
2. A. Kosnik, W. Carroll, A. Cunningham, R. Modras, J.
Schulte, *Human Sexuality: New Directions in Catholic Thought. A
Study Commissioned by the Catholic Theological Society of America* (New York/Toronto: Paulist, 1977) 241.
3. Cf. M. Kehl, "Hans Urs von Balthasar: A Portrait," *The von
Balthasar Reader* (eds. M. Kehl and W. Löser; New York: Crossroad, 1982) 8–11.
4. It has also been noted that the scholars quoted in the study
tended to represent an overbalance of liberal and progressive
views.
5. It would be unfair to suggest that the authors of *HS* were
unaware of this. Indeed, after presenting and explaining the values (self-liberation, etc.) which should characterize sexual behav-

ior, they add: "Again let it be recalled that all of these values must be enlightened and permeated by the core principle of Christian conduct, the Gospel law of love. It is in the light of the life of the Lord that each of these values or qualities is illuminated by a unique Christian dimension or motivation. In the light of the life of the Lord the Christian has the potential to take each of these values and transcend the temporal to contribute thereby to the coming of the kingdom to give human living a Christic dimension" (*HS* 95). To this we must add the essential qualification that the core principle of Christian conduct is the Gospel law of love *with its specific mode of realization in the paschal mystery*. We must also point out that this remark appears as something of an afterthought in *HS*. It is not integral to the method of *HS* or to the "several levels of moral evaluation as one moves from abstract principle to concrete decision" (*HS* 96). This is clear as one reads through the rest of *Human Sexuality*.

Appendix

Appendix

A METHODOLOGY
FOR APPLYING
BIBLICAL TEXTS
TO ETHICAL DECISIONS

Prenote:

Between the years 1977 and 1980 this statement was formulated and reformulated again and again by James Fischer. Over those years it passed through extensive discussion and refinement at the hands of members of the task force and of others as well. In the spring of 1983 it was slightly edited (mostly by way of additional comment and explanation) by Robert Daly for inclusion in this book. Its various authors consider it to be the clearest statement they can make at this time, but also one which they assume can still be extensively improved and refined.

1. LOCATING THE IMAGES WITHIN WHICH THE PROBLEM IS EXPRESSED

a. It is presumed that most decision-making arises out of images more than out of abstract reasoning; i.e., it is pre-discursive or only implicitly discursive; it proceeds from a non-discursive awareness, decision, commitment. Some ethicists express the image function in terms of "value-centered judgments."

b. For the hermeneutic of biblical ethics to occur, the images must be located both in the text and in the decision-maker. *It is presumed that a scholarly analysis of the text* (as, e.g., via the historical-critical method) *and a cross-reference to scientific ethics*

289

shall be involved. Beyond this, however, lies an *art* of applying both the experience of scientific study and the experience of Christian living to the specific problem. (For an outline of these relationships see above, Figure 1 in the section "The Science and the Art of Christian Biblical Ethics" 114–138). The ethician must be personally involved; but this involvement must also be balanced with enough distance to be aware of where and how he/she is entering into the hermeneutical circle.

c. The problem of connecting the biblical text to the contemporary decision (getting from "there" to "here"), or of discovering how the biblical texts or, more broadly, "Christian Biblical Revelation" influences the decision-making process, is concentrated in the images which are trans-temporal and trans-cultural. Since the images are shared both by the text and the exegete, a dynamic flow back and forth is involved until, ideally, both the text and the decision-maker are satisfied.

d. The first step in the methodology is an "artistic" decision about the selection of the biblical passage(s) which most closely approximate the decision-maker's own images. "Artistic" is an abbreviation or code word for what will often be a largely non-discursive process inevitably involving the hermeneutic circle and the reception and influence of a tradition.

2. IDENTIFYING THE CHALLENGE WHICH THE CONFLICTING IMAGES ESTABLISH

a. In decision-making by images, at least two conflicting images are involved.

By "*image*" is meant:

1. Literary expressions which are based on images, such as metaphors, similes, parables, stories, sym-

bols, etc. Since the Semitic mentality is usually concrete, many apparently abstract statements are actually based on images rather than on abstract reasoning. Moreover, each literary form must be examined on its own merits to determine its *function* within society, or the *role* it plays in the particular and overall stories/actions in which it is found. Similar attention must be paid to the way in which we finally express our communication of the insight we have.

2. *Psychological* self-images. Such internal pictures exist within both the individual and society. The resources of psychology, sociology, history, archaeology, linguistics, comparative religion, mythology, etc., must be employed to define such self-images within the milieu or story of the text and of the contemporary commentator.

3. *Ontological images.* Various other terms are used to express this category—e.g., "nature," "character," "root of being," "vision," "value," etc. The basic emphasis of these terms is on the reality of the thing imaged.

In this paper the term "image" is employed consistently as being the most appropriate biblical term. However, the following nuance should be kept in mind with regard to historical contexts and eschatological contexts. In historical recollections the images bear the marks of pain and sin since they miss (at least partially) or fall short of the authentic image and are to a certain extent a caricature of the good. In eschatological contexts the images are always a "dream" or "vision" in the sense of a reality on the way to becoming authentic. But although images are essentially partial and imperfect, and thus misleading if they are absolutized or not contextualized, they are also concrete, and therefore effective.

b. The images challenge one another.

1. In the literary text a challenge emerges from the multiple use of images which are most often set

against one another in antitheses and paradoxes. So also in narrative, the stories are often ironic: in tradition history one biblical theme is often contrasted with another without conscious effort at reconciliation; in proverbs and prophetic preaching there are often hidden questions and conflicting messages.

2. In the decision-maker there are often conflicting images which are not observed until brought into contact with the biblical text.

3. THE DYNAMISM IN THE CONFLICT EVENTUALLY CONCENTRATES ON A NECESSITY FOR A CONSCIOUS ACT OF FAITH WHICH IN TURN LEADS TO DEEPER UNDERSTANDING (IF NOT RESOLUTION) OF THE PROBLEM

a. *At the literary level* of images the challenge is finally made by admitting the mysteriousness of the text (or recognizing the hermeneutical principle that texts in themselves are open to an infinite range of interpretations). Various terms have been employed by exegetes for signifying this stage of the procedure—e.g., "the mysterious parable," "the challenge of discipleship," "the messianic secret," "the book of signs and the book of glory" in John, etc.

b. *At the psychological level* the challenge is made by defining the *Sitz im Leben* of the biblical community and the function of the challenge presented to it to re-examine accepted ways. Some of these challenges are outright on the basis of specific actions; others are challenges to the underlying insights.

(Biblical study indicates that almost all of the legal or parenetic materials were taken over from existing mores.

Acceptance of the existing mores *is a necessary stage of growth in any society; it is Paul's "tutor stage." The methodology used here acknowledges the validity of such declarations as ethical standards whether termed "natural law," customary law, authoritative mandates, norms of character formation, etc. However, the terminal function of biblical ethics is not the mandating of rules but the quest for deeper understanding—as a means to a deeper, more conscious entry into life in Christ. For example, Paul accepts the usual picture of a well-ordered household in his* Haustafeln; *yet he also challenges these pictures by another picture of the Christian acting "in Christ" while performing the same acts. This involves the challenge to the psychological images of the Christian and of God.)*

    c. *At the ontological level* this challenge reveals more of the true nature of the Christian who must make a faith declaration of the impossibility of achieving his/her true nature of image by oneself. It is at this level that a new understanding of truth becomes possible. What is achieved is not total understanding nor understanding accomplished by compromise or reconciliation of opposites in logical fashion; what is perceived is the area of potential growth which leads into mystery.

[handwritten margin note: need for salvation (or for God)]

4. THIS ACT OF FAITH REVEALS THE PRESENCE OF GOD/CHRIST IN THE BIBLICAL AUTHOR AND, BY CONTINUING REVELATION, WITHIN THE LEARNING CHRISTIAN

---

    a. At the level of the text the literary analysis reveals that the author was primarily involved in defining how the presence of God/Christ was seen in the "Way" of community living.

(The specific ethical decision in the biblical text may have been accepted from common custom, law, philosophy, au-

thority, etc; it may e converso *have been accepted as a Christian rejection of worldly wisdom. In either case, what was terminal was not the precise decision for acting in a certain way, but the interpretation of how God/Christ was present in such decision-making. The specific decision may be reformable or only one of several alternative right ways of acting; the need for finding the presence of God/Christ in the situation is an absolute. This is also true for value-centered ethics in which the absolute value is the defining of self. From a biblical viewpoint such absolutes begin with a recognition of the goodness of God and creation and the absolute drive toward knowing and loving. The Christian does not simply imitate such qualities; the Christian is constituted Christian by them, is "divinized" or, in the older terminology, Christ is both exemplary and efficient cause.)*

    b. It is presumed that revelation in the broader sense has always operated within the faith community both in the acceptance of the text (canonizing) and in the interpretation (magisterium). This action of the Holy Spirit has affected the author of the text and continues to affect the reader.

(Neither the author nor the community works in isolation. What the biblical author wrote arose from the community and was destined for the community. So also the reader must be aware of the community as a source of interpretation and as recipient of communication from the reader. Such community influence on the decision-maker extends beyond one's immediate community to the historical and Catholic community which must have a voice in witnessing to and interpreting the action of the Holy Spirit.)

    c. This revelation is recognized not by scientific means or other rational processes, but by faith. The former are indeed part of the community's experience and a necessary presupposition at varying levels of expertise. However, the distinctively Christian aspect of the decision-making process lies in the at least implicit perception of the operation of faith at all stages in the decision-making process from composition to individual decision in act. Authentic Christian decision-making is not limited to scholars.

d. The final test of rightness of the decision can be found only within community acceptance (the *sensus fidelium* or rule of faith, i.e., one's being with and in the Church). For only in the community can one have contact with the "absolute"; only in the community, in ways often mysterious and hard to recognize, can be realized the promise to be "with you always, to the close of the age" (Mt 28:20). Nevertheless, no proof, however logical, no appeal to objectivity can ever give infallible assurance to rightness. The acceptance by the community cannot be measured by an *ad hoc* sampling of opinion; indeed, on a biblical model, popular opposition may be as valid a criterion for rightness as popular acceptance. Only over a long period and in the totality of Christian communities can the final decision emerge. Dialogue within the community is essential for specific decisions and yet it does not achieve totality of Christian acceptance. The Word of God must be accepted as a single Word, and this can occur only infrequently and on major issues. More often than not the individual Christian is alone in specific decision-making and must recognize the partial and fallible nature of the process. The only criterion for the individual Christian is perfect honesty with the self or, in Lonergan's term, full and open "authenticity."

Epilogue

THE ROAD TRAVELED
THE GOALS APPROACHED
THE WORK AND THE CHALLENGES
REMAINING

In its early years of existence from 1975 on, the continuing seminar, and then from 1977 the task force, spoke often and sometimes idealistically of its goal of developing or teasing out a method for doing Christian biblical ethics. We wanted to bridge both the historical and cultural gap between the literature of the Bible and contemporary ethics and Christian life, and the gap between biblical scholarship and the other theological disciplines. Our path toward these goals has been interesting, often exciting and, at least for those making the journey, very educational. We have not, of course, reached our goal in any absolute sense, but that does not surprise us. We did not presume that we would in a few years find definitive solutions to problems that have bedeviled Christian theology from its outset. However, we do believe that we have made some advances. And whenever we have found someone willing to listen to us talk about them, we were encouraged to share them with the rest of the community of scholars. Hence this book.

It is an *interim report.* Whether it will eventually lead to something more complete and more final, either by us or by others who will build on our work, will depend on how it is received. Our decision to publish now and in this form was determined by the fact that the work of the task force and its method sub-group had run its course. It was time to make a report.

Our topic is so comprehensive that almost any conceivable work on it would be of an interim nature. This is particularly true of our work, as the reader has doubtless

299

noticed already. It was theoretically possible for us to package our "product" more handsomely: to pursue the numerous loose ends we could have tied up, to cover several major omissions of which we are now aware, to offer a systematic, selected bibliography on the topics treated in or related to the book, to order and integrate the whole into a much more complete and consistent unity. We did not have to "decide" not to do this—we knew that all this exceeded our currently available resources. And even if we could see our way to making our work more complete in this way, we would be talking about a significant delay, perhaps of years. In the meantime, others who might profit from our work might be laboriously following paths we had already explored.

There is also a further consideration. The time and effort needed to make our work more perfect would be well spent only if we are on the right track, or at least a helpful track. If we are, and it will be our readers who tell us this, then the needed follow-ups and completions, by us or by others, will surely follow. If we are not on the right track, our readers' reactions will presumably keep us from further pursuing a fruitless dead-end.

All this concerns the task we have undertaken. However, *how* we have undertaken it could be just as important as the subject itself. The teamwork aspect of this project has been critical. There is absolutely no question that we have come to levels of knowledge and understanding and to communicative ways of expressing this that quite exceed the individual capacities of any of its authors and editors. If we have worked out a practical, effective way of overcoming some of the limitations that come from increasing specialization in theology, this might turn out to be our most valuable contribution.

But one final reflection—perhaps the most important and most challenging. If we meet with significant agreement that the road we have traveled is the right road, then we face a serious, fundamental challenge about the nature of theological research and theological education. If the road indicated here is the road to travel, or at least an important road to travel, we have to ask ourselves if our professional theological societies are really organized and do really operate in such a way as to support us effectively on this road. We have to ask ourselves if the way we teach theology in our colleges, universities, seminaries and divinity schools is really suited to help students learn to practice the science and the art of Christian biblical ethics.

LAUS DEO SEMPER
April 28, 1983

SCRIPTURE INDEX

Old Testament

Genesis
1:26   212
2:24   98, 251, 252, 253

Exodus
20:1–17   108

Leviticus
17—25   108, 111

Deuteronomy
5:6–12   108
22:13–19   252
22:28–29   252
24:1   232
24:1–4   252

Numbers
11   *161–164*

1 Kings
21:1–16   161

Psalms
49:2   64 n.10

Proverbs
4:9   232
5:15–23   251

Qoheleth
9:1–3   110
9:13–15   104

Isaiah
6:9–10   263
65:2   263

Jeremiah
31:31–34   80

Ezekiel
34   80

Hosea
4   64 n.10

Amos
3:6b   271

Sirach
25:25   251

New Testament

Matthew
5   109
5—7   174, *200–210*
5:1–12   198
5:3–10   198
5:17   252
5:17–20   101
5:32   249, 252
5:35–38   213
5:38–48   212, 214, 215, 216, 219
5:39   217
5:39–41   214
5:39–48   198
5:48   252
8:1—9:34   197
11:19   210
11:25–30   210
19:4–5   252
19:9   249, 252
26:34–39   210

28:19	218	10		196
28:19–20	212	10:1–16		196
28:20	207, 295	10:1–24		193
		10:2		194
Mark		10:9		194
8:35	105	10:16		194
10:6–8	252	10:22		194
10:11	253	11:22		194
14:36	237	11:2b		194, 196
16	167	11:2b–4		193
		11:3		194
Luke		11:4		195
1:3	192	11:13		193, 196
1:26–38	193	11:20		193, 194, 196
1:32–35	193, 194	12:12		193, 196
1:39–80	193	14:1		194
1:43	194	14:14		194
1:76	194	15:1–32		195
2:41–52	193	16:17		252
3:1—4:13	193	16:18		252, 255 n.11
3:16	193, 194	17:21		196
3:21–22	193, 194	20:36		193
3:22	193, 194	22:42		194
3:22–23	194	22:67–71		193
3:38	194	22:70–71		193, 195
4:1–13	193	23:34		194
4:3	194	24:49		193, 194
4:9	194			
4:14–44	193	*John*		
4:18	194	8:1–11		252
4:18–19	144	13:27–33		238
4:18–22	193	15:1–11		52
4:22	194			
4:31–44	193	*Acts*		
5:21	196	1:8		212
5:25	194	2:3–4		193, 194
6:17–49	*179–199*	2:4–5		193
6:20—8:3	198	2:17		193
6:27–36	212, 213, 214, 216, 219	2:23–24		238
6:29	214	2:36		193, 199
7:11–17	194	3:1–10		194
8:21	194, 196	3:14–15		199
8:49–56	194	5:31		199
9:21–36	193	9:32–35		194
9:27	194	9:36–42		194
9:28–36	193	12:12		194

13:13	193, 194, 199	12:3	232
14:8–10	194	12:3–8	269
20:7–10	194	12:6	232
		12:14	212, 213, 216
Romans		12:17	213
1:1	231	12:19	213
1:1–6	243	12:19–20	269
1:5	232	12:19–21	212
1:16–17	268	12:21	182, 216
3:24	232	13:1–7	177, *266–277*
4:4	232	13:8	269, 276 n. 8
4:16	232	13:8–10	269
4:25	238	13:11–12	229, 230
4:25—7:25	64 n. 11	13:11–14	269
5:2	232	13:18	275
5:4	138	14:1–22	269
5:10	229	14:12	229
5:12–17	220	14:22	268
5:15–17	232	15:1–13	269
5:20–21	232	15:9	244 n. 17
6—7	64 n. 11	15:15	232
6:1–4	64 n. 11	16:26	227
6:5–14	64 n. 11		
6:11	227	*1 Corinthians*	
6:14	231, 232	1—16	*221–224*
6:17	230	1:1	237
6:17–18	231	1:1—4:21	268
6:23	232	1:4	232
7—8	71	1:11	233
7:1–6	64 n. 11	1:14	239
7:6	230	1:17–18	240
7:24–25	71	1:18	234, 239
8:2	64 n.11, 230	1:23	239, 241
8:12–17	53, 64 n.11	1:25	105, 239, 268
8:18–23	229	2:2	220, 239, 241
8:21	230	2:3–5	234
8:22	221	2:8–9	241
8:29	239	2:14–15	239
8:34	238	2:16	235
8:34–39	71	3:1–2	234
9—11	177, 244 n.17, 256–265	3:3	233
11:6	232	3:10	232
11:33	272	3:18	239
12—15	268, 276 n.11	3:21–22	236
12:1–2	102, 138, 268	4:5	229

4:6	233	9:23	236
4:8	234	10	235
4:10	239	10:23	237
4:12–13	216	10:31	237, 241
4:16	235, 237	11:1	73, 235, 237
4:18	233	11:10	271
4:19	233	11:17	235
4:19–20	234	11:18–19	233
5:2	234	11:19	236
5:9–13	104	11:26	237
6:12	237	12:7	237
6:13–14	229	12:27	52
6:14	241	13	53
6:19–20	228, 243	13:4	234
6:20	221, 227, 235, 237, 241	14:4	236
7	245, 255 n. 11	14:12	236
7:4	235	14:26	236
7:6	227	14:40	268
7:8	244	15	239–241
7:8–16	246, 247	15:3–4	238
7:8–24	*245–255*	15:10	231, 232
7:9b	247	15:12	238
7:10	226, 245, 246, 254 n. 3,	15:20–26	239
	255 n. 11	15:23	239
7:11	246	15:24	271
7:12	246	15:24–26	229
7:13	246	15:36	239
7:15b	247	15:43	234, 241
7:17	242, 254 n. 3	15:44–46	239
7:17–24	246, 247	15:50–52	230
7:19	247		
7:24	246	*2 Corinthians*	
7:25	226, 227, 234	1:12	232
7:25–35	249	3:17	230
7:25–40	250	4:7	220
7:35	235	5:1–11	230
7:36–40	249	5:2	229
8:1	234	5:10	229
8:2	234	5:15	238
8:5–6	268	5:17	53, 229
8:10	273	5:17–18	229
9:10	268	5:19–20	212
9:16–17	237	5:21	53
9:21	226, 227	7:1	228
9:22	236	8:8	227

8:9	232	*Colossians*	
12:9	232	1:16	271
12:10	106	2:15	271
		2:18	234
Galatians		3:18—4:1	154 n. 36
1:15	232		
2:9	232	*1 Thessalonians*	
2:16	233	4:11	245
2:20	221, 228	4:14	238
2:21	232	4:15	230
3:13	238		
4:6–7	220, 233	*2 Thessalonians*	
4:8	230	3:4	245
4:26	230	3:6	245
5:1	221, 230, 233	3:10	245, 246
5:4	232	3:12	245, 246
5:13	228, 231, 243		
5:25	221, 228, 229	*1 Timothy*	
6:10	229	2:8–15	154 n. 36
6:15	64 n. 12, 229		
6:17	237	*Titus*	
		2:1–10	154 n. 36
Ephesians			
2:2	271	*1 Peter*	
2:13–16	64 n. 12	2:12	216
3:10	271	2:18–25	215
4:22–24	53	2:18—3:7	154 n. 36
5:21—6:9	154 n. 36	2:23	216
5:22–23	253	3:9	216
6:12	271	3:16	216
1:7	232	4:4	216
1:20	230	4:14	216
2:9–11	138		
2:12	220, 227	*2 Peter*	
4:9	228	1:4	196

INDEX OF AUTHORS CITED OR REFERRED TO

Alonso-Schökel, L., 157, 168
Alter, R., 168, 169
Auer, A., 80, 152

Bacon, B. W., 183, 198
Balch, D. L., 255
Balthasar, H. U. von, 153, 166, 169, 281, 284
Barth, K., 267, 276
Bartsch, H. W., 198, 218
Beavin, J. H., 154
Betti, E., 63
Bevilacqua, A. J., 255
Birch, B. C., 73, 265
Bläser, P., 198
Bloch, E., 87
Böckle, F., 80, 82, 94, 153, 244
Bondi, R., 65
Bonino, J. M., 142, 155
Bornkamm, G., 210
Braun, H., 212, 214
Brentano, 83
Bresnahan, J., 97
Broad, C. D., 153
Brooks, C., 169
Brown, R. McAfee, 144, 155
Brown, Raymond, 30, *33*, 63, 65, 198
Brunner, E., 276
Bultmann, R., 141, 142, 212, 214
Burrell, D., 65

Cahill, L. S., *117–118*, 151, 154
Carroll, W., 284
Chase, S. J., 56

Chesterton, G. K., 107
Chevignard, B. M., 197
Chiavacci, E., 95, 96, 122–124, 154
Chirico, P., *49–53*, 63, 64
Collingwood, R. G., 63
Conzelmann, H., 244
Coreth, E., 63
Cousins, E. H., 169
Creed, J. M., 197
Croatto, J. S., 146, 155
Crouzel, H., 255
Culliton, J. T., 218
Cullmann, O., 267, 276
Cunningham, A., 284
Curran, C. E., 5, 60, 64, 65, 90, 143, 152, 153, 155, 255

Daly, R., 65, 114, 154, 155, 289
Danker, F., 197
Defarrari, R. J., 275
Diem, H., 198
Dilthey, W., 28
Dodd, C. H., 226–227, 243, 244
Donfried, K. P., 63, 276
Dornisch, L., 187
Dostoevski, F., 55
Dungan, D. L., 255
Dupont, J., 179, 197, 210

Easton, 197
Edwards, R. A., 219
Eliade, M., 168, 169
Elliott, J. E., 22, 32, 254
Ellis, E. E., 197

Ernst, J., 190–191, 198
Everding, H. E., 265
Ewing, A. C., 152

Finance, J. de, 153
Fisher, J. A., 107, 114, 156, 169, 177, 198, 245, 256, 264, 266, 276, 283, 289
Fitzmyer, J. A., 63, 154, 195, 254, 255
Frankemölle, H., 198
Freud, S., 54, 60
Fuchs, J., 90
Funk, R. W., 265

Gadamer, H.-G., 18, 28, 33, 63, 186, 201
Gager, J., 22
Gandhi, M., 55, 133
Gerstenberger, 110–111
Gilmer, H. W., 255
Gladstone, W. E., 166
Good, E. M., 169
Griffin, D., 243
Grundmann, W., 64, 181, 182, 183, 192, 193, 205, 209, 210
Gustafson, J., 92, 148, 151, 155, 265

Hahn, G. L., 197, 198
Hare, D., 210
Häring, B., 76, 152
Harrington, D., 5, 197, 210
Hauck, 197
Hauerwas, S., 65, 73, 92, 151, 154, 155
Hefling, C., 63, 130, 154
Hegel, G. W. F., 54, 104
Heidegger, M., 63, 104, 186, 187
Hengel, M., 267, 276
Hirst, E. W., 182, 198
Hobbes, T., 54
Hodgson, L., 57
Hoffman, P., 198
Hörmann, K., 152
Hyers, M. C., 169

Jackson, D. D., 154
Jeremias, J., 72, 197
Jurkowitz, P., 23

Kaklefeld, H., 181, 198
Kant, I., 78, 79, 83, 84, 87, 187
Karris, R. J., 276
Käsemann, E., 265
Kee, H. C., 219
Keegan, T., 114, 169, 220, 283
Kehl, M., 169, 284
Kelsey, D., 46–48, 57, 58, 60, 63, 130, 147, 148, 155
Kierkegaard, S., 54
Kingsbury, J. D., 210
Kissinger, W. S., 197, 210
Klostermann, E., 197
Knauer, P., 153
Knaus, 83
Koch, K., 210
Kosik, A., 284
Küng, H., 63

Lagrange, M.-J., 197, 198
Lamb, M., 63
Laun, A., 152
Lawrence, F., 63
Leaney, A. R. C., 197
Locke, J., 54
Lonergan, B., 18, 63, 122, 130, 186, 295
Löser, W., 169
Lührmann, D., 198

Macquarrie, J., 152
Maier, G., 57, 65
Marx, K., 54, 60
Marxsen, W., 222, 243
McCormick, R., 64, 90, 91, 93, 94, 95, 96, 97, 104, 152–154, 255
McEleney, N., 203, 210
McLuhan, M., 56
Meier, J., 203, 206, 209, 210
Merklein, H., 78, 152
Metz, J. B., 63

Mieth, D., 153
Modras, R., 284
Mongillo, D., 153
Montefiore, C. G., 197, 198
Moore, G. E., 83
Murphy, F. X., 274, 276
Murphy, R., 37, 63
Musurillo, H., 277

Nietzsche, F., 55, 71
Nineham, D., 54, 55, 57, 64

O'Neill, J. C., 267, 276

Palmer, R. E., 186–187
Paulsen, 83
Perkins. P., 3, 5, 218
Perrin, N., 197
Pius IX, 266
Pius XII, 27, 29, 33
Polanyi, M., 63
Popishil, V. J., 255
Purser, J., 169

Rahner, K., 92, 97
Ramsey, I. T., 151, 152
Ramsey, P., 75
Rashdall, H., 83
Rasmussen, L. L., 73, 265
Rengstorf, K. H., 197
Reumann, J., 63
Ricoeur, P., 28, 30, 33, 186, 187,
    198, 201
Rigali, N., 92
Rigaux, B., 182, 197
Roberts, R. L., 254
Robinson, J. A. T., 265, 267, 276
Rose, A., 197
Rousseau, J. J., 54
Ruf, A. K., 77, 152
Ryan, T. J., 65

Sabourin, L., 255
Sanders, J., 183
Sauer, J., 152
Schanz, 197

Scheler, M., 87
Schelkle, C. H., 267
Schelkle, K. H., 276
Schlatter, A., 197
Schleiermacher, F., 28, 33, 186
Schnackenburg, R., 203, 209,
    210
Schneiders, S., 30
Schottroff, L., 64, 214, 216–219
Schroeder, D., 153
Schuele, F., 64, 99, 174, 200,
    211, 217
Schüller, B., 80, 84, *86–89,* 90,
    91, 101, 152–154
Schulte, J., 284
Schumacher, 166, 169, *223–226,*
    227, 231, 233, 238, 243–244,
    283
Schürmann, H., 179, 182, 189,
    191, 196, 197, 214, 219
Schweizer, E., 202–203, 209, 210
Segundo, J. L., 139–140, 146,
    148, 149, 150, 154
Smith, J. E., 152
Sobrino, J., 150–151, 154
Soncino, R., 110, 154
Sonnenschein, E. A., 198
Strecker, G., 210
Stuhlmacher, P., 65
Stuhlmueller, C., 197
Swidler, L., 63, 255

Tambasco, A., 114, 139, 154
Teresa, Mother, 161, 242, 244
Theissen, G., 22
Thompson, W. G., 197, 210
Tinsley, E. J., 197
Tittle, E. F., 183
Topel, L. J., 49, 174–175, 179,
    211, 217
Tracy, D., 29, 30, 33, 63
Truhlar, K., 198
Turner, N., 276
Tyson, J., 197

Van Unnik, W. C., 197, 198

Walter, J., 91–93
Watzlawick, P., 104–105, 106, 154
Weiss, B., 197
Whybray, R. N., 255
Wilbanks, D., 265
Wilder, A., 54, 64

Wright, A. G., 255
Wuellner, W., 276

Yoder, J. H., 267, 276

Zimmerli, W., 244
Zwingli, H., 57

INDEX OF SUBJECTS

Abba, 53, 192, 194, 196, 220

Abnormal reasoning, 105

Abortion, 159, 160

Absolute (ultimate), 77, 82, 100, 129, 130, 151, 167, 294, 295

Absurdity, 106

Abuse, 216

Access to Christ, 71–73, 74

Action imperative, 77, 78

Action principle, 77, 78, 100, 102

Acts of the Apostles, 192, 196, 206, 256

Acts of the Martyrs, 132, 270, 276

Adam and Eve, 109

Adequate/inadequate, 130, 139, 186, 200, 202, 223, 281–283

Administration, administrative, 246, 252

Admonition, admonish, 235, 246, 252, 259, 262

Adolescent, 224, 228

Adultery, 252

Advice, 111, 248, 253

Aesthetic(s), 50, 53, 54, 159, 185–186

Agathos, 269

Agent (of God), 275

Agere sequitur esse, 52, 70, 71, 81, 180, 189, 221, 228

Akathartos, 249

Akrobustia, 250

Alcoholics Anonymous, 106

Alexander VIII, 266

Alexandria, 15–16

Allegory, 15, 16

Alpha, 137, 281

Altruism, 127

American(s), 95, 126, 134, 135, 137, 152, 230

Amorality, 227

Analogy, analogical, 159, 221

Analytical philosophy/ philosophers, 87

Anecdote(s), 134

Angel, angelic, 195

Anglo-American ethics, 84

Animal (human being), 225

Anthropology, anthropological, 81, 279

Antinomian, 206, *226–227*

Antiocheans, 16

Antiquity, 215

Antithesis, antithetical, 175, 176, 246–247, *257–258,* 262, 263, 269, 270, 292

Aphiēmi, 249

Apocalyptic, 161

Apocrypha, apocryphal, 13, 132

Apologetic(s), 129, 134

Apostle(s), 204, 263

Apostolic age, 119

Apostolic community, 222

Appropriation of biblical revelation, 96

Appropriation (personal) of Christ, 71–73

Aquinas, 83, 185

Aramaic, 15

Archaeology, 113, 291

Aristotelian-Thomism, 81, 103

Aristotelians, the, 67

Aristotle, Aristotelian, 157, 158, 168–169, 224
Art, artist, artistic, 66, 115–116, 120, 157–160, 187, 188, 290
Art of Christian biblical ethics, 96, *116–117,* 119, 120, 280
Ascetic, 255
Atheist, atheism, 113
Athenagoras, 215
Attitude, 214–216, 250, 269
Audience, 216
Augustine, 64, 104
Autarchy, 74, *80,* 102
Authentic/inauthentic, 128–130, 146, 158, 181, 188, 257, 291, 295
Author(s), 216, 263, 300
   biblical, 104, 164, 168, 174–176, 293, 294
   human (of the bible), 26–32, 98–99, 202, 216
   literary, 160
Authoritative ethic, *97, 100–102*
Authoritative kerygma, 100, 101
Authority, authoritative, 76, 79, 86, 88, 100, 129, 130, 144, 147, 158, 205, 209, 211, 213, 216, 253, 267, 269–273, 293
Autobiographical, 134
Autonomy, autonomic, autonomous, 36, 74, *78–80,* 81, 181, 212, 224, 230–231, 233, 241, 244, 283
Avenger, 269, 275
Average, 75

Babel, Tower of, 58
Bankruptcy (of historical-critical method), 27, 57
Baptism, baptize, 52, 53, 64, 193, 194, 196, 249
Baptists, 57
Barnaby Jones, 133
Basic Christian communities, 148

Beatitudes, 52, 83, 180, 184, 188, 189, 198, 204, 210
Behavior, 74, 75, 77, 221, 222, 230, 234, 236, 241, 279, 282, 284
Being (Christian), 184–185. See Existence, Christian
Belief, 92, 259
Bible, the, *13–17,* 115, 116
Bible/exegesis and theology/dogma, 186, 203
Biblical criticism/research, 202
Biblical history, 27
Biblical language, 111
Biblical literature, 110
"Biblical meaning," 34, 65, 98
Biblical revelation, 14
Biblical Scholar(s), 114, 120, 167
Biblical studies, 45, 72, 73, 114, *116–117,* 120, 124, 176
Biblical theology/theologian, 9, 26, 39, 40–44, 62, 75, 114, 118, 167, 202, 209, 211
Biblicism, biblicist, 17, 20, 27, 39, 44
Binding, 76, 85, 86, 98, 100, 102
Biographical, 134
Bishops, 126
Blessing(s), 181, 216, 258
Boast, 259
Body, 220, 227, 229, 237, 284
Body of Christ, 52, 53, 86, 129, 137, 182, 196, 253
Bonaventure, 104
Boniface VIII, 266
Book of Glory, 292
Book of Signs, 292
Bound/not bound, 250
Branches, 259
Breaking of the bread, 182. See Eucharist
Brotherhood (of love) 206
Buffoonery, 166
Builder (the good), 189

Bypass mode of doing
Christian biblical ethics,
73, *116–117,* 120, 124, 136,
177

Call, Calling, 100–102, 209, 247,
250
Calvin, J., 57
Canon, canonical, canonical
sense, 14, 31, 34, 57, 65, 254
Canonist (canon lawyer), 254
Canon within the canon, 70, 72
Canonization (of a saint), 242,
264
Canons (rules), 159
Captive(s), Captivity, 144–145,
230
Casuistry, 160, 181
Catchword, 162–163, 246, 247,
269
Catechism, 134, 135
Categorical imperative, 84
Catholic, 25, 26, 78, 82, 92,
134–137, 158, 279, 283, 294
Catholic Conference, U.S., 63
Catholic ethic(s), 90, 92
Catholic theology, 29, 80, 84, 92,
125. See also Theology
CBA (Catholic Biblical
Association), 3, 5, 9, 17, 27,
30, 284
Ceremonial laws, 108
Certitude, 49
Challenge, 129–131, 145, 175,
176, 180–181, 209, 251, 257,
258, *262,* 284, 290–293,
299–300
Character, 121, 137, 147, 148,
158, 160, 165, 167, 168, 175,
224, 257, 291
Character-formation, 69, 73,
293
Charis, 231–232
Charism(s), charisma,
charismatic, 52, 112
Charity, 122

Child, children, 245, 250
Child/children of God, 185, 206,
207. See also Sons, sonship
Children of the Father, 205,
207, 217
Choice, 262
Chōrizō, 249
Chosen people, 168, 264
Christ (in), 111, 133, 293
Christian(s), a/the 113–116,
121, 123, 124, 126, 129, 132,
136, 146, 174–177, 182,
189–190, 196–198, 200, 203,
206, 207, 214–217, 219, 221,
222, 228–229, 232, 237, 241,
242, 249, 250, 254, 256, 258,
269, 272–275, 285, 293, 294
Christian being in Christ,
101–102
Christian Biblical Revelation,
7, 8, *14,* 29, 32, 38, 39, 41, 44,
45, *46,* 58, 61, 65, 67, 68, 72,
73, 91, 96, 97, 114, *116–117,*
119, 120, 124, 128, 131, 136,
137, 177, 278, 280–282, 290.
See also Revelation.
Christian ethic(s). See Ethic(s)
Christocentricity, *38, 68–73,* 74,
137, 150
Christology, Christological,
192–194, 202, 204, 205,
209
Chronicle, 156
Chronicler, the, 15
Church, 25, 26, 29, 37, 38, 44,
59, 65, 72, 79, 91, 98, *117,*
128–129, 132, 136, 137, 147,
177, 193, 194, 204, 206, 207,
209, 213, 226, 253, 254, *256,*
269, 295
Eastern, 253
life of the, 34, 47, 98
Western, 253
Church and State, 266–277
Circularity, 119
Circumcision, 246, 250

Circumstances, 81, 83, 103, 160,
167, 215, 248, 251
Citizens, 273
Civil Legislation, 109
Civil rights, 108, 137
Civil servant, 274
Clan wisdom, 110–111, 113
Clarification of images/values,
128–131, 133
Class consciousness, 108
Classics, Classical, 71, 215
Classical world view, 93
Clemency, 215
Clement of Alexandria, 64
Climax, 167, 168, 248
Code of Holiness, 108, 111
Code of laws/precepts/
behavior, 221, 227
Codification, 108, 109
Co-existence, 250
Coincidentia oppositorum, 104
Colleges, 301
College students, 44
Comedy, 165, 166, 169
Comic Character, 166
Command(s),
commandment(s), 64, 74,
85, 89, *97–103,* 105, 111, 148,
180, 182, 183, 189, 190, 201,
205, 207, 208, 212, 218,
226–227, 229, 235, 245, 247,
269
Comment, commentary,
commentator, 100, 104, 108,
144, 180, 197, 201, 257, 291
Commitment, 61, 235, 289
Communication,
communicative, 51, 103,
294, 300
theological or religious, 24,
58, 59, 291
Communion, 253
with God, Christ, the Father,
182
Communion breakfast, 135

Community, communal, 14, 17,
46, 59, 61, 62, 67, 69, 72, 79,
91, 96, 97, 101, 103, 114, *117,*
118–122, 124–138, 147, 159,
176, 182, 183, 192, 201, 204,
207–209, 213, 215, 216, 219,
233, 235, 249, 250, 253, 254,
258–265, 292–295
ethic of and for, 59
Comparative religion, *22,* 32,
291
Compassion, compassionate,
189–191, 195–197, 208
Compromise, 105, 224, 293
Compulsive, 105
Concept(s), 147, 148, 151
Conception of Jesus, 193, 194,
196, 197
Conclusio, 205
Conclusion(s), 274
Concrete universal, 281
Condemn, 252
Condition, conditional, 100, 250
Conduct (Christian), 285
Conflict, conflicting, 126, 158,
167–168, 176, 177, 257,
261–263, 290–293
Confront, confronting,
confrontation, 130–131,
159–160, 224, 236, 262
Congregationalists, 57
Conscience, 74, 254, 267, 269,
273
Consecrated, 249
Consequences, 81–84
Consequentialism, *82–83*
modified, 70, 150
Conservative, 283
Contemporary moral problems,
118
Continence, 248
Contingent, 82
Contradiction, 104
Contrast(s), 104, 126
Controlling, 76

Convention, 79
Converge, convergent
  problems/solutions
  224–225, 227, 236, 283, 284
Conversion, convert, 124, 129,
  130–131, 181, 214, 216, 270
  intellectual, moral, religious,
  45, 60–61
Convictious, moral, 94
"Core"/"constant quantum" of
  Christian doctrine, 56
Corinth, Corinthian, 52–3, 104,
  106, 220, 255
Cosmic, 187
Cosmic forces, 267
Councils, 253
Counsel, 100
Counselor, 128, 263
Court(s), 109, 252
Cowardice, 113
Creation, 77, 166, 230, 251, 294
Creative growth toward
  integration, 280–283
Crisis, 242
Critical biblical scholarship,
  279
  studies, 222
Cross, crucifixion, etc., 105,
  118, 238–240, 284
CTSA (Catholic Theological
  Society of America), 5,
  278–279
Cult, cultic, 249, 271, 279
  legends, 20
Culturally conditioned, 150, 279
Culture, cultural, 36, 126, 132,
  136, 142, 167, 175, 183, 279,
  299
Curses, 181
Custom(s), 79, 103, 108, 293
Cycle of sin, etc., 202
Cyril of Alexandria, 64

Dante, 166
Dasein, 182

Davidic-Solomonic society, 251,
  255
Deacon, 269, 273
Dead Sea Scrolls, 15
Death, 130, 166, 220, 221
Decay, 225, 238
Decalogue, 111, 112
Deception, 107
Decision, decision-making, 61,
  67, 77, 103–107, 115, 116,
  120–122, 125–127, 131, 161,
  167–168, 175–177, 185, 246,
  248, 257, 258, 262, 264, 272,
  280, 285, 289–290, 292–295
Declaration, declarative, 111, 255
Decrees, 253
Deduction, 60
Definitive, 76
Deistic, 230
Democracy, 230
Democrat, 236
Demythologization, 62, 134, 135
Deontological, deontology, 74,
  81–84, 86, 109, 111
Depersonalization, 142
Descending revelation, 119. See
  also Revelation
Descriptive, 62
Descriptive norm, 75, 76
Despot, 112
Detective story, 20
Determinism, 79
Deux ex machina, 165
Deutero-learning, 149, 151
Deuteronomy, Deuteronomist,
  Deuteronomic, 15, 19, 109,
  110, 251, 252, 255, 263
Deutero-Pauline epistles, 101
Development, developmental,
  44, 45
Dialectic, 70, 97, 149
Dialogue, 147, 151, 162, 186,
  209, 295
Dialogue (biblical literary
  genre), 20

Diatessaron, 15, 132
Diatribe, *261*
Didachē, 253
Didactic, 159
Dilemma, 105, 168
Diocesan, 256
Directing norm. See Norm
Direction, 225
Directives, 74, 77, 220, 221
Disbelief, 259
Disciples, 193–195, 208, 212, 218, 226
Discipleship, 209, 292
Discipline, 224
  theological, 37, 299
Discrimen, 48, 57, 60, 62, 64, 71, 77, *94–97,* 121, 122, *125–130,* 135, 136, 283
Discursive, 289
Disenfranchised, the, 141
Disposition(s), 91–92
Disraeli, B., 166
Dissent, *256–265*
Dissolve (paradoxes), 241
Distinctive(ly) *93–94,* 176, 183, 221
Distinctiveness of Christian Ethics, 64, 69, 70, *90–97,* 180, 294
Diverge, divergent problems/ solutions, 116, *224–225,* 227, 235–236, 283, 284
Diversity, 235–236
Divina Commedia, 166
Divine positive law, 107
Divine sonship theme, 180
Divinity schools, 301
Divinization, 16, 52, 71, 73, 294
Divino afflante Spiritu, 36
Divorce, 108, *245–255*
Docetism, docetic, 121
Doctrine, doctrinal, 54, 56, 62
Documentary (two-source) theory, *218–219.* See also "Q"
Dogma, dogmatic, 36, 97, 185
Dominical, 248, 251, 253

Dominion, 217
Double-bind, 105–106
Double effect, 103
Double truth, theory of, 67
Dove, 236
Doxology, 71, 259, 262
Drama, 160, 161, 167
Dream(s), 49, 291
Drugs, 227
Dualism, 244
Duty, 109, 249
Dying/rising, death and resurrection of Jesus, *220–244,* 281, 284
  See also Paschal mystery, Resurrection
Dying to oneself, 226
Dynamism, dynamic, 225, 234, 238–241, 250, 257, 290, 292

Early Christians/Christianity, 56, 214, 215, 218, 219
Early Church, 101, 204
Easter, 222
Eastern Church. See Church
Eastern Orthodoxy, 38
Eating, 166
Ecclesial moral experience See Experience
Ecclesiology, ecclesial, 24, 25, 72, 73, 90, 95, 137, 206
Economics, economist, 144, 150, 223
Ecumenical, ecumenism, 63, 136
Eden, 98
Edification, 236
Education, 45
  ministerial, 37
  pastoral, 37
  theological, 37, 43, 300
Egocentric, 226
Eisegesis, 73, 80, 141, 263
Eldad, 163
Eleos, 231–232, 244
Elijah, 161

Elohist (E), 15, 19, 108
Emotion(s). Emotional, 142,
    158–160, 186, 260
Empirical sciences, 67, 68, 118,
    278
Empowerment, 102
Enemy, 216, 217, 219, 229, 230,
    259
Enforce, enforcement, 109, 252
Enigma, 217, 249
Enlightenment, the, 17, 132
Enslave, 250
Envelope story, 164
Epictetus, 87
Epistemology, epistemological,
    67, 72, 81, 224
Epistles, the, 109
Eschatology, eschatological,
    160, 161, 182, 193, 195–197,
    199, 202, 204–207, 219, 274,
    291
    realized, 161, 204
Esoteric, 247
Essene, 252
Essential Christian ethics, *93,*
    102
Essential ethic, *93*
Establishment, the, 266
E. T., 55, 133
Ethic(s) *92–93,* 94, 184–185, 189,
    191, 195, 198, 199, 203, 224
    Christian, 87, 90, 91, *93,* 97,
    116–117, 120, 124
    existential, *93*
    existential Christian, 93
    existential ground of,
    188–197
    fundamental, 66, 81
    social, 182, 183
Ethical advance, the, 225, 231,
    233, 235
Ethicist, 118, 157–161, 164, 167,
    168, 289
Ethnic, ethnicity, 133–135, 260,
    262
Ethos, 74, 183, 184

Eucharist, 63, 182, 235, 237, 249.
    See Breaking of the Bread.
Eudaimonism, 74, *83*
European, 152
Euthanasia, 103
Evangelical revival, 57
Evangelical tradition, 202
Evangelists, 55, 131
Example, 100
Exclusive, exclusivity, 93, 95,
    96, 122–124
Exegesis, exegete, exegetical, 8,
    9, 16–19, 21, 23–25, 27, 29,
    31, 39–45, 47, 51, 52, 54, 62,
    64, 74, 76, 77, 85, 91, 97, 98,
    101, 114, 118, 140, 142, 144,
    174, 179–182, 185, 187, 195,
    203, 213, 217, 266, 276, 290,
    292
Exemplar, Christ as, 69, 73
Exemplar stories, 159
Exhortation(s) 74, *85–86,*
    100–102, 190, 214, 219, 229,
    246, 248
Existence, Christian, 52, 58–61,
    68, 69, 92, 147, 181, 182, 187,
    195, 205, 221, 223, 231,
    233–234, 236–242, 282, 284
    human, 68, 81, 92, 107, 167,
    225, 230, 241, 282, 284
Existential Christian ethics.
    See Ethic
Existential ethic. See Ethic
Existential ground(s) of
    ethic(s). See Ethic
Existentialism, existential, 20,
    59, 72, 142, 189, 195
Exodus, 110, 111, 148
Exousia, 277
Expedient, 237
Experience, 14, 40, 43, 45, 49,
    50, 51, 56, 60, 67–71, 94, 97,
    104, 105, 106, 118, 119, 132,
    134, 140, 142–146, 167, 168,
    186, 187, 209, 248, 272, 279,
    290, 294

ecclesial moral, 95–96, 120, 123, 124
faith, 95, 123, 209
Judaeo-Christian, 275
Extra-temporal, 267
Extraterrestrial forces, 277

Fable(s), 85
Faith, 14–17, 20, 27, 44–46, 52, 60, 62, 67, 70, 74, 87–89, 91, 94, 95, 105, 106, 110, 114, 118, 122–124, 127, 160, 168, 177, 181, 200, 208, 212, 213, 222, 227, 229, 258–260, 262, 273, 293, 294
act of, 176, 177, 258, 292, 293
Christian biblical, 9
community, 14, 46, 119, 294
decision, 90, 166, *168,* 264
ethics, 61, 87
tradition, 168
Faith and praxis/practice, 54, 67
Faith and reason, 88, 90
Family, 72, 125
Family ethics, 4
Fatherhood of God, 205–206
Feel, 126
Feeling(s), 103, 115, 137, 164, 187
Fellowship, 202
Feminist theology, 6
Fiction, fictitious, 134, 167
Fides quae creditur, 87
Fideism, 89
Fidelity, 118, 181, 279, 280, 283
Figure(s) of speech, figurative, 50, 53, 175, 186, 188, 190
Film drama, 55
Flaw (of character), 165
Flesh, 251, 260
Following/follower (imitation) of Christ, 73, 129, 201, 207, 208, 279
Folly of the cross, 71, 239
Foolish(ness), folly, 181, 268
Forensic, 71

Forgiveness, 118, 194, 202, 208
Formal Norm(s), 100, 102
Formalistic (=deontological), 83, 84
Form criticism, *20,* 21, *98—100,* 167, 169, 203
Fortress Church, 129
Foundations, 61
Fourteenth St. Bridge, 241
Freedom, free, 74, 100, 101, 113, 224–226, *230–233,* 237, 238, 245–247, *248—251,* 253, 254, 258, 268, 275
Friend(s)/Quaker(s), 57
Fulfillment, 83
Function (of the text), 251–254
Functional specialty, 122
Fundamental ethics. See Ethic moral theology, 91
theology, 10, 36
Fundamentalism, fundamentalist, 15, 17, 39, 44, 57, 74

Galatians, Galatia, 220, 231, *232–235,* 242
Gallicanism, 266
Generation (sexual), 83
Genesis, book of, 251, 279
Genesis of moral insights, *86–90*
Genre, literary, 20, 251, 252
Gentile(s), 239, 259, 261, 263
German biblical scholars/ scholarship, 202, 209
German Catholic moral theologians, 79–80
Germany, 85
Ghetto mentality, 134
Glory (doxa), 239–242, 259, 284
Gnomic, 98, 100, 180, 246, 247, 254, 271, 272, 275
Goals (of the task force), *8–9*
God-centered, 230
God-directed/direction, 226, 231, 235, 239, 241, 242

God-talk, 221–223
Golden rule, 181–184, 198
Good news, 212
Goods, 82
Gospel(s), 15–17, 59, 74, 85, 86,
    100, 105–106, 130, 131, 150,
    204, 205, 232, 236–237, 268
Governance, 261
Government, civil, 267
Government, governmental,
    267, 270–276
Grace, 79, 100, 114, 123–124,
    127, 130, 133, 135, 137,
    231–232
Grace, sufficient, 232
Greco-Roman, 192
Greek, 15, 18, 111, 198, 245, 246,
    254
  drama, 165
  Fathers, 64, 71, 73
  freedom, 230–231, 233
  philosophy/philosophers,
    115, 230
Ground (or grounding) of
    ethics, 91, *92–93,* 94, 102,
    123, 182, 188–191, 198
Growth, 225, 238
Guide, guiding, guidelines, 76,
    77, 280

Haggadah (exhortation), 98,
    100
Halakah (law), 98, 100
Hammurabic law, 108
Happiness, 83
Harmonization, 15, 54, 132
Hate, 181
Haustafeln, 100, 101, 109, 293
Hawk, 236
Hazeroth, 162
Healing, 196
Hearers, 262
Hebrew, Hebrew bible, 13, 18,
    231
Hedonism, hedonist, 74, 83, 126
Hellenistic, 191

Hermeneutical circle, 48, 72,
    73, 121, 123, 139–140, 145,
    146, 200, 284, 290
Hermeneutics, hermeneutical,
    4, 8, 9, 17, 18, 23–26, 30, 33,
    40, *45–54,* 56, 57, 62, 69, 70,
    72, 96, 119, 139–141, 143,
    145, 146, 148, 174, 177,
    186–188, 198, 200, 203, 209,
    262, 289, 292
Hero, heroic, 109, 125, 130, 208,
    241, 242
Hero-story, 165–166, 169
Hesed, 231–232
Heteronomy, heteronomic, 74,
    78, 79, 80, 81, 212, 244, 283
Hierophany, 168
Higher level/form of being/
    existence/reality, 224–225,
    231, 235–237, 284
Historian, 62
Historical books of the bible, 13
  conditionedness, 143, 149,
    150, 280
  consciousness, 92
  criticism, 16, 222
  Jesus, 20, 69, 71–73, 98, 99,
    121–122, 217, 222
  meaning, 15, 16
Historical-critical method, 5, 9,
    17–34, 45, 56, 62, 65, 72, 73,
    141, 142, 144, 145, 151, 174,
    177, 201, 289
Historicity, 59
Historicize, 151
Historiography, 57
History, historical, 14, 16, 17,
    55, 56, 58, 72, 132, 134, 149,
    156, 157, 193, 196, 201, 251,
    266, 279, 291, 294, 299
  of ideas, 186
  of Religions, *22*
Hitler, 161, 267
Holy, 249
Holy Spirit. See Spirit
Homosexuality, 118

Honesty, 280, 283, 295
Hope, 182
Horizon of understanding, 146
Human
    author(s) (of the bible). See
        Author
    dignity, 212
    goods, 82
    rights, 150
    sexuality, *278–285*
Humanism, 16, 112
Humility, 201
Hunger, 188
Husbands, 274
Hybris, 161–164
Hymns, 20
Hyperbole, hyperbolic, 98, 208
Hypocritical, 208
Hypotasso, 276

Ideology, ideological, 140–144,
    149
Illogical, 221, 227
Image(s), imagery, 50, 52, 54,
    64, 71, 102–105, 121,
    125–137, *156–169,* 175,
    188–190, 208, 253, 257,
    259–260, 270–271, 275,
    289–292
Imagination, imaginative, 17,
    46–48, 54, 56, 57, 59, 62, 64,
    70, 94, 122, 125–137, 147,
    157, 158, 186, 282
Imitation, 195, 237
Imperating norm. See Norm
Imperative(s), 52, 74, 77, 85,
    100–102, 108, 110, 111, 113,
    190–191, *228–230,* 233–234,
    238, 251, 254, 267
Imperative mode, *58–59*
Impotence, cognitive and/or
    moral, 71, 79, 102
Imprisonment, 145
Inadequate. See Adequate
Inauthentic. See Authentic
Incarnation, 39, 121

Incarnationalism, 16
Incestuous, 104
Inclusion (*inclusio*), 246, 248,
    250, 268
Incorporation into Christ, 59,
    71, 281
Indicative(s), 52, 74, 100–102,
    130, 190, *228–230,* 233–234,
    238, 241
Indicative mode, *58*
Individualistic, individuality,
    137, 150
Individual rights, 142
Indwelling of the Spirit, 212
Infallible, infallibility, 5, 88,
    295
Inference, 60
Injunction, injunctive, 105,
    109–111, 185, 216, 276
Injustice, 215, 217
Inscrutability of God, 272
Insight(s), 102, 104, 105, 107,
    143–146, 149, 203, 248, 250,
    252, 253, 262, 268, 278–280,
    291, 292
Inspiration, 15, 36, 158, 168,
    216, 254
Instinct, 115
Instruction, 103, 105
Insurrectional, 217
Integration, spiritual and
    intellectual, 45, 280–283
Intelligence, 224
Intentionality, Christian, *94–97*
Intentions, 91–92
Interim-ethic, 214, 219
Interiorize, interiorization, 225
Internal forum, 254
Interpolate, 252
Interpretation(s), interpreter,
    interpret, 14–17, *50–52,* 55,
    63, 112, 113, 139–140,
    142–144, 156, 160, 174,
    186–188, 196, 198, 200–202,
    205, 212–215, 226–227, 253,
    270–274, 279, 294

infinite range of, 28, 292
plurality/superfluity of, 29,
   201–202, 271–274
Irenicism, 37
Irony, ironic, 104, 175, 176, 292
Irrational, 67, 106
Irreconcilable, 225
Isaac, 259
Isaiah, 31, 263
Isolation, 202
Israel, Israelite, 258, 260–262
Israelite religion, 108

Jacob, 259
Jahwist (J), 19, 108
Jails, 145
Jansenism, 232
Jefferson, Thomas, 230
Jehu, 161
Jeremiah, 263
Jesus, lives of, 128
Jesus-talk, 223
Jew(s), Jewish, 57, 112, 119,
   191, 192, 195, 215, 239, 247,
   256, 258–260, 262–263, 267,
   268, 276
Jewish
   Christianity, 101
   meaning, 15
   war, 206
Jezebel, 161
Jezreel, 161
Job, 272
John, Johannine, 112, 196, 204,
   209, 292
Joke(s), 134, 166
Joshua, 163–164
Joy, 280, 283
Judaism, 206, 232, 252
Judaizers, 233
Judas, 165
Judgment(s), judging, 74, 93,
   103, 147, 158, 189, 191, 269,
   272, 276, 289
Judgment(s), moral, 82, 94, 95,
   104, 158–160

Judgmental, 208
Judgment to come, Last
   judgment, 85, 86, 101–102,
   148, 160
Judicial, judiciary, 109, 275
Juridic(al), 100, 182, 251
Justice, 232, 275
Justice of God, 232
Justification, 195, 227, 229,
   232–234
Justification by faith, 234
Justin, 185
Justness, 262
Just war theory, 126

Kakos, 269
Kalos, 245
Kantian ethics, 69, 70, 80
Keleuō, 245
Kerygma, 86, 100, 146
Killing, 83
King, 165
Kingdom of God, 78, 130, 150,
   180–181, 184, 193–194, 196,
   285
Kingdom of heaven, 86
Knowledge, 149
Knowledge and virtue, 115
Koinōnia, 104
Kojak, 133

Language (3 levels of), 169
   biblical, 111
   of Christian ethics, 221–223
   disclosure-, 222
   empirical, 221
   ethical, 103
   figurative, 180
   limit-, 222
   literary, 103
   non-discursive, 221–223
   scientific, 103, 107, 111
Law, 13, 64, 74, 76, 78, 85, 100,
   101, 104, 128, 152, 176, 204,
   205, 206, 208, 230, 233, 246,

252, 254, 259, 260, 263, 267, 273, 293
-abiding, 270
of Christ, 76, *226–227*
code, 108, 207
of the cross, 283
divine, 76
-giving texts, 55
and Gospel, 76, 85, 86, 202
of love, love command, 77, 78, 102, *211–219,* 281, 283, 285
positive, 76
and the Prophets, 205
Roman, 253
texts (early), 98
and wisdom, 5, *107–114*
"Learning to learn," 149
Legal, 292
forms, 104, 253
principle, 110
process, 109
statement, 252, 255
text, 110–113
Legalism, 112, 208, *226–227*
Legality, 252, 253
Legend, legendary, 216
Legion (Roman), 270
Legislation, 108, 109, 252, 254
Leitourgos, 273
Leitwort, 169
Leniency, 215
Lex,
moralis (praecipiens vel prohibens), 86
poenalis, 86
praemians, 86
talionis, 183
Liberal, 129, 284
Liberalism, 19th Century, 222
Liberation, 64, 71, 118
Liberation theology, 6, *139–151,* 267
Liberty, 144
Life, Christian, 52, 54, 94, 96, 97, *116–117,* 119–122, 124, 128, 134, 136, 138, 174, 187,

206, 211, 213, 220, 227, 228, 241–243, 245, 281, 282, 290, 299
eternal, 227
human, 156, 159
in/of Christ, 7, 59, 62, 72, 102, 281, 284, 293
situation (*Sitz im Leben*), 174, 200, 204
Linguistics, 62, 291
Literal, 17
interpretation, 16, 39, 207
meaning or sense, 15, 16, *28–34,* 36, 47, 65, *97–98,* 174, 177, 202
Literalism, 15
Literary, 175, 176, 282, 290–292
analysis, *259–260,* 293
artist, 104, 105
criticism, *21,* 56, 62, 100, 186
figure, 195
form, *97–103,* 104, 109, 110, 203, 208, 246, 247, 252, 291
image, 175
language, 110
trick, 104
writing, 107
Literature, 10, 53, 103, 114, 168
biblical, 107
Liturgical minister, 269, 275
Liturgy, liturgical, 65, 98, 253
Lives of the saints, 132, 134
Local church, 256
Logic, logical, 104–109, 113, 119, 157, 164–165, 166, 185, 221, 223–225, 227, 232, 248, 263, 284, 293, 295
Logicity (of a text), 98
Logion/logia, 246, 248, 251–254
Logos, 16
Long-suffering, 184
Lord's Prayer, 205
Lord's Supper. See Eucharist
Love, 181–183, 198, 225, 242, 269, 274

command, 52, 104, 105,
    180–181, 184, 188, *190–191,*
    211–219
of enemies, 64, 180–181, 184,
    190, 211
    ethic of, 84
    of neighbor, 182, 195, 267
    self-transcending, 70, 92, 102
Loving kindness, 231–232
Lukan Sermon, 4, 49, 52,
    174–175, *179–199,* 200–210,
    211
Luke, 19, 145, 206, 210, 211, 213
Luke-Acts, 184, 192–193
Luther, 104
Lutherans, 63
Lutheran World Federation,
    National Committee for, 63
Lying, 83, 107

M (Gospel source), 204
Machiavelli, 112
Magisterium (teaching
    authority of the Church),
    33, 67, 254, 294
Makarism, 188
Managerial, 247
Man-centered, 230
Mandate, 253, 258, 269, 293
Manipulate, 264
Many, the, 107
Marcion, 227
Marginated, the, 141, 142, 145
Mark, Markan, 19, 192, 204,
    209, 253
Marriage, *245–255*
Martin Luther King, Jr., 217
Martyrs, 270
Material and formal, *94*
Material content of ethics, 97
Material norm, 100, 102
Mathematics, 104, 186, 224
Matthaean Sermon (see
    Sermon on the Mount)
Matthew, Matthaean, 19, 31,
    200–210, 211, 213, 253

Mature, maturity, 107, 113, 224,
    234, 283
Maxim(s), 226
Meaning, 201
Meaning(s), excess/plurality/
    superfluity of, 30, 146,
    201–202
Measure, 76
Medad, 163
Media (Communications), 133
Mediator (Christ), 73
Medieval, 99
Melancthon, 57
menō, 251
Mercy, 231–232, 244, 260, 262
Mesopotamia, 110
Messianic secret, 292
Meta-economics, 223
Metaethics, metaethical, 72
Metanoia, 61, 181
Metaphors, 49, 196, 223, 290
Metaphysics, metaphysical, 50,
    63, 185–188, 192, 194
Method, methodology,
    methodological, 4, 8, 9, 16,
    17, 42, *45–54,* 63, 66, 74, 104,
    114, 120, 139, 140, 143–145,
    150, *174–177,* 179, 187–188,
    192, 200, 203, 209, 256, 257,
    267, 270, 275, 276, 278, 280,
    282, *289–295,* 299
Methodists, 57
Middle Ages, 185
Middle Class, 274
Milieu, 168, 291
Military, 270
Minister of God, 275
Ministry of Jesus, 193, 194, 204,
    258
Minority, 219
Miracle story/stories, 20, 99, 166
Mission(s), 134, 135, 194, 262–264
Missionary attitude/activity,
    216, 219
    command, 212
    love, 217–218

Mode(s) of communicating
    Christian existence, *58–62*
Model, 74, 75, 100
Model, Christ as, 69, 73
"Moments," 3 major moments
    of Christian theology, 39,
    45, 67, 68
Monogamy, monogamous, 98,
    251, 252
Moral law, 109
Morals, *92–93,* 94, 102
Moral theology/theologian, 67,
    77, 80, 82, 84, 120, 128, 207,
    209, 280–282, 284. See also
    Fundamental moral
    theology
Mores 253, 292
Moses, 162–164, 262
Motivation, 86, 94, 110, 113, 135,
    285
Mourning, 188
Murder, 103, 108
Murder story, 161
"Murmuring tradition," 162
"Must," 165
Mysterium Ecclesiae, 36
Mystery, 63,104,241,259,263,270,
    272,273,282,284,292,293
    of faith, 87
    story, 164
Mystical, 112, 137, 164
Mystical mode, *61–62,* 72, 122
Mysticism, 122
Myth, 62, 63
Mythology, 168, 291

NAB (New American Bible),
    245, 246, 254, 276
Naboth, 161
Narrative, 20, 55, 74, 109, 111,
    113, 147, 148, 151, 164, 184,
    185, 219, 251, 292
Narrative ethics, 157
Natural ethics, 87
Natural law, 67, 69, 74, 76, 107,
    118, 143, 293

Natural order, 92
Naturally good, 127
Nature and Grace, *91–92,* 124
Near Eastern languages, 18
Necessity, 269, 273
Neurosis, 144
New creature/creation, 53, 64,
    135, 231
New level/mode/state of
    existence, 206, 221, 227,
    228, 232
New life, 221
Nicholas of Cusa, 104
Nineteenth century, 16, 222
Non-baptized, 250
    -discursive, 221–223, 231, 244,
    289, 290
    -hearer, 262
    -Jew, 260
    -resistance, 64, 183–184, 217
    -violence, 64, 183, *211–219*
"No people"-"my people,"
    259–260, 264
Norm, normative, 25, 47, 67, 68,
    74–90, 102, 118, 143, 144,
    148, 151, 152, 180, 213, 216,
    241, 280, 293
    directing, 75, 76
    imperating, 75, 76
Norma normans, 75
Normative ethic, *97, 100–102*
Normatively human, 118
Norming norm, 75, 76
North American, 150
Novena, 135
Nuclear medicine, 24

Obedience, civil, 266
Obedience, Obedient, Obey, 74,
    90, 104, 207, 227, 267, 269, 272
Objective(ly), 74, *81,* 103, 119,
    143, 201, 264
Objectivity, 16, 159, 295
Obligation(s), 74, 75, 76, 102,
    212, 220, 227, 241, 251
Observation, 100, 248

Officials of the state, 267, 271, 273, 275
Old man, the, 53
Omega, 137, 281
One, the, 107
Ontology, ontological, 53, 54, 80–81, 109, 175, 186–187, 190, 193, 195, 205, 224, 291, 293
Ontonomy, 70, 74, *80–81*
Opinion, 250
Opponent(s), *261*
Opposite(s), opposition, opposing, 224, 225, 228, 231, 234–236, 238, 240, 262, 272, 293, 295
Oppressed, oppression, 144–145, 150, 217
Opprobrium, 188
Optional, 100, 102
Oral teaching, 204
Oral tradition/transmission, 19, 182, 204
Order, 100, 101, 112, 225, 238, 272, 275, 293
Ordinance(s), 101
Origen, 15–16, 58, 64, 185
Origin(s) of moral judgments, 94
Orthodox Church, 57
Other-enrichment, 280, 283
Outside-direction, 234
Overconfidence, 262

Pacifism, pacifist, 113
Pagan, 274
Papyrus, 18
Parable(s), 20, 32, 56, 59–61, 85, 98, 99, 130, 134, 148, 221, 223, 290, 292
Parabolic, 100, 180
Parabolic mode, *59–61*
Paradigm(s), 20, 74
Paradox, paradoxical, 5, 69, 73, *103–107,* 175, 176, 180–181, 188, 189, 198, 211, 221–223, 225, 231, 234, *235–242,* 246,

254, *257–258,* 260, 262, 268, 270, 283, 284, 292
Paraggelō, 245, 246
Parakaleō, 246
Paraphrase, 271–274
Parenesis, parenetic, 52, 74, *85–86,* 95, 96, 99–103, 105, 109, 120, 123, 124, 180, 219, 268, 274, 292
Parenetic mode, *58–59*
Parent(s), 224, 228
Parousia, 213, 229–230
Partakers of the divine nature,196
Paschal mystery, 69, 281, 283, 285
Passing over
    Christ's, 122
    our, 69, 96, 122
Passion narrative, 166
Passive, Passivity, 214, 217, 227, 272
Passover, 58
Pastor, pastoral, 128, 278
Pastoral counseling, 254
Patience, 215
Patriarchal society, 279
Patristic, 73, 179, 253, 270, 274
Pattern(s), 191, 200
Paul, Pauline, 64, 101, 105–106, 111, 138, 192, 194, 196, 202, 206, 209, 213, 220, 253, 256, 257, *260–265,* 280, 293
Pauline Privilege, 253
Peace, peaceably, 202, 215, 250, 251
Penalty, 109, 252, 255
Penance, public, 253
Pentateuch, 19
Perfect, 208, 252
Peritomē, 250
Permissible, 237
Persecution, persecutor, 188, 194, 196, 212–217, 219
Person(s), personalist, 107, 113, 142, 150
Personal involvement, 260, 290
    morality, 151, 254

Personhood, 279
Peter, 194
Petrine Privilege, 253
Pharisee(s), 128, 205, 206, 207, 208
Phases in the dynamic of Christian existence, 60–61
Phenomenology, 92
Phenomenon, phenomena, 76, 115, 132, 193
Philology, 16, 17, *18*
Philosophical ethics, 87, 89, 107
Philosophy, philosopher, philosophical, 10, 17, 53, 63, 76, 81, 87, 89, 104, 112, 122, 124, 141, 142, 148, 183, 185, 192, 195, 216, 223, 293
Physical sciences, 186
Physics, physicist, 232, 244
Picture, 257
Plato, 54, 60, 117
Platonist, 185
Play (drama), 167
Plot, 158, 165
Pluralistic, plurality, 136, 150, 279
Pneumatikos (spiritual), 239
Poetics (Aristotle), 168–169
Poetry, poetic, 32, 56, 187, 191
Polemic, polemicist, 186, 276
Police forces, 271
Policemen, 109
Police proceeding, 252
Political theory, *274–275*
Politics, political, 144–145, 215, 217, *266–277*
Pontifical Biblical Commission, 203
Poor, the, 141, 142, 144, 242–243
Porneia, 209, 249
Portrait gallery, 107
Positivism, 89
  theonomic/moral, 74, 79
Post-apostolic, 99
  -Bultmannians, 222
  -Constantine, 253

Pot, potter, 259
Poverty, 188
Power(s), 222, 229, 234, 239, 267, 270, 275, 276
Powerful/powerless, 214–217
Power of the cross, 239–240
  of God, 258, 284
Practical norm, 75, 76, 79
Praiseworthy, 245
Praxis, 54
Prayer, praying, 181, 208, 216, 236
Preach, preaching, preacher, 39, 44, 58, 88, 105–106, 130, 132, 134, 181, 194, 196, 212, 215, 259–263, 292
Precept(s), 226, 248, 280
Precomprehension, 141
Preconscious, 49, 50, 52, 53, 71, 125, 131, 188, 190
Pre-discursive, 64, 94, 104, 125, 128, 134, 289
  —existent, pre-existence, 55, 192, 194
  —legal Church, 253
  —Lukan, 192
  —reflective, 64
  —synoptic, 192
Prejudice, 134
Presbyterian(s), 57
Prescriptions, 98, 131, 279
Presence of God/Christ, 147, 176, 193, 206, 208, 258, 260, 293, 294
Presuppositions, 16, 20, 75, 141–145, 149, 200, 203, 223, 281, 294
Preunderstanding, 142
Priestly Writers, 15, 19
Primitive community, 20, 99
Principle(s), 61, 74–77, 81, 91, 93, 100, 102, 104, 108, 110, 128, 148, 183, 189–191, 223, 224, 241, 268, 270, 274, 279–283, 285, 292
Privatized, 137

Problem, 175, 257, 260, 262, 266, 272, 289, 290, 292
Problem, convergent, 224–225
divergent, 224–225
solving, 149
Process Christology/ Christologists, 222
Process of doing theology/ ethics, *41–45,* 96, 114, *116–117,* 119, 120, *122–131,* 136, 138, 143, 145, 146, 147, 149, 176, 177, 279–283, 290, 294, 295
Professional societies, 37
Progressive, 284
Prologue (Johannine), 112
Promise, 260
Proof-texting, 29
Prophet(s), prophetical, 13, 15, 205, 256, 259–260, 262, 263, 264, 292
Proposition(s), Propositional, 148
Prostitution, 235
Protestant, 25, 73, 78, 134, 137
Protester, 264
Proto-learning, 149
Proverb(s), Proverbial, 20, 98, 99, 103, 113, 247, 248, 251, 252, 264, 274, 275, 292
Psalmist, Psalms, 15, 263
Pseudepigrapha, 13, 132
Psychic, 187
Psychikos (natural), 239
Psychological interpretation, 28, 33, 49
Psychology, psychological, 50, 59, 62, 75, 107, 130, 134, 142, 164, 175, 176, 257, 264, 291–293
Psychotherapy, 104
Public, 217
Public morality, 137
Punishment(s), 110, 164, 269, 273
Pythagoras, 104

"Q", 19, 179, 192, 194, 204, 213, *218–219,* 252, 255
Quail, 164
Quincy, 133
Qumran, 15, 18, 252

Rabbi(s), Rabbinic, 112, 252
Racist, 126
Rational, 60, 62, 78, 89, 94, 95, 132, 135, 141, 166, 294
Rational ethics, 61, 67, 74, 79, 166, 195
Rationalism, 15, 17, 89
Rationalizing, 257
Reaction(s), 215, 264, 300
Reader(s), 160, 261, 263, 294, 300
Realism, 67, 188
Reason, reasoning, 60, 67, 68, 71, 74, 87–89, 96, 143, 144, 186, 289, 291
moral, 64, 257, 258
practical, 77, 79
Rebellion, rebellious, 217, 269, 272
Recommendations, 101
Reconciliation, reconcile, 118, 202, 208, 224–225, 229, 231, 233, 248, 293
Redaction, redactional, redactor, 51, 132, 179, 199, 201, 202, 204, 214, 278
Redaction criticism, 17, *21,* 99, 100, 218
Redemption, 227, 269
Reductio ad absurdum, 106
Reduction, reductionism, 20, 43, 135
Reflection, ethical, 115–117, 120–122, 125, 127, 136, 144
Reformation, 99, 185
Rejection, 262–264, 294
Regulation, regulating, 76, 101, 102, 251, 252, 254
Relative, 100
Religion, 79, 223

Religionswissenschaft, 22
Remnant, 259, 262
Remythologization, 135
Renaissance, 16
Renewed, renewal, 268, 275
Repression, 144
Republican, 236
Research, 185, 300
Resistance, 184, 215, 217
Resolution (of problem), 292
Resolve/resolving (tensions),
    284
Resources, 224
Resurrection, 69, 118, 132, 137,
    166, 192, 193, 194, 220–244
Retreat, 134
Retribution, 86, 110, 161, 165
Revelation, reveal, 14, 36, 39,
    45, 77–79, 118, 146, 156, 168,
    196, 254, 258, 275, 279, 293,
    294. See also Christian
    biblical revelation
Revelation, continuing, 14, 46,
    119, 176, *263–264, 293–295*
Revelatory, revelational, 112,
    166–167
Revenge, 202, 215, 216
Reversal, 238
Reverse logic, 166
Revolution, revolutionary, 183,
    217, 272
Reward(s), 110, 189, 190, 195,
    199, 264
Rhetorical criticism, *21*, 100,
    190
Rhythmic, 191
Rich, 243
Right, 245
Rights, personal/property, 252
Rising (see Dying/Rising)
Risk-taking, 105
Ritual, 50, 62
Roman Catholics/Catholicism,
    47, 57, 67, 84, 90, 129, 133,
    142, 150, 223, 253, 266, 283
Romans, the, 215, 270

Romantic, 28, 133
Rome, 144
Root of being, 175, 257, 291
"Roots" (TV drama), 55, 133
Royal sonship, 193
Rule(s), 74, 76–78, 100–102, 106,
    115, 128–129, 134, 138, 149,
    214, 234, 246, 280, 282, 283,
    293
Rule of faith. See *sensus
    fidelium*

Sacramentality, 137
Sacred Congregation for the
    Doctrine of the Faith, 36
Sacred science, 203
Sacrifice, 63, 118
Salvation, 229, 233, 259
    history, 58, 59
    story, 160
Samson, 168
Sanction, 253
Sapiential, 247, 251, 270, 272,
    275
Saul, 165
Saying(s), dominical/of Jesus,
    20, 98, 211, 213, 218, 226,
    251, 252, 253, 255, 280
Scandal, 238, 259
Schizophrenic, 105
Scholarship, scholars,
    community of, 37, 90,
    124–125, 130, 132, 136–138,
    204, 289, 295, 299
Scholasticism, scholastics, 81,
    221
Science, scientific, 16, 17, 62,
    103, 110, 111, 113, 120, 142,
    157–159, 203, 223, 232, 255,
    294
    age of, 79, 142
    and art (of ethics), 8, 64, 66,
    68, *114–138*, 177, 278, 280,
    290, 301
    of Christian biblical ethics,
    116–117, 120

fiction, 164
theological, 136
Scientific ethics, 103, 289
Scillitan martyrs, 276
Script, 167
Scripture and tradition, 25, 32
Self-awareness, 225, 238
-conscious(ness), 144
-directed/direction, 225, 231,
    233, 235, 239
-fulfillment, 283
-giving, 127
-identity, 147
-image, 165, 175, 257, 263,
    264, 283, 291
-interest(s), 263
-liberation, 280, 282–284
-preservation, 105
-sacrificing, 126
-sufficiency, 230
-understanding, human
    ethical, 96, 147, 263
Seminaries, 301
Semitic, 230, 291
Sense, 126
Sense, biblical, 177
Sensitivity, 94, 225, 238
Sensus fidelium, 106, 295
Separation (see Divorce)
Septuagint, 13, 15, 112, 231–232
Sermon, 134
Sermon on the Mount, 4, 52, 98,
    174, 179–199, *200–210*, 211,
    219
Servant of Jahweh, 193
Service, 118
Service to life, 280, 283
Sex, Sexual, Sexuality, 166, 227,
    231, 247, *278–285*
Sex act, 83
Sexism, sexist, 126, 159
Sexual ethics, 4
Shopkeeper, 189
Siger of Brabant, 67
Simile, 223, 290
Similitudes, 20, 85

Sin, 202, 220, 231–231, 291
Sinfulness, 118, 208
Situation(s), 76, 128, 145, 146,
    149, 209, 219, 242, 253, 268,
    294
Sitz im Leben, 28, *97–103*, 176,
    247, 251, 252, *270*, 276, 292
Skepticism, 89
Slave(s), slavery, 64, 94, 112,
    230–232, 245–247, 274
Social analysis, 140–141,
    143–146
criticism, 143
differences, 215, 216
ethics, 148, 185
event, 214
group, 75, 112, 217
justice, 137, 144, 148
morality, 137
order, 150
psychology, 77
relationship, 215
responsibility, 280, 283
sciences, 10, 114
situation(s), 215, 216
structures, 143
system, 112
values, 150
Society, Societal, 113, 137, 142,
    216, 217, 225, 251, 254, 268,
    275, 291
Sociological analysis/criticism/
    exegesis, *22*, 30, 32, 33, 211
Sociology, 77, 141, 291
Socio-political, 144, 149
Socrates, 117, 215
Sola Scriptura, 24
Soldier (Roman), 271, 275
Solution, 222–223
Sonship (of Jesus), 205
Sonship (our) from the Father,
    182, 185, *190–199,* 205–206
Sons of God, 53, *189–199,* 217,
    233
Sophocles, 54
Soteriology, 73

Source, the (Q), 183
Source criticism, *19,* 20, 21, 111,
　179, 200, 213
Source(s) of theology/ethics/
　Christian life, *41–45,* 47,
　67–68, 77, 78, *117–118,* 145,
　213
Sources of revelation, 25
Specialization, 37, 114, 300
Specific, specificity, 91, *93–95,*
　122–124
Spirit (Holy), 96, 123, 196, 212,
　220, 221, 228, 230, 233, 237,
　254, 294
Spirit, life in the, 206, 220
Spiritual captivity, ills, 144–145
　director/direction, 128
　meaning/sense, 15, 144, 185
Spiritualism, 15
Spirituality, 122
Stage (drama), 167
Stance (theological or
　confessional), 27, 60, 68,
　102, 158, 176, 258, 263, 264,
　268, 270–272
Standard (of a legion), 270
Star Wars, 55, 133
Stoic, 181, 185, 230, 276
Stone, to, 252
Story, stories, 54–62, 65, 85,
　102–104, 109, 112, *131–137,*
　146, 148–151, *156–169,*
　290–292
　ethical, 160
　pronouncement, 252
　-teller, 109, 147, 157–161, 164,
　167, 168
　within a story, 59, 60
Strabo, 247
Strong/powerful, the, 214–215
Strophe, strophically, 190–191
Structural criticism/analysis,
　21, 100, 190–191, 198
Structuralism, 62
Structure(s), 144
Subconscious, 131

Subjective, *81,* 103, 113, 119,
　159, 263
Subjectivity, 17
Suffering, 221
Surd, 49, 51, 70, 71, 73
Supernatural existential, 92
Supernatural order, 92
Suspicion, exegetical, 140
Suspicion, ideological, 139–140
Sword, 271, 273
Symbol, symbolism, symbolic,
　49, 50, 53, 62, 71, 184–187,
　192, 194, 195, 270–271,
　290–291
Synagogue(s), 206, 256
Synoptic(s), 193, 205
Synthesis, 51, 187, 279
System(s), systematic, 50–52,
　66, 67, 75, 76, 87, 108,
　110–112, 158, 160, 183–185,
　187, 188, 198, 203, 232,
　279–282, 300
System, systematic theology,
　10, 40, 43, 44, 186

Taberah, 162
Tassō-antitassō, 269
Tatian, 15, 132
Tax collector, 271, 273–274
Taxes, 166, 271, 274
Teacher(s), 113, 205
Teacher (Christ), 205, 206
Teaching, 129
　authority of the Church, 25
　of Jesus, Dominical teaching,
　56, 201, 206–209, 217
Tease, teasing, 223, 225, 227,
　234, *235–237,* 239, 242, 299
Techniques, 115
Technology, 142
Teleology, teleological, 74,
　81–84, 86, 109, 111, 150
Television (TV), 55, 126, 135,
　165
Temple, 206
Temptation, 221

Ten commandments,
  decalogue, 108, 109
Tension(s), 103, 104, 107, 115,
  125–131, 221, 225, 227,
  228–234, 237, 238, 241, 249,
  254, 283, 284
Tertullian, 205, 217, 219
Textbook, 224
Text criticism, 16, *18*, 19, 245
Theodramatik, 167
Theology, theologian,
  theological, 18, 76, 81, 85,
  87, 88, 90, 114, 118, 124,
  136–138, 142, 143, 145–149,
  191, 193, 202–204, 212–214,
  221, 222, 232, 278–280, 301.
  See also Fundamental
  Theology
  Christian *38–45*, 65–67, 73,
  89, 94, 98, *116–117*, 120, 122,
  124, 129, 145, 160, 232, 299.
  See also Catholic Theology
  and exegesis *35–65*. See
  Bible and theology
  philosophical or natural, 41
  scientific, 104
Theonomic, 74, 80, 212
  human autonomy, 80, 244
Theoretical norm, 75, 76
Theory, 104
Therapy, therapeutic, 106
Third world, 66
Third world ethics, 5, *139–151*
Thirteenth century, 67
Thomas, Gospel of, 218
Time-conditioned, 274
Toll agent, 271
Tools (historical-critical),
  18–23, 73, 98, 167, 222
Torah, 112, 208, 226
Tractarians, 57
Tradition, 6, 67, 69, 72, 111, 112,
  118, 128, 146, 148, 179, 192,
  202–203, 210, 215, 216, 217,
  219, 225, 226, 253, 254, 264,
  270, 276, 278, 279, 281, 282, 290

criticism *19–20*, 21, 213
history, 292
history and, 39, 43, 46
Traditionsgeschichte, 20
Tragedy, 158, 165, 169
Tragic figure, 165
Transcendence,
  transcendental, 92
Transcendentals, ontological,
  67
transcultural, 290
Transforming power, 270, 275
Transitus (passing over), 121
Translation, translator, 15, 111,
  271
Trans-temporal, 263, 290
Treatise, 260
Tree, good, 189
Trent, Council of, 13, 57
Truth, 62, 157, 159, 254
Truth-value of moral insight,
  86–90
Tutor, 113, 176, 293
Two-source theory, 19, *218–219*

Überlieferungsgeschichte, 20
Ultimate, absolute, 79, 83, 147,
  281
Unbeliever/non-believer,
  unbelief, 250, 259, 263
Unclean, 249
Unconscious, 141, 144
Underdog, 215
Unintelligibility, 49, 51
Universal (ethic/principle
  etc.), 215, 280, 281
Universities, 301
Unmarried, 248
Utilitarianism, 74, *83*, 84

Valuable, 245
Value(s), 61, 74, *76–78*, 79, 94,
  100, 102, 121, 125–130, 133,
  135, 149–151, 175, 183, 254,
  257, 278–280, 283–285, 289,
  291, 294

Value-centered, 150
Vatican I, 67
Vatican II, 27, 29, 32, 33
Vengeance, 161, 269
Vessels of wrath/mercy, 260
Vice, 225
Victims, 144, 150
Vietnam War, 95, 126
Villain, 109, 208
Violence, 108, 113
Virgin, 245
Virtue(s), 184, 188–189, 195, 225
Virtue-lists, 100, 101, 109. See
    Haustafeln
Vision, 175, 257, 291
Vision, integrating, 115
Vocation, 100, 232, 237, 242

Waltons, The, 133
War, 159
Weakness, the weak/powerless,
    214–215, 234, 239, 259, 284
Weltanschauung, 52, 60, 122,
    141
Western, 142, 274
  (story, drama), 164
  Church. See Church
Widow, 245, 248

Will of God, 79, 167, 181, 196,
    208, 272, 275, 276
Will of the Father, 205, 206, 207
Wisdom, 100, 188, 194, 205, 236,
    239, 240, 247, 251, 252, 254,
    255, 268, 294. See also Clan
    wisdom
  genre, 253
  law and, *107–114*
  tradition, 219
  writer/writing, 104, 246
Wishes, 111
Wives, 269, 274
Women's ordination, 75
Wonderworking,
    wonderworker, 192, 194
Word study, 269–270
Works, 232, 242–243, 259, 260, 262
World view, 186–187, 198. See
    Weltanschauung
Wrath, -of God, -to come, 262,
    268–270, 272, 273, 275
Writings, 13

Yahweh, 55
Yahwist (J), 15, 251, 255

Zealot, 214